LONGMAN LITERATUR

Three plays: The Wild Duck, Ghosts and A Doll's House

Henrik Ibsen

Editor: Jacqueline Fisher

Longman Literature
Series editor: Roy Blatchford

Short stories

Angelou, Goodison,
Senior & Walker *Quartet of Stories* 0 582 28730 8
Thomas Hardy *The Wessex Tales* 0 582 25405 1
Susan Hill *A Bit of Singing and Dancing* 0 582 09711 8
George Layton *A Northern Childhood* 0 582 25404 3
Twisters: stories from other centuries 0 582 29253 0

Poetry

Poems from Other Centuries edited by Adrian Tissier 0 582 22585 X
Poems in my Earphone collected by John Agard 0 582 22587 6
Poems One edited by Celeste Flower 0 582 25400 0
Poems Two edited by Paul Jordan & Julia Markus 0 582 25401 9
Voices of the Great War edited by Geoff Barton 0 582 29248 4

Plays

Alan Ayckbourn *Absent Friends* 0 582 30242 0
Ad de Bont *Mirad. A Boy from Bosnia* 0 582 24949 X
Oliver Goldsmith *She Stoops to Conquer* 0 582 25397 7
Henrik Ibsen *Three plays: The Wild Duck, Ghosts and A Doll's House* 0 582 24948 1
Ben Jonson *Volpone* 0 582 25408 6
Christopher Marlowe *Doctor Faustus* 0 582 25409 4
Terence Rattigan *The Winslow Boy* 0 582 06019 2
Jack Rosenthal *Wide-Eyed and Legless* 0 582 24950 3
Willy Russell *Educating Rita* 0 582 06013 3
Shirley Valentine 0 582 08173 4
Peter Shaffer *Equus* 0 582 09712 6
The Royal Hunt of the Sun 0 582 06014 1
Bernard Shaw *Androcles and the Lion* 0 582 29252 2
Arms and the Man 0 582 07785 0
The Devil's Disciple 0 582 25410 8
Pygmalion 0 582 06015 X
Saint Joan 0 582 07786 9
R B Sheridan *The Rivals* and *The School for Scandal* 0 582 25396 9
J Webster *The Duchess of Malfi* 0 582 28731 6
Oscar Wilde *The Importance of Being Earnest* 0 582 07784 2

Other titles in the Longman Literature series are listed on page 356.

Contents

The writer on writing

Ideas and ideals

> *Every new work has had as its purpose for me that of serving as a process of spiritual emancipation and purification; for no man ever stands quite without some responsibility and some complicity in the society to which he belongs. That was why I once wrote the following lines in a copy of one of my books as a dedication:*
>
> *To* **live** *is to war with the trolls*
> *in the vaults of the heart and the brain.*
> *To* **write***: that is to sit*
> *in judgement over one's self.*
>
> From a letter to Ludwig Passarge, 16 June 1880

For Ibsen these trolls represent the enemies of mankind – evil supernatural beings from Norwegian folklore: the dark forces exercising power over a human's soul. Ibsen's lines serve well in portraying a writer analysing his own literary powers and they illustrate his constant battle against what he considered to be the ills of society – hypocrisy, compromise, irresponsibility and self-delusion.

In Act 2 of Ibsen's play ***Peer Gynt***, the trolls show Peer the difference between living as a human and merely existing as a troll. The motto for the trolls is 'Troll, to thyself be – *enough*'. For humans, however, it is 'Man, to thyself be *true*.'

This central quest for spiritual evolution and revolution pervades Ibsen's dramatic works and his own plentiful private correspondence to family, friends, publishers, and critics.

> *I must confess that the only thing I love about liberty is the fight for it... All that we have been living on until now is but scraps from the table of the last century's revolution... liberty, equality and fraternity* [ideals from the 1789

> French Revolution] *are no longer the same as they were in the days of the lamented guillotine. That is what the politicians refuse to understand, and that is why I hate them. These fellows only want individual revolution, external revolutions, political etc. What matters is the revolution of the spirit…*
>
> Letter to his friend Georg Brandes, 20 December 1870

Ibsen is seen – as are his characters (particularly in ***Ghosts***) – to be living within a claustrophobic society:

> *I have never really had any strong liking for solidarity; I have always regarded it as just another traditional dogma… The whole human race is on the wrong track…*
>
> Letter to Georg Brandes, 24 September 1871

> *There is still much to be done in this country before we can be said to have achieved full freedom… An element of aristocracy must enter into our political life, our government, our members of parliament and our press. I am not thinking of aristocracy of wealth, of learning, or even of ability or talent. I am thinking of aristocracy of character, of mind and of will.*
>
> Speech to local Workers' Association in Trondheim, 14 June 1885

Such 'aristocracy of will' is *not* the uncompromising mission of Gregers Werle in ***The Wild Duck***; Ibsen makes a clear distinction between iron-willed ideals and living a *humane* life. He had read the free-thinking philosopher, Kierkegaard, whose distrust of dogma led to a belief in individual choice but Ibsen denied his plays were consciously influenced by Kierkegaard. In his play ***Brand***, the eponymous hero requires 'All or Nothing – no half-measures' and goes through life unwilling to make any 'cowardly compromise' in the belief that man can be 'transformed' only by 'will'. These ideals are attacked by Agnes, Brand's wife:

> *It is easy to be strong in the storm*
> *Easy to live the warrior's life.*
> *But to sit alone in silence, nursing one's grief*
> *Performing dull and humble tasks, is harder.*

Ghosts in particular considers the arguments between the free-thinkers and the rest of society, but all three plays in this volume explore what it is to be a human being.

I believe that an age is impending where the political and social concepts will cease to exist in their present forms, and from these two things a unity will emerge containing within itself conditions for the potential happiness of mankind.

On various occasions people have said about me that I am a pessimist. And this I am, in so far as I do not believe in the eternal validity of human ideals. But I am also an optimist, in so far as I believe with full confidence in the propagatory powers of ideals and in their capacity for development.

From a speech at a banquet in Stockholm, 24 September 1887

The art of the dramatist

William Archer, who translated many of Ibsen's plays and championed Ibsen in the face of hostile criticism, notes a conversation with the playwright in August 1887:

I tried to get at the genesis of a piece in his head... it seems that the **idea** *of a piece generally presents itself before the characters and incidents... He has to incarnate the ideas as it were, in character and incident, before the actual work of creation can be said to have fairly begun. Different plans and ideas, he admits, often flow together, and the play he ultimately produces is sometimes very unlike the intention with which he set out. He writes and re-writes, scribbles and destroys, an enormous amount, before he makes the exquisite fair copy... As for symbolism, he says that life is full of it, and that, consequently, his plays are full of it...*

Published in ***Monthly Review***, June 1906

In conversation with M.G. Conrad, editor of ***Die Gesellschaft***, Ibsen also comments on his own methods for creating his characters:

Before I write one word, I must know the character through and through, I must penetrate into the last wrinkle of his soul. I always proceed from the individual; the stage setting, the dramatic ensemble, all of that comes naturally and causes me no worry, as soon as I am certain of the individual in every aspect of his humanity. But I have to have his exterior in mind also, down to the last button, how he stands and walks, how he bears himself, what his voice sounds like. Then I do not let him go until his fate is fulfilled.

In a letter to Edmund Gosse, 15 January 1874, regarding his first play in prose, Ibsen gives us an insight into the drafting process:

As a rule, I make three drafts of my plays, which differ greatly from each other – in characterization, not in plot. When I approach the first working-out of my material, it is as though I knew my character from a railway journey; one has made a preliminary acquaintance, one has chatted about this and that. At the next draft I already see everything much more clearly, and I know the people roughly as one would after a month spent with them at a spa; I have discovered the fundamentals of their characters and their little peculiarities; but I may still be wrong about certain essentials. Finally, in the last draft, I have reached the limit of my knowledge; I know my characters from close and long acquaintance – they are my intimate friends, who will no longer disappoint me; as I see them now, I shall always see them.

and his use of language:

The illusion I wanted to produce is that of reality. I wished to produce the impression on the reader that what he was reading was something that had really happened. If I had employed verse, I should have counteracted my own intention... what I desired to depict were human beings, and therefore I would not let them talk in 'the language of gods'.

Regarding symbolism, Ibsen said:

Every notable human being is symbolic, both in his career and in his relationship with history... [symbolism should exist] *hidden in the work, like a vein of silver ore in a mountain...*

From a review in ***Illustreret Nyhedsblad***, 20 & 27 December 1857

The writer defends his plays

Ibsen began work on ***The Wild Duck*** on 20 April 1884. Writing to his publisher, Frederik Hegel, he was mindful of the criticism some of his previous plays had aroused:

The play doesn't touch on political or social problems, or indeed any matters of public import. It takes place entirely within the confines of family life. I dare say it will arouse some discussion; but it can't offend anyone.

14 June 1884

In a subsequent letter to a young poet, Theodor Caspari, Ibsen touches on an idea central to the play itself:

...I have long ceased to make universal demands of people because I no longer believe that one has any inherent right to pose such demands. I believe that none of us can have any higher aim in life than to realise ourselves in spirit and in truth. That, in my view is the true meaning of liberalism, and that is why the so-called liberals are in so many ways repugnant to me.

27 June 1884

Having completed the play, he wrote to Frederik Hegel:

I enclose the manuscript of my new play, **The Wild Duck**, *which has occupied me daily for the past four months, and from which I cannot part without a certain feeling of loss... This new play occupies, in some ways, a unique position among my dramatic works... The critics will... find something to argue about, something to construe. I believe, too, that* **The Wild Duck** *may possibly tempt some of our younger dramatists to explore new territories, and this I regard as a desirable thing.*

2 September 1884

Ibsen's comments about the subject material and critical reception of the other two plays in this collection had been more passionate out of sheer necessity:

Ghosts *will probably cause alarm in some circles: but that can't be helped. If it didn't, there would have been no necessity for me to have written it.*

Letter to Hegel, 23 November 1881

*My new play [***Ghosts***] has come out, and has created a violent commotion in the Scandinavian press. Every day I receive letters and newspaper articles, some for, some against. A copy will be sent to you very shortly; but I feel it is quite impossible that the play should be performed in any German theatre at*

> *this time; I hardly think they'll dare to stage it even in Scandinavia for some little time* [owing to the references to syphilis].
>
> Letter to Hegel, 22 December 1882

With increased public hostility towards the play, Ibsen became more enraged and wrote to Georg Brandes:

> *What is one to say of the attitude of the so-called liberal press?… These leaders who talk and write of freedom and progress, and at the same time let themselves be the slaves of the supposed opinions of their subscribers?*
>
> 3 January 1882

In another letter, to Sophus Schandorph, he wrote:

> *I was prepared for some commotion. If for nothing else, certain of our Norwegian reviewers have an undeniable talent for completely misunderstanding and misinterpreting the authors whose books they presume to judge… My intention was to try and give the reader the impression of experiencing a piece of reality… And they say the book advocates nihilism. By no means. It does not set out to advocate anything at all. All it does is to point out that nihilism is fermenting under the surface, at home as everywhere else…*
>
> 6 January 1882

The germ of the idea for ***A Doll's House*** came from the circumstances of an acquaintance of Ibsen's, Laura Kieler, whose husband had contracted tuberculosis and who secretly obtained a loan, the result of which included forged cheques for repayment. When thinking about the play, Ibsen wrote ***Notes for a Modern Tragedy*** which, in reflecting the plot of the play, has been heralded as a revolutionary defence of women:

> *There are two kinds of moral laws, two kinds of conscience, one for men and one, quite different, for women. They don't understand each other; but in practical life, woman is judged by masculine law, as though she weren't a woman but a man.*
>
> *The wife in the play ends by having no idea what is right and what is wrong; natural feelings on the one hand and belief in authority on the other lead her to utter destruction.*
>
> *A woman cannot be herself in modern society. It is an exclusively male*

society, with laws made by men and with prosecutors and judges who assess feminine conduct from a masculine standpoint.

She has committed forgery, and is proud of it; for she has done it out of love for her husband, to save his life. But this husband of hers takes his standpoint, conventionally honourable, on the side of law, and sees the situation with male eyes.

Moral conflict. Weighed down and confused by her trust in authority, she loses faith in her own morality, and in her fitness to bring up her children. Bitterness. A mother in modern society, like certain insects, retires and dies once she has done her duty by propagating the race. Love of life, of home, of husband and children and family. Now and then, as women do, she shrugs off her thoughts. Suddenly anguish and fear return. Everything must be borne alone. The catastrophe aproaches, mercilessly, inevitably. Despair, conflict and defeat.

Notes made in Rome, 19 October 1878

Ibsen himself had made quite radical proposals (to indignant opposition) at the Scandinavian Club – for women to be employed as the club's librarian and that women should vote on all club matters. Yet, inviting as it may be to think of ***A Doll's House*** only as a defence of women within society, Ibsen made the following point in a famous speech to the Norwegian Society for Women's Rights:

I have been more of a poet and less of a social philosopher than people generally tend to suppose. I . . . must disclaim the honour of having consciously worked for women's rights . . . To me it has been a question of human rights . . . Of course it is incidentally desirable to solve the problems of women; but that has not been my whole object. My task has been the portrayal of human beings.

26 May 1898

Above all Ibsen wanted his plays to make us look at ourselves. His writing is provocative, revolutionary, controversial – and intentionally so:

My plays make people uncomfortable because when they see them they have to think, and most people want to be effortlessly entertained, not to be told unpleasant truths . . . People who are afraid of being alone with themselves, thinking about themselves, go to the theatre as they go to the beach or to parties – they go to be amused. But I find that people's eyes can be opened as well from the stage as from a pulpit.

Introduction

> *Anyone who wishes to understand me fully must know Norway. The spectacular but severe landscape which people have around them in the north, and the lonely, shut-off life – the houses often lie miles from each other – force them not to bother about other people, but only their own concerns, so that they become reflective and serious, they brood and doubt and often despair. In Norway every second man is a philosopher. And those dark winters, with the thick mists outside – ah, they long for the sun!*
>
> In conversation, quoted 27 October 1902

Henrik Ibsen was born on 20 March 1828 in the small town of Skien on the east coast of Norway, the second and eldest surviving of six children. His mother had a great interest in the theatre and arts in general; his father was a prosperous merchant who ran the local general store and a large schnapps distillery.

In 1834 the Ibsen family suffered a dramatic reversal of fortune when the authorities closed the distillery and Ibsen's father was made all but bankrupt. The family moved from its large town residence to a small country house at Venstøp, just outside Skien, suffering financial and social ruin. Also during Ibsen's childhood there were rumours that his real father was a friend of his mother's. Unsubstantiated though they were, and with evidence to the contrary, these rumours nevertheless left their mark. Interestingly, although Ibsen's drama is not overtly autobiographical, themes of financial loss, social standing, inheritance and legitimacy are explored throughout his plays.

At fifteen, Ibsen left school to work as an apothecary's apprentice in the coastal town of Grimstad, painting, writing and reading avidly during rare spare time. In 1846 he fathered an illegitimate son by the older maid of the house in which he worked and stayed.

For the next two years he studied hard at night for university, began to write poetry seriously and became deeply affected by the enormous political changes in Europe from the many uprisings in 1848 across the continent. Reflecting his concerns that Republicanism should be the only effective form of government, his unsuccessful first play ***Cataline*** (1849), which was set in ancient Rome, centred on political disillusionment.

In 1850 Ibsen went to the university in Christiania (now Oslo). His poetry began being published, he wrote a second play: ***The Warrior's Barrow***, and he became involved with a student magazine, a new independent literary and political paper, and a radical newspaper. Instead of completing university, in 1851 Ibsen accepted an invitation to assist as dramatic author at the newly-formed National Theatre at Bergen, staying for six years in antiquated theatrical conditions and in comparative poverty, directing, designing costumes and writing mostly historical verse plays with more failure than success: ***St John's Night, Lady Inger of Østraat, The Feast at Solhaug*** and ***Olaf Llijekrans***.

Dispirited, Ibsen agreed a contract as artistic director and stage instructor with the Norwegian Theatre at Christiania which, having fed audiences on French farces or Danish vaudeville, was looking for new drama; influenced by old Icelandic sagas, Ibsen wrote ***The Vikings at Helgeland***. Its first night, in November 1858, was successful but it failed to attract audiences much to the disappointment of Ibsen who had recently married and whose only son of the marriage, Sigurd, was born in the following year.

Growing increasingly depressed with his new post and with Norway itself, Ibsen found himself unable to write and when he finally managed another play – ***Love's Comedy*** in 1862 – it was rejected by the theatre which itself became bankrupt. He was sacked, blamed quite unfairly in some quarters for the financial failure but managed to secure a part-time position as literary adviser to the same theatre following its reorganisation. His new play – ***The Pretenders*** – achieved some success.

The turning point came in 1864 when Ibsen left Norway to settle in Rome. Personal despair about Norwegian theatres and politics, the hostility with which his plays were received, together with the aid of a grant, led to what was to become a self-imposed, almost total exile to central Europe for the next twenty-seven years. It was to be a revelation for him: the sun, the beauty, the artistry, and the literature. During this period abroad Ibsen wrote his greatest drama starting with the verse plays ***Brand*** and ***Peer Gynt*** in 1865 and 1867 – successful in the published form but not staged for some years, and each forerunners of his more mature work. In ***Brand***, the eponymous hero's mission of the 'will' is continued by Gregers Werle in ***The Wild Duck*** in his destructive 'claims of the ideal'. When the Provost tells Brand:

The surest way to destroy a man
Is to turn him into an individual

Act 5

the redeeming features of Relling's 'life-illusion' become clear echoes of the same sentiment. In contrast, something of the character of Peer Gynt – as the epitome of compromise, laziness, lies, avoidance of true relationships – can be seen in Hialmar Ekdal, amongst other characters.

Ibsen moved to writing in prose – ***The League of Youth*** and his last historical play ***Emperor and Galilean***. His most fruitful period then began with ***The Pillars of Society*** in 1877, but it was Ibsen's next play, ***A Doll's House*** in 1879, which established him as the innovator of modern drama. ***Ghosts*** followed in 1881, and ***An Enemy of the People*** in 1882 – a play concerning the dilemma faced when the main character discovers contamination at the baths in a spa town which threatens to destroy the town's livelihood. Then came ***The Wild Duck*** (1884), ***Rosmersholm*** (1886), ***The Lady from the Sea*** (1888) and ***Hedda Gabler*** (1890). Many of these 'middle period' Ibsen plays broke the barriers of convention of what was then thought permissable on the stage, with their portrayals of family relationships, marriage, sexual tensions, venereal disease, illegitimacy and the human psyche.

Upon returning permanently to Norway in 1891, Ibsen wrote his four last plays: ***The Master Builder*** in 1892 (considered to be based on

Ibsen's own infatuation with the eighteen-year-old Emilie Bardach, whilst on holiday in 1889), ***Little Eyolf*** (1894), ***John Gabriel Borkman*** (1896) and ***When We Dead Awaken*** (1899). These last plays are considered to form an epilogue to Ibsen's writing, with three of them concerned with an uplifting spiritual journey followed by a physical journey towards death. Ibsen's own death came in 1906 following a serious stroke which had left him severely disabled.

Critical responses to the three plays

Ibsen's influence as a dramatist cannot be underestimated, and productions of his plays are now plentiful; yet at the time of publication or performance they provoked violent reactions. Studying such criticism helps to understand something of the playwright and his society.

As was common practice, Ibsen's plays were published in book form before staging; in each case readers, audiences and critics across Europe were enormously divided in their views. There is no doubt, however, that Ibsen changed the face of European drama with his plots, subject matter, characterisation and themes. Playwrights such as George Bernard Shaw and Arthur Miller have paid homage to his influence in their own writing and many other twentieth-century dramatists owe much to the frontiers crossed and devices used by him.

In England Ibsen was lionised, against the bulk of society's opinions, by eminent literary men – Edmund Gosse, George Bernard Shaw and William Archer. Gosse aroused the interest of a wider reading public with great praise for Ibsen in prominent periodicals; apart from reviewing many of the plays, Shaw delivered an influential lecture, later expanded into a book in 1891: ***The Quintessence of Ibsenism***. Archer, who had met Ibsen in Rome in 1881, not only translated and reviewed many of the plays but ensured their production. Such good fortune for Ibsen, however, was not always in evidence from all circles!

The publication of ***The Wild Duck*** on 11 November 1884 and its première in Bergen were met with bewilderment. When first staged in London on 4 May 1894 by the Independent Theatre Society, critics received it with a degree of scorn:

> *The poor* **Wild Duck** *was, as epicures would say, a trifle fishy... There is no need to enter into the details of so commonplace and suburban a story. In essence it is trivial... To call such an eccentricity as this a masterpiece, to classify it at all as dramatic literature... is to insult dramatic literature and outrage common sense.*
>
> ***Daily Telegraph***, 18 May 1897

By contrast Bernard Shaw, in an article headed 'Ibsen Triumphant', wrote:

> *Where shall I find an epithet magnificent enough for* **The Wild Duck**! *To sit there getting deeper and deeper into your own life all the time; until you forget you are in a theatre; to look on with horror and pity at a profound tragedy, shaking with laughter all the time at an irresistable comedy; to go out, not from a diversion, but from an experiment deeper than real life ever brings to most men, or often brings to any man: that is what* **The Wild Duck** *was like last Monday...*
>
> ***The Saturday Review***, 22 May 1897

Still, controversy surrounding ***The Wild Duck*** was mild compared with the utter furore at the publication of ***Ghosts*** on 13 December 1881, causing Ibsen's faithful publisher to write:

> *As you will know from the reviews,* **Ghosts** *has caused a great sensation and has been the literary event of the winter, like* **A Doll's House** *two years ago. This is only as one would expect. But, amazingly, there ensued almost at once great indignation at the circumstances which are portrayed in* **Ghosts** *and which people wish at all costs not to have as family literature...*
>
> 10 January 1882

Bookshops had to return copies to the publisher due to lack of sales, theatres in Scandinavia refused to stage the play, it was banned in Germany and there were petitions in London to have the play censored and banned. One amusing anecdote by the Danish novelist

Herman Bang tells of students at a production of **A Doll's House** seen throughout the performance secretly reading copies of **Ghosts** as they dared not read it at home!

Ghosts eventually was premièred in Chicago, America, on 20 May 1882 and had its London opening on 8 April 1891. William Archer noted the choicest comments:

> *An open drain; a loathsome sore unbandaged; a dirty act done publicly ... candid foulness ... offensive cynicism ... gross, almost putrid indecorum ... (leading article of* **The Daily Telegraph***). Unutterably offensive.... prosecution under Lord Campbell's Act ... abominable piece ... scandalous ... (***The Standard***). Morbid, unhealthy, unwholesome and disgusting story ... a piece to bring the stage into disrepute and dishonour with every right-thinking man and woman ... (***Lloyd's***). As foul and filthy a concoction as has ever been allowed to disgrace the boards of the English theatre ... (***Era***)*
>
> **Pall Mall Gazette**, 8 April 1891

On the other hand, the critic A. B. Walkey, with great gusto, hailed the play as a revolutionary masterpiece, coining the phrase 'Drama of revolt':

> *Well, the awful, the unspeakable thing has happened. The 'nameless horror' has been – perpetuated – yes, really and truly seen ... Hold tight! Don't faint! Ibsen's* **Ghosts** *was played last night on the boards of a London theatre. Shall I get you a glass of water?...* **Ghosts** *actually played; and yet we are all still alive and (some of us) kicking! ... What! Do these people really find nothing in* **Ghosts** *but a mere hospital ward play? Is it really for them nothing but a painful study of disease? Have they no eyes for what stares them in the face: the plain and simple fact that* **Ghosts** *is a great spiritual drama? Like nearly all other great masterpieces of the stage, it is a drama of revolt – the revolt of the 'joy of life' against the gloom of hide-bound conventional morality, the revolt of natural man and woman, against the law-made, law-bound puppet, the revolt of the individual against the oppression of social prejudice ...*
>
> **The Star**, 14 March 1891

A Doll's House, the first of Ibsen's plays to cause a public sensation, was published on 4 December 1879 with a certain amount of success. Its première in the same month at the Royal Theatre Copenhagen attracted the following comments:

> *It is long since any new play was awaited with such excitement, and even longer since a new play brought so much that is original to the stage, but it is beyond memory since a play so simple in its action and so everyday in its dress made such an impression of artistic mastery...*
>
> Erich Bogh, **Folkets Avis**

It took ten years for the play to reach London in its original state because of the shock caused by the final stage direction. Ibsen even had to send a draft of an altered version as an emergency to Germany to prevent another writer changing the original ending. In this alternative, Nora, forced by her husband to look at her sleeping children, remains in the family home in great despair. In a letter to a Danish newspaper on 17 February 1870 Ibsen voiced his anger:

> *I myself described this alteration to my translator as a 'barbaric outrage' against the play. If it is used, it is therefore completely against my wishes.*

The first London production, on 7 June 1889 at the Novelty Theatre in Kingsway, provoked comments such as:

> *It would be a misfortune were such a morbid and unwholesome play to gain the favour of the public* (**The Standard**)*... unnatural, immoral...* (**The People**) *The works of the Norwegian playwright are not suitable for dramatic representation – at any rate on the English stage...* (**St James's Gazette**).

The criticism, which attacked the fact that a wife decides to leave her husband and children, was in turn attacked by the likes of Bernard Shaw and William Archer, whose translation was used in the first unabridged version of the play in England.

Structure of the plays

On face value these three plays are social dramas about family life, set in the home, with a balanced structure of the 'well-made' play of three or five acts. In effect, however, Ibsen presents audiences with a time-bomb waiting to explode by employing particular dramatic devices.

Plot and sub-plot

Ibsen juxtaposes main and sub-plots in the same way as he interlocks main and secondary characters to perfection. By employing relatively few characters, he takes a microcosm of society (the family) to explore human lives, desires, fears and secrets.

In each play the characters are found to be more linked by their pasts than at first imagined:

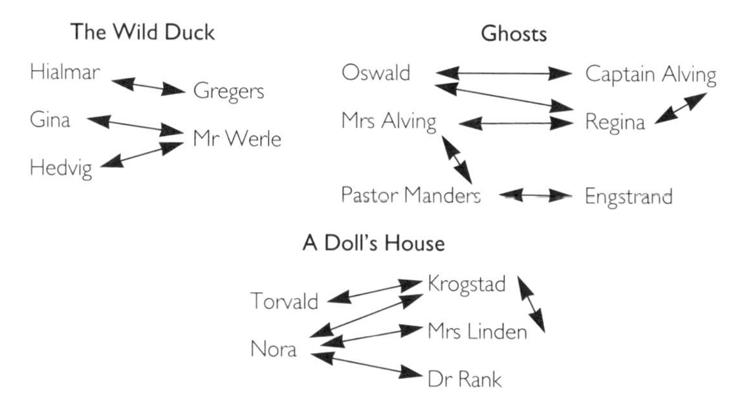

Ibsen also skilfully uses the device of suspense to sustain the tension and keep the audience wondering:

- what will happen after the private, off-stage talk between Hialmar and Gregers?
- what will happen when Hedvig goes into the garret with the shotgun?
- how will matters be resolved once Pastor Manders knows the truth about Regina and Oswald?
- will Mrs Alving reveal the truth about her husband to Oswald?

- how will Nora get the money she needs?
- will Nora be able to keep Torvald away from the letter box?

Stage directions are essential as well. As you read the plays look out for who does what – even the minutest detail – and who is on or off stage when something is said or done.

The past

Present action is revealed in terms of the past, very much like a lot of Ancient Greek drama in which the unravelling on stage of past events and relationships provides much of the action. Snippets of information about the past are presented to involve the audience from the opening moments of each play.

The past actions of Mr Werle underpin the entire action, lives and relationships of the characters, and the shocking consequences in ***The Wild Duck***; the 'ghost' of Captain Alving, deceased ten years before the action of the play, casts a tragic shadow over all the characters in ***Ghosts***; in ***A Doll's House***, Nora's past actions, again well before the present stage action, lead to blackmail, gripping tension and a climatic final stage direction which shocked Europe.

Ibsen manages to reveal the past very slowly so that when, even by the end of Act 1, information and facts emerge, the stage action then becomes relentless. Very often information about the past is given as early on as the opening lines.

Dramatic irony

The construction of each play works not only because of actual action on the stage, but also because of Ibsen's constant use of irony. This is the device whereby something is known by some characters (and the audience) but not others, or where something is said in which the significance is understood only by certain characters (and the audience) at the expense of others. Dramatic irony becomes the gap between what is *thought* and what is *known* to be the case. This is what creates conflict and dramatic tension.

The plays make great use of irony as Ibsen strips away all illusions: the real extent to which Mr Werle has been at the centre of the Ekdal family in ***The Wild Duck***; the actual facts relating to Captain Alving's past and Oswald's true inheritance in ***Ghosts***; the consequences of Nora's past actions leading to the present dilemmas in ***A Doll's House***. In each case, the irony is used subtly until all characters are in full knowledge of everything.

As you read the plays, look in particular for this heavily used device to see how Ibsen constructs each act.

Contrast and conflicts

Each play has contrasting characters, for example:

The lazy self-deluded Hialmar	◄——►	Gregers, with his 'claims of the ideal'	(T.W.D.)
Mrs Alving, torn between love and duty	◄——►	The rigid code of conduct of Pastor Manders	(G)
Helmer's 'honour' and 'morality'	◄——►	Krogstad's expediency in the face of ruin	(A.D.H.)

Using the characters, Ibsen considers conflicts in different ways of life and explores various abstract concepts:

illusion	truth
'claims of the ideal'	'life-lies'
duty	'joy of life'
iron will	compromise
guilt	spiritual emancipation
ideas	action
marriage	relationships

Symbolism

A symbol is an object, token or sign which stands for something else. The titles of all three plays here are actual objects but are also used by Ibsen to represent something else: the wild duck in the play *is* an actual wounded duck, but it also symbolises Hedvig, Hialmar, and the whole family's idea of living an illusion. As the play progresses Ibsen makes the symbol of the wild duck work even harder in the overall effect of the plot.

Ghosts are constantly present for each character in ***Ghosts*** and the symbol is utilised in all parts of the action. With the symbolic title of ***A Doll's House***, Ibsen makes the audience wonder just whose doll's house the audience sees: Nora's or Torvald's. Even this symbol has its complexities in the ways it is used by Ibsen.

Themes

A theme is an idea which runs through a piece of work. As you read the plays think about the following themes which are central to all three:

marriage	legitimacy
parents and children	light and dark
money	honour
duty	truth and illusion
social standing	the individual society

Some of the characters help to make these themes explicit:

> *If I could choose, I should like best to be a clever dog... one that goes to the bottom after wild ducks when they dive and bite themselves fast in tangle and seaweed, down among the ooze.*
>
> Gregers Werle, ***The Wild Duck***, Act 2, pages 45–46

> *Rob the average man of his life-illusion, and you rob him of his happiness at the same time.*
>
> Relling, ***The Wild Duck***, Act 5, page 105

Do not despise ideals, Mrs Alving; they will avenge themselves cruelly.

Pastor Manders, ***Ghosts***, Act 2, page 161

I almost think we're all of us Ghosts... It's not only what we have inherited from our father and mother that 'walks' in us. It's all sorts of dead ideas, and lifeless old beliefs, and so forth. They have no vitality, but they cling to us all the same, and we can't get rid of them... And then we are... so pitifully afraid of the light.

Mrs Alving, ***Ghosts***, Act 2, page 163

Mrs. Helmer, you evidently do not realise what you have been guilty of. But I can assure you it was nothing more and nothing worse that made me an outcast from society.

Krogstad, **A Doll's House**, Act 1, page 234

... in such an atmosphere of lies home life is contaminated in every fibre. Every breath the children draw contains some germ of evil.

Helmer, **A Doll's House**, Act 1, page 238

HELMER: *...But no man sacrifices his honour, even for one he loves.*

NORA: *Millions of women have done so.*

A Doll's House, Act 3, page 290

Reading log

One of the easiest ways of keeping track of your reading is to keep a log book. This can be any exercise book or folder that you have to hand, but make sure you reserve it exclusively for reflecting on your reading, both at home and in school/college.

As you read the plays, stop from time to time and think back over what you have read.

- Is there anything that puzzles you? Note down some questions that you might want to research, discuss with your friends or ask a teacher. Also note any quotations which strike you as important or memorable.
- Does your reading remind you of anything else you have read, heard or seen on TV or the cinema? Jot down what it is and where the similarities lie.
- Have you had any experiences similar to those occurring in the plays? Do you find yourself identifying closely with one or more of the characters? Record this as accurately as you can.
- Do you find yourself really liking, or really loathing, any of the characters? What is it about them that makes you feel so strongly? Make notes that you can add to.
- Can you picture the locations and settings? Draw maps, plans, diagrams, drawings, in fact any doodle that helps you make sense of these things.
- Now and again try to predict what will happen next in the plot. Use what you already know of the playwright and the characters to help you do this. Later, record how close you were and whether you were surprised at the outcome.
- Write down any feelings that you have about the plays. Your reading log should help you to make sense of your own ideas alongside those of the playwright.

The Wild Duck

Gina (Nicola McAuliffe) and Hialmar (Alex Jennings): The Phoenix Theatre, 1990

Characters

WERLE, *a merchant, manufacturer, etc.*
GREGERS WERLE, *his son*
OLD EKDAL
HIALMAR EKDAL, *his son, a photographer*
GINA EKDAL, *Hialmar's wife*
HEDVIG, *their daughter, fourteen years old*
MRS. SÖRBY, *Werle's housekeeper*
RELLING, *a doctor*
MOLVIK, *ex-student of theology*
GRÅBERG, *Werle's bookkeeper*
PETTERSEN, *Werle's servant*
JENSEN, *a hired waiter*
A FLABBY GENTLEMAN
A THIN-HAIRED GENTLEMAN
A SHORT-SIGHTED GENTLEMAN
Six other gentlemen, dinner-guests at Werle's
Several hired waiters

The first act passes in Werle's house, the four following acts at Hialmar Ekdal's.

(Pronunciation: Gregers Werle = *Grayghers Verlë*; Hialmar Ekdal = *Yalmer Aykdal*; Gina = *Gheena*; Gråberg = *Groberg*; Jensen = *Yensen)*

Act One

At Werle's house. A richly and comfortably furnished study; bookcases and upholstered furniture; a writing-table, with papers and documents, in the centre of the room; lighted lamps with green shades casting a dim light. In the background, open folding doors with curtains drawn back. Within is seen a large and elegant room brilliantly lighted with lamps and branching candlesticks. In front, on the right (in the study), a small baize door leads into Werle's office. On the left, in front, a fireplace with a glowing coal fire, and farther back a folding door leading into the dining-room.

Werle's servant, Pettersen, in livery, and Jensen, the hired waiter, in black, are putting the study in order. In the large room, two or three other hired waiters are moving about arranging things and lighting more candles. From the dining-room the hum of conversation and laughter of many voices are heard; a glass is tapped with a knife; silence follows, and a toast is proposed; shouts of 'Bravo!' and then again a buzz of conversation.

PETTERSEN (*lights a lamp on the chimney-piece and sets a shade over it*): Just listen, Jensen; now the old man's on his legs proposing Mrs. Sörby's health in a long speech.

JENSEN (*pushing forward an armchair*): Is it true, what people say, that there's something between them?

PETTERSEN: Lord knows.

JENSEN: I'm told he's been a lively customer in his day.

PETTERSEN: May be.

JENSEN: It's in honour of his son that he's giving this dinner-party, they say.

PETTERSEN: Yes. His son came home yesterday.

JENSEN: I never knew till now that Mr. Werle had a son.

PETTERSEN: Oh yes, he has a son. But he's always up at the Höidal works. He's never once come to town all the years I've been in service here.

A WAITER (*in the doorway of the other room*): Pettersen, here's an old fellow wanting –

PETTERSEN: (*mutters*): The devil – who's this now?

(*Old Ekdal appears from the right, in the inner room. He is dressed in a threadbare overcoat with a high collar; he wears woollen mittens, and carries in his hand a stick and a fur cap. Under his arm, a brown-paper parcel. Dirty red-brown wig and small grey moustache.*)

PETTERSEN (*goes toward him*): Good Lord – what do *you* want here?

EKDAL (*at the door*): Must get into the office, Pettersen.

PETTERSEN: The office was closed an hour ago, and –

EKDAL: So they told me at the door. But Gråberg's in there still. Let me slip in this way, Pettersen; there's a good fellow. (*Points towards the baize door.*) I've been in this way before.

PETTERSEN: Well, you may pass. (*Opens the door.*) But mind you go out again the proper way, for we've got company.

EKDAL: I know – h'm. Thanks, Pettersen, good old friend! Thanks! (*Mutters softly.*) Ass!

(*He goes into the office; Pettersen shuts the door after him.*)

JENSEN: Is he one of the office people?

PETTERSEN: No, he's only an outsider that does odd jobs of copying. But he's been a gentleman in his time, has old Ekdal.

JENSEN: You can see he's been through a lot.

PETTERSEN: Yes; he was a lieutenant, you know.

JENSEN: The devil he was!

PETTERSEN: No mistake about it. But afterwards he went into the timber trade or something of that sort. They say he once played Mr. Werle a very nasty trick. They were in partnership at the Höidal works at the time. Oh, I know old Ekdal well, I do. Many's the glass of bitters and bottle of ale we two have drunk at Madam Eriksen's.

JENSEN: He can't have much to stand treat with.

PETTERSEN: Why, bless you, Jensen, it's me that stands treat. You see I always think one must be a bit civil to folks that have seen better days.

JENSEN: Did he go bankrupt, then?

PETTERSEN: No, worse than that. He went to prison.

JENSEN: To prison!

PETTERSEN: Or perhaps it was the Penitentiary – (*listens*). Hush, they're leaving the table.

(*The dining-room door is thrown open from inside, by a couple of waiters. Mrs. Sörby comes out conversing with two gentlemen. Gradually the whole company follows, amongst them Werle. Last come Hialmar Ekdal and Gregers Werle.*)

MRS. SÖRBY (*in passing, to the servant*): Pettersen, we'll have the coffee in the music-room.

PETTERSEN: Very well, Mrs. Sörby.

(*She goes with the two gentlemen into the inner room, and then out to the right. Pettersen and Jensen go out the same way.*)

A FLABBY GENTLEMAN (*to a Thin-haired Gentleman*): Whew! What a dinner! – It was a stiff bit of work!

THE THIN HAIRED GENTLEMAN: Oh, with a little goodwill one can get through an astonishing lot in three hours.

THE FLABBY GENTLEMAN: Yes, but afterwards, afterwards, my dear Chamberlain!

A THIRD GENTLEMAN: I hear the coffee and maraschino are to be served in the music-room.

THE FLABBY GENTLEMAN: Bravo! Perhaps Mrs. Sörby will play us something.

THE THIN-HAIRED GENTLEMAN (*in a low voice*): If only Mrs. Sörby doesn't play us a tune we don't like!

THE FLABBY GENTLEMAN: Oh no, not she! Bertha will never turn against her old friends.

(*They laugh and pass into the inner room.*)

WERLE (*in a low voice, dejectedly*): I don't think anybody noticed it, Gregers.

GREGERS (*look at him*): Noticed what?

WERLE: Didn't you notice it either?

GREGERS: Why, what do you mean?

WERLE: We were thirteen at table.

GREGERS: Indeed? Were there thirteen of us?

WERLE (*glances towards Hialmar Ekdal*): Twelve is our ordinary party. (*To the others.*) This way, gentlemen!

(*Werle and the others, all except Hialmar and Gregers, go out by the back to the right.*)

HIALMAR (*who has overheard the conversation*): You oughtn't to have invited me, Gregers.

GREGERS: What! Not ask my best and only friend to a party supposed to be in my honour – !

HIALMAR: But I don't think your father likes it. You see I'm quite outside his set.

GREGERS: So I hear. But I wanted to see you and talk with you, for I certainly shan't be staying long. Ah, we two old schoolfellows have drifted far apart from each other. It must be sixteen or seventeen years since we met.

HIALMAR: Is it so long?

GREGERS: It is indeed. Well, how goes it with you? You look well. You've grown stout and almost portly.

HIALMAR: H'm, 'portly' you can scarcely call it; but I daresay I look a little more of a man than I did.

GREGERS: Yes, you do; your outer man's in first-rate condition.

HIALMAR: Ah, but the inner man! That's another matter, I can tell you! Of course you know of the terrible catastrophe that has befallen me and mine since we last met.

GREGERS (*more softly*): How is your father getting on now?

HIALMAR: Don't let's talk of it, old fellow. Of course my poor unhappy father lives with me. You see he hasn't another soul in the world to care for him. But you can understand that this is a miserable subject for me. Tell me how you've been getting on up at the works.

GREGERS: I've had a delightfully lonely time of it; plenty of leisure to reflect on things in general. Come over here; let's make ourselves comfortable.

(*He seats himself in an armchair by the fire and pulls Hialmar down into another alongside of it.*)

HIALMAR (*sentimentally*): After all, Gregers, I thank you for inviting me to your father's table; for I take it as a sign that you've got over your feeling against me.

GREGERS (*surprised*): How could you imagine I had any feeling against you?

HIALMAR: You had at first, you know.

GREGERS: How at fiirst?

HIALMAR: After the great misfortune. It was natural enough that you should. Your father was within an ace of being drawn into that – well, that terrible business.

GREGERS: Why should that give me any feeling against you? Who put that into your head?

HIALMAR: I know it did, Gregers; your father told me so himself.

GREGERS (*starts*): My father! Oh indeed. H'm – was that why you never let me hear from you – not a single word.

HIALMAR: Yes.

GREGERS: Not even when you took to photography?

HIALMAR: Your father said I'd better not write you about anything.

GREGERS (*looking straight before him*): Well, well, perhaps he was right. But tell me now, Hialmar: are you pretty well satisfied with your present position?

HIALMAR (*with a little sigh*): Oh yes, I am; I've really no cause to complain. At first, you know, I felt it a little strange. It was such a totally new state of things for me. But of course my whole circumstances were totally changed. Father's utter, irretrievable ruin – the shame and disgrace of it, Gregers –

GREGERS (*affected*): Yes, yes; I understand.

HIALMAR: I couldn't think of remaining at college; there wasn't a shilling to spare; on the contrary, there were debts; principally to your father, I believe –

GREGERS: H'm –

HIALMAR: Well, you see, I thought it best to break once for all with my old surroundings and associations. It was your father that specially urged me to it; and since he interested himself so much in me –

GREGERS: Father did?

HIALMAR: Yes, you knew that, didn't you? Where do you suppose I got the money to learn photography, and to furnish a studio, and make a start? All that costs a pretty penny, I can tell you.

GREGERS: And my father provided the money?

HIALMAR: Yes, my dear fellow, didn't you know? I understood him to say he had written to you about it.

GREGERS: Not a word about *his* part in the business. He must have forgotten it. Our correspondence has always been purely a business one. So it was my father that – !

HIALMAR: Yes, certainly. He didn't wish it to be generally known; but he it was. And of course it was he too that put me in a position to marry. Don't you – don't you know about that either?

GREGERS: No, I haven't heard a word of it. (*Shakes him by the arm.*) But, my dear Hialmar, I can't tell you what pleasure all this gives me – and regret too. I've perhaps done my father injustice after all – in some things. This proves that there's some good in his nature. It shows a sort of compunction –

HIALMAR: Compunction – ?

GREGERS: Yes, or whatever you like to call it. Oh, I can't tell you how glad I am to hear this of father. – And so you're married, Hialmar! That's farther than I shall ever get. Well, I hope you're happy in your married life?

HIALMAR: Yes, thoroughly happy. She's as good a wife as a man could wish for. And she's by no means without education.

GREGERS (*rather surprised*): No, surely not.

HIALMAR: You see, life is itself an education. Her daily intercourse with me – And then we know one or two rather remarkable men, who come a good deal about us. I assure you you'd hardly know Gina again.

GREGERS: Gina?

HIALMAR: Yes; have you forgotten that her name's Gina?

GREGERS: Whose name? I really don't know –

HIALMAR: Don't you remember that she used to be in service here?

GREGERS (*looks at him*): Is it Gina Hansen – ?

HIALMAR: Yes, of course it's Gina Hansen.

GREGERS: – who kept house for us during the last year of my mother's illness?

HIALMAR: Yes, exactly. But, my dear friend, I'm quite sure your father wrote you that I was married.

GREGERS (*who has risen*): Oh yes, he mentioned it; but not that – (*walking about the room*). Stay – perhaps after all – now that I think of it. My father always writes such short letters. (*Half seats himself on the arm of the chair.*) Now, tell me, Hialmar – this interests me – how did you come to know Gina – your wife?

HIALMAR: The simplest thing in the world. Gina didn't stay here long; everything was so much upset at that time, with your mother's illness and so forth, that Gina wasn't equal to it all, and so she gave notice and left. That was the year before your mother died – or perhaps it was the same year.

GREGERS: It was the same year. I was up at the works then. But afterwards?

HIALMAR: Then Gina lived for a year at home with her mother, a Madam Hansen, an excellent hardworking woman, who kept a little eating-house. She had a room to let too; a very pretty, comfortable room.

GREGERS: And I suppose you were lucky enough to secure it?

HIALMAR: Yes; it was your father that recommended it to me. So you see it was there I really came to know Gina.

GREGERS: And then you got engaged?

HIALMAR: Yes. It doesn't take young people long to fall in love –; h'm –

GREGERS (*gets up and walks about a little*): Tell me, was it after your engagement – was it then that my father – I mean was it then that you began to take up photography?

HIALMAR: Yes, precisely. I wanted to get on and be able to set up house as soon as possible; and your father and I agreed that this photography business was the readiest way. Gina thought so too. Oh, and there was another thing in its favour, you know: it happened, luckily, that Gina had learnt to retouch.

GREGERS: That chimed in marvellously.

HIALMAR (*pleased, rises*): Yes, didn't it? Quite marvellously, you know!

GREGERS: Yes, no doubt. My father seems to have been almost a kind of providence for you.

HIALMAR (*with emotion*): He didn't forsake his old friend's son in the hour of his need. He has a good heart, you see.

MRS. SÖRBY (*enters, arm-in-arm with Werle*): Nonsense, my dear Mr. Werle; you mustn't stop there any longer staring at the lights. It's not good for you.

WERLE (*lets go her arm and passes his hand over his eyes*): I believe you're right.

(*Pettersen and Jensen come round with refreshment trays.*)

MRS. SÖRBY: (*to the guests in the other room*): This way, gentlemen; if any one wants a glass of punch, he must be so good as to come in here.

THE FLABBY GENTLEMAN (*comes up to Mrs. Sörby*): Surely it isn't possible that you've suspended our cherished tobacco-privileges?

MRS. SÖRBY: Yes. No smoking in Mr. Werle's quarters, Chamberlain.

THE THIN-HAIRED GENTLEMAN: When did you enact these stringent amendments on the cigar law, Mrs. Sörby?

MRS. SÖRBY: After the last dinner, Chamberlain, when certain persons permitted themselves to overstep the mark.

THE THIN-HAIRED GENTLEMAN: And may one never overstep the mark a little bit, Madam Bertha? Not the least little bit?

MRS. SÖRBY: Not in any way, Mr. Balle.

(*Most of the guests have assembled in the study; servants hand round glasses of punch.*)

WERLE (*to Hialmar, who is standing beside a table*): What are you studying there, Ekdal?

HIALMAR: Only an album, Mr. Werle.

THE THIN-HAIRED GENTLEMAN (*who is wandering about*): Ah, photographs! They're quite in your line of course.

THE FLABBY GENTLEMAN (*in an armchair*): Haven't you brought any of your own with you?

HIALMAR: No, I haven't.

THE FLABBY GENTLEMAN: You ought to have; looking at pictures is good for the digestion.

THE THIN-HAIRED GENTLEMAN: And it contributes to the entertainment, you know.

THE SHORT-SIGHTED GENTLEMAN: And all contributions are thankfully received.

MRS. SÖRBY: The Chamberlains mean that when one is invited out one should do something to earn one's dinner, Mr. Ekdal.

THE FLABBY GENTLEMAN: Where one dines so well, that duty should be a pleasure.

THE THIN-HAIRED GENTLEMAN: And of course when it's a question of the struggle for life –

MRS. SÖRBY: I quite agree with you!

(*They continue the conversation, with laughter and joking.*)

GREGERS (*softly*): You must join in, Hialmar.

HIALMAR (*writhing*): What am I to talk about?

THE FLABBY GENTLEMAN: Don't you think, Mr. Werle, that Tokay may be considered a tolerably safe wine – from the medical point of view, I mean?

WERLE (*by the fire*): I can answer for the Tokay you had today, at any rate; it's of one of the very finest seasons. Of course you would notice that.

THE FLABBY GENTLEMAN: Yes, it had a remarkably delicate flavour.

HIALMAR (*shyly*): Is there any difference in the seasons?

THE FLABBY GENTLEMAN (*laughs*): Come! That's good!

WERLE (*smiles*): It really doesn't pay to set fine wine before you.

THE THIN-HAIRED GENTLEMAN: Tokay is like photographs, Mr. Ekdal; it must have sunshine. Isn't that so?

MRS. SÖRBY: And it's exactly the same with Chamberlains – they, too, need sunshine, as the saying is.

THE THIN-HAIRED GENTLEMAN: Oh fie! That's a very stale sarcasm!

THE SHORT-SIGHTED GENTLEMAN: Mrs. Sörby is coming out.

THE FLABBY GENTLEMAN: – and at our expense. (*Threatening her.*) Oh, Madam Bertha, Madam Bertha!

MRS. SÖRBY: Yes, and there's not the least doubt that the seasons differ greatly. The old vintages are the finest.

THE SHORT-SIGHTED GENTLEMAN: Do you reckon me amongst the old?

MRS. SÖRBY: Oh, far from it.

THE THIN-HAIRED GENTLEMAN: There now! But *me*, dear Mrs. Sörby – ?

THE FLABBY GENTLEMAN: Yes, and me? What vintage do you think we belong to?

MRS. SÖRBY: I think you belong to the sweet vintages, gentlemen.

(*She sips a glass of punch. The gentlemen laugh and flirt with her.*)

WERLE: Mrs. Sörby can always find a loop-hole – when she wants to. Fill your glasses, gentlemen! Pettersen, will you attend to – ! Gregers, suppose we have a glass together. (*Gregers does not move.*) Won't you join us, Ekdal? I couldn't find a chance of drinking with you at table.

(*Gråberg, the bookkeeper, looks in through the baize door.*)

GRÅBERG: Excuse me, sir, but I can't get out.

WERLE: Have you been locked in again?

GRÅBERG: Yes, and Flakstad had gone away with the keys.

WERLE: Well, you can pass out this way.

GRÅBERG: But there's some one else –

WERLE: All right; come through, both of you. Don't be afraid.

(*Gråberg and Old Ekdal come out of the office.*)

WERLE (*involuntarily*): Ugh! Pah!

(*The laughter and talk among the guests cease. Hialmar shrinks back at the sight of his father, puts down his glass, and turns towards the fireplace.*)

EKDAL (*does not look up, but makes little bows to both sides as he passes, murmuring*): Beg pardon, come the wrong way. Door locked – door locked. Beg pardon.

(*He and Gråberg go out by the back, to the right.*)

WERLE (*between his teeth*): Confound that Gråberg!

GREGERS (*open-mouthed and staring, to Hialmar*): Why surely that wasn't – !

THE FLABBY GENTLEMAN: What's that? Who was it?

GREGERS: Oh, nobody; only the bookkeeper and some one with him.

THE SHORT-SIGHTED GENTLEMAN (*to Hialmar*): Did you know that man?

HIALMAR: I don't know – I didn't notice –

THE FLABBY GENTLEMAN: What the deuce is the matter?

(*He goes over to some others who are talking softly.*)

MRS. SÖRBY: (*whispers to the Servant*). Give him something outside; – something good, mind.

PETTERSEN (*nods*): I'll see to it. (*Goes out.*)

GREGERS (*softly and with emotion, to Hialmar*): So that was really he!

HIALMAR: Yes.

GREGERS: And yet you could stand there and deny that you knew him!

HIALMAR (*whispers vehemently*): But how could I –

GREGERS: – acknowledge your own father?

HIALMAR (*with pain*): Oh, if you were in my place –

(*The conversation amongst the guests, which has been carried on in a low tone, now swells into constrained boisterousness.*)

THE THIN-HAIRED GENTLEMAN (*approaching Hialmar and Gregers in a friendly manner*): Aha! Reviving old college memories, eh? Don't you smoke, Mr. Ekdal? Have a light? Oh, by-the-by, we mustn't –

HIALMAR: No, thank you, I won't –

THE FLABBY GENTLEMAN: Haven't you a nice little poem you could recite for us, Mr. Ekdal? You used to recite so charmingly.

HIALMAR: I'm sorry I can't remember anything.

THE FLABBY GENTLEMAN: Oh, that's a pity. Well, what shall we do, Balle?

(*Both gentlemen move away and pass into the other room.*)

HIALMAR (*gloomily*): I'm going, Gregers! When one has felt the crushing hand of Fate on one's head, you know – Say goodbye to your father for me.

GREGERS: Yes, yes. Are you going straight home?

HIALMAR: Yes. Why?

GREGERS: Oh, because I may perhaps look in on you later.

HIALMAR: No, you mustn't do that. You mustn't come to my home. Mine is a melancholy dwelling, Gregers; especially after a splendid banquet like this. We can always meet somewhere in the town.

MRS. SÖRBY (*who has approached softly*): Are you going, Ekdal?

HIALMAR: Yes.

MRS. SÖRBY: Remember me to Gina.

HIALMAR: Thanks.

MRS. SÖRBY: And say I'm coming up to see her one of these days.

HIALMAR: Yes, thank you. (*To Gregers.*) Stay here, I'll slip out unobserved.

(*He saunters away, then into the other room, and so out to the right.*)

MRS. SÖRBY (*softly to the servant, who has come back*): Well, did the old man get something to take with him?

PETTERSEN: Yes; I gave him a bottle of cognac.

MRS. SÖRBY: Oh, you might have thought of something better than that.

PETTERSEN: Oh no, Mrs. Sörby; cognac is what he likes best in the world.

THE FLABBY GENTLEMAN (*in the doorway, with a sheet of music in his hand*): Shall we have a little music, Mrs. Sörby?

MRS. SÖRBY: Yes, by all means, let us.

THE GUESTS: Bravo, bravo!

(*She goes with all the guests through the back room, out to the right. Gregers remains standing by the fire. Werle is looking for something on the writing-table, and appears to wish that Gregers would go; as Gregers does not move, Werle goes towards the door.*)

GREGERS: Father, won't you stop a moment?

WERLE (*stops*): What is it?

GREGERS: I must have a word with you.

WERLE: Can't it wait till we're alone?

GREGERS: No, it can't; for perhaps we'll never be alone together.

WERLE (*comes nearer*): What do you mean?

(*During the following, pianoforte music is heard from the distant music-room.*)

GREGERS: How has that family been allowed to go so miserably to the wall?

WERLE: I suppose you mean the Ekdals.

GREGERS: Yes, I mean the Ekdals. Lieutenant Ekdal and you once stood in such close relations.

WERLE: Unfortunately our relations were too close; that I have felt to my cost for many a year. It's thanks to him that I, yes *I*, have had a kind of slur cast upon my reputation.

GREGERS (*softly*): Are you sure that he alone was to blame?

WERLE: Who else do you suppose – ?

GREGERS: You and he acted together in that affair of the forests –

WERLE: But wasn't it Ekdal that drew up the map of the forest tracts – that fraudulent map? It was he who cut down timber illegally on Government ground. In fact, the whole management was in his hands. I was quite in the dark as to what Lieutenant Ekdal was doing.

GREGERS: Lieutenant Ekdal seems to have been in the dark himself as to what he was doing.

WERLE: That may be. But the fact remains that he was found guilty and I acquitted.

GREGERS: Yes, of course I know that nothing was proved against you.

WERLE: Acquittal is acquittal. Why do you rake up these old troubles that turned my hair grey before its time? Is that the sort of thing you've been going and brooding over all these years? I can assure you, Gregers, here in the town the story's been forgotten long ago – so far as I am concerned.

GREGERS: But that unhappy Ekdal family!

WERLE: What would you have had me do for the people? When Ekdal came out of prison he was a broken-down man, fit for nothing. There are people in the world who sink to the bottom the moment they get a couple of shot in their body, and never come to the surface again. You may take my word for it, Gregers, I've done all I could without positively exposing myself, and giving rise to all sorts of suspicion and gossip –

GREGERS: Suspicion – ? Oh, yes, I see.

WERLE: I've given Ekdal copying to do from the office, and I pay him far, far more for it than his work is worth –

GREGERS (*without looking at him*): H'm, I don't doubt that.

WERLE: You laugh? Perhaps you doubt me? Well, I certainly can't refer you to my books, for I never enter payments of that sort.

GREGERS (*smiles coldly*): No, there are certain payments it's best not to keep any account of.

WERLE (*starts*): What do you mean by that?

GREGERS (*mustering up courage*): Havc you entered what it cost you to have Hialmar Ekdal taught photography?

WERLE: I? How entered it?

GREGERS: I've learnt that it was you who paid for it. And I've learnt, too, that it was you who generously enabled him to make a start in life.

WERLE: Well, and yet you say I've done nothing for the Ekdals! I can assure you these people have cost me enough in all conscience.

GREGERS: Have you entered any of these expenses in your books?

WERLE: Why do you ask?

GREGERS: Oh, I have my reasons. Now tell me: when you interested yourself so warmly in your old friend's son – wasn't that just when he was going to get married?

WERLE: Why, how the deuce – after all these years, how can I – ?

GREGERS: You wrote me a letter about that time – a business letter, of course; and in a postscript you mentioned – quite briefly – that Hialmar Ekdal had married a Miss Hansen.

WERLE: Yes, that was quite right. That was her name.

GREGERS: But you didn't tell me that this Miss Hansen was Gina Hansen, our former housekeeper.

WERLE (*with a forced laugh of derision*): Well, upon my word, it didn't occur to me that you were so particularly interested in our former housekeeper.

GREGERS: No more I was. But (*lowers his voice*) there were others in this house who were particularly interested in her.

WERLE: What do you mean by that? (*Flaring up.*) You can't be alluding to me?

GREGERS (*softly but firmly*): Yes, I am alluding to you.

WERLE: And you dare – you presume to – ! How can he – that thankless hound – that photographer fellow – how dare he go making such insinuations?

GREGERS: Hialmar has never hinted a word of it. I don't believe he has the faintest suspicion of such a thing.

WERLE: Then where have you got it from? Who can have told you anything of the kind?

GREGERS: My poor unfortunate mother told me, and that the very last time I saw her.

WERLE: Your mother! I might have known as much! You and she – you always held together. It was she who first turned you against me.

GREGERS: No, it was all the suffering she had to go through, until she broke down and came to such a pitiful end.

WERLE: Oh, she had no suffering to go through; not more than most people, at all events. But there's no getting on with morbid, overstrained creatures. I've found that often enough. And so you could go and nurse such a suspicion – go and burrow into all sorts of old rumours and slanders against your own father! I must say, Gregers, I really think that at your age you might be doing something more useful.

GREGERS: Yes, it's high time.

WERLE: Then perhaps your mind would be easier than it seems to be now. What can be your object in remaining up at the works, year out and year in, drudging away like a common clerk, and not receiving a farthing more than the ordinary monthly wage? It's absolute folly.

GREGERS: Ah, if I were only sure of that.

WERLE: I understand you well enough. You want to be independent, and not beholden to me for anything. Now there just happens to be an opportunity for you to become independent, your own master in everything.

GREGERS: Indeed? In what way?

WERLE: When I wrote you insisting on your coming to town at once – h'm –

GREGERS: Yes, what do you really want me for? I've been waiting all day to know.

WERLE: I propose to offer you a partnership in the firm.

GREGERS: I! In your firm? As partner?

WERLE: Yes. It wouldn't involve our being constantly together. You could look after the business here, and I should move up to the works.

GREGERS: *You* would?

WERLE: Yes. You see I'm not so fit for work as I once was. I'm obliged to spare my eyes, Gregers; they've begun to be rather weak.

GREGERS: They've always been so.

WERLE: Not as they are now. And besides – circumstances might possibly make it desirable for me to live up there – for a time, at any rate.

GREGERS: I could never have imagined such a thing.

WERLE: Listen, Gregers: there are many things that form a barrier between us; but we're father and son after all. It seems to me we might manage to come to some sort of understanding with each other.

GREGERS: Outwardly, you mean, of course?

WERLE: Well, even that would be something. Think it over,

Gregers. Don't you think we might, eh?

GREGERS (*looking at him coldly*): There's something behind all this.

WERLE: How so?

GREGERS: You want to make use of me in some way.

WERLE: In such a close relationship as ours, each can always be useful to the other.

GREGERS: Yes, people say so.

WERLE: I want to have you at home with me for a time now. I'm a lonely man, Gregers; I've always felt lonely, all my life through; but most of all now that I'm getting up in years. I need to have somebody beside me –

GREGERS: You have Mrs. Sörby.

WERLE: Yes, I have her; and she has become, so to speak, almost indispensable to me. She is bright and even-tempered; she enlivens the house; and that's such a great thing for me.

GREGERS: Well then, you have everything just as you wish.

WERLE: Yes, but I'm afraid it can't last. A woman so placed may easily find herself in a false position, in the eyes of the world. For that matter, it does a man no good either.

GREGERS: Oh, when a man gives such dinners as you give, he can risk a great deal.

WERLE: Yes, but she, Gregers? I'm afraid she won't accept the situation much longer; and even if she did – even if, out of attachment to me, she were to disregard gossip and scandal and all that – ? Do you think, Gregers – you with your highly developed sense of justice –

GREGERS (*interrupts him*): Tell me in one word: are you thinking of marrying her.

WERLE: Suppose I was thinking of it? What then?

GREGERS: That's what I say: what then?

WERLE: Would you be inflexibly opposed to it?

GREGERS: Not at all. Not by any means.

WERLE: I didn't know whether your devotion to your mother's memory –

GREGERS: I am not overstrained.

WERLE: Well, whatever you may or may not be, at all events you've lifted a great weight from my mind. I'm extremely pleased that I can reckon on your concurrence in this matter.

GREGERS (*looking intently at him*): Now I see what you want to do with me.

WERLE: To do with you? What an expression!

GREGERS: Oh, don't let us be nice in our choice of words – not when we're alone together, at any rate. (*With a short laugh.*) Well well! This is the reason why I had to come to town in person. For the sake of Mrs. Sörby, we're to get up a pretence at family life in the house – a tableau of filial affection. That'll be something new indeed.

WERLE: How dare you speak in that tone!

GREGERS: Was there ever any family life here? Never since I can remember. But now I suppose you require something of the sort. No doubt it'll have an excellent effect when it's reported that the son has hastened home, on the wings of filial piety, to the grey-haired father's wedding-feast. What'll remain of all the rumours as to the wrongs the poor dead mother had to put up with? Not a vestige. Her son annihilates them at one stroke.

WERLE: Gregers – I believe there's no one in the world you dislike as much as me.

GREGERS (*softly*): I've seen you at too close quarters.

WERLE: You've seen me with your mother's eyes. (*Lowers his voice a little.*) But you should remember that her vision was clouded now and then.

GREGERS (*trembling*): I see what you're hinting at. But who was to blame for mother's unfortunate weakness? Why, you, and all these – ! The last of them was that woman you palmed off upon Hialmar Ekdal, when you no longer – Ugh!

WERLE (*shrugs his shoulders*): Word for word as if it were your mother speaking!

GREGERS (*without heeding*): And there he sits now, with his great confiding, childlike mind, in the midst of the deception – lives under the same roof with such a creature, and does not know that what he calls his home is built upon a lie! (*Comes a step nearer.*) When I look back upon your past, I seem to see a battle-field with shattered lives on every hand.

WERLE: I almost think the chasm that divides us is too wide.

GREGERS (*bowing, with self-command*): So I have observed; and therefore I take my hat and go.

WERLE: You're going! out of the house?

GREGERS: Yes, for at least I see my mission in life.

WERLE: What mission?

GREGERS: You would only laugh if I told you.

WERLE: A lonely man doesn't laugh so easily, Gregers.

GREGERS (*pointing towards the background*): Look, father, – the Chamberlains are playing blind-man's buff with Mrs. Sörby. Goodnight and goodbye.

(*He goes out by the back to the right. Sounds of laughter and merriment from the company, who appear in the outer room.*)

WERLE (*muttering contemptuously after Gregers*): Ha – Poor wretch – and he says he's not overstrained!

Act Two

Hialmar Ekdal's studio, a good-sized room at the top of the house. On the right, a sloping roof of large panes of glass, half covered by a blue curtain. In the right-hand corner, at the back, the entrance door; further forward, on the same side, a door leading to the sitting-room. Two corresponding doors on the opposite side, and between them an iron stove. At the back a wide double sliding-door. The studio is plainly but comfortably fitted up and furnished. Between the doors on the right, standing out a little from the wall, a sofa with a table and some chairs; on the table a lighted lamp with a shade; beside the stove an old armchair. Photographic instruments and apparatus of different kinds lying about the room. Against the back wall, to the left of the double door, stands a bookcase containing a few books, boxes, and bottles of chemicals, instruments, tools, and other objects. Photographs and small articles, such as camel's-hair pencils, paper, and so forth, lie on the table.

Gina Ekdal sits on a chair by the table, sewing. Hedvig is sitting on the sofa with her hands shading her eyes and her thumbs in her ears, reading a book.

GINA (*glances once or twice at Hedvig, as if with secret anxiety; then says:*): Hedvig! (*Hedvig does not hear. Gina repeats more loudly.*) Hedvig!

HEDVIG (*takes away her hands and looks up*): Yes, mother?

GINA: Hedvig dear, you mustn't sit reading any longer now.

HEDVIG: Oh, mother, mayn't I read a little more? Just a little bit?

GINA: No, no, you must put away your book now. Your father doesn't like it; he never reads himself in the evening.

HEDVIG (*shuts the book*): No, father doesn't care much about reading.

GINA (*puts aside her sewing and takes up a lead pencil and a little account-book from the table*): Can you remember how much we paid for the butter today?

HEDVIG: It was one crown sixty-five.

GINA: That's right. (*Puts it down.*) It's terrible what a lot of butter we get through in this house. Then there was the smoked sausage, and the cheese – let me see – (*writes*) – and the ham – h'm. (*Adds up.*) Yes, that makes just –

HEDVIG: And then the beer.

GINA: Yes, of course. (*Writes.*) How it mounts up! But we can't do with less.

HEDVIG: But then you and I didn't need anything hot for dinner, as father was out.

GINA: No, that was a good thing. And then I took eight crowns fifty for photographs.

HEDVIG: Really! So much as that?

GINA: Exactly eight crowns fifty.

(*Silence. Gina takes up her sewing again. Hedvig takes paper and pencil and begins to draw, shading her eyes with her left hand.*)

HEDVIG: Isn't it jolly to think that father's at Mr. Werle's big dinner party?

GINA: You can't say that he's exactly Mr. Werle's guest. It was the son that invited him. (*After a pause.*) We've nothing to do with that Mr. Werle.

HEDVIG: I'm longing for father to come home. He promised to ask Mrs. Sörby for something nice for me.

GINA: Yes, there are plenty of good things going in that house, I can tell you.

HEDVIG (*continues drawing*): I believe I'm rather hungry too.

(*Old Ekdal, with the paper parcel under his arm and another parcel in his coat pocket, comes in through the entrance door.*)

GINA: How late you are today, grandfather!

EKDAL: They'd closed the office. Had to wait in Gråberg's room. And then they let me through – h'm.

HEDVIG: Did you get some fresh copying, grandfather?

EKDAL: This whole packet. Just look.

GINA: That's capital.

HEDVIG: And you've got another parcel in your pocket.

EKDAL: Eh? Oh, nonsense, that's nothing. (*Puts his stick away in a corner.*) This work'll keep me a long time, Gina. (*Opens one of the sliding-doors in the back wall a little.*) Hush! (*Peeps into the room for a moment, then pushes the door carefully to again.*) Hee-hee! They're fast asleep, all the lot of them. And she's gone into the basket herself. Hee-hee!

HEDVIG: Are you sure she's not cold in that basket, grandfather?

EKDAL: Not a bit of it! Cold? With all that straw? (*Goes towards the farther door on the left.*) There are matches in here, I suppose.

GINA: The matches are on the drawers.

(*Ekdal goes into his room.*)

HEDVIG: It's nice that grandfather's got all that copying.

GINA: Yes, poor old father; it means a bit of pocket-money for him.

HEDVIG: And he won't be able to sit the whole forenoon down at that horrid Madam Eriksen's.

GINA: No more he will.

(*Short silence.*)

HEDVIG: Do you suppose they're still at the dinner-table?

GINA: Goodness knows; very likely.

HEDVIG: Think of all the delicious things father's having to eat! I'm certain he'll be in splendid spirits when he comes. Don't you think so, mother?

GINA: Yes; and if only we could tell him that we'd got the room let –

HEDVIG: But we don't need that this evening.

GINA: Oh, we'd be none the worse of it, I can tell you. It's no use to us as it is.

HEDVIG: I mean that we don't need it this evening, for father'll be in a good humour anyhow. We'd better save up the room for another time.

GINA (*looks across at her*): Are you glad when you've some good news to tell father when he comes home in the evening?

HEDVIG: Yes; for then we have a pleasanter time.

GINA (*thinking to herself*): Yes, there's something in that.

(*Old Ekdal comes in again and is going out by the foremost door to the left.*)

GINA (*half turning in her chair*): Do you want something out of the kitchen, grandfather?

EKDAL: Yes, I do, yes. Don't you trouble. (*Goes out.*)

GINA: He's not raking away at the fire, is he? (*Waits a moment.*) Hedvig, go and see what he's about.

(*Ekdal comes in again with a small jug of steaming hot water.*)

HEDVIG: Are you getting some hot water, grandfather?

EKDAL: Yes, I am. Want it for something. Want to write, and the ink has got as thick as porridge, – h'm.

GINA: But you ought to have supper first, grandfather. It's laid in there.

EKDAL: Can't be bothered with supper, Gina. Very busy, I tell you. No one's to come to my room. No one – h'm.

(*He goes into his room; Gina and Hedvig look at each other.*)

GINA (*softly*): Can you imagine where he's got money from?

HEDVIG: From Gråberg, I daresay.

GINA: Not a bit of it. Gråberg always sends the money to me.

HEDVIG: Then he must have got a bottle on credit somewhere.

GINA: Poor grandfather, who'd give him credit?

(*Hialmar Ekdal, in an overcoat and grey felt hat, comes in from the right.*)

GINA (*throws down her sewing and rises*): Why, Ekdal, are you here already?

HEDVIG (*at the same time, jumping up*): Fancy your coming so soon, father!

HIALMAR (*taking off his hat*): Yes, most of the people were coming away.

HEDVIG: So early?

HIALMAR: Yes, it was a dinner-party, you know. (*Is taking off his overcoat.*)

GINA: Let me help you.

HEDVIG: Me too.

(*They draw off his coat; Gina hangs it up on the back wall.*)

HEDVIG: Were there many there, father?

HIALMAR: Oh no, not many. We were about twelve or fourteen at table.

GINA: And you had some talk with them all?

HIALMAR: Oh yes, a little; but Gregers took me up most of the time.

GINA: Is Gregers as ugly as ever?

HIALMAR: Well, he's not very much to look at. Hasn't the old man come home?

HEDVIG: Yes, grandfather's in his room, writing.

HIALMAR: Did he say anything?

GINA: No, what should he say?

HIALMAR: Didn't he say anything about – ? I fancy I heard that he'd been with Gråberg. I'll go in to him for a moment.

GINA: No, no, better not.

HIALMAR: Why not? Did he say he didn't want me to go in?

GINA: He doesn't want to see anybody this evening –

HEDVIG (*making signs*): H'm – h'm!

GINA (*not noticing*): – he's been in to fetch hot water –

HIALMAR: Aha! Then he's – ?

GINA: Yes, I suppose so.

HIALMAR: O God! my poor old white-haired father! – Well, well; there let him sit and get all the enjoyment he can.

(*Old Ekdal, in an indoor coat and with a lighted pipe, comes from his room.*)

EKDAL: Got home? Thought it was you I heard talking.

HIALMAR: Yes, I've just come.

EKDAL: You didn't see me, did you?

HIALMAR: No; but they said you'd passed through – so I thought I'd follow you.

EKDAL: H'm, kind of you, Hialmar. Who were they, all those fellows.

HIALMAR: Oh, all sorts of people. There was Chamberlain Flor, and Chamberlain Balle, and Chamberlain Kaspersen, and Chamberlain – this, that, and the other – I don't know who all –

EKDAL (*nodding*): Hear that, Gina! He's been with nothing but Chamberlains.

GINA: Yes, I hear they're terribly genteel in that house nowadays.

HEDVIG: Did the Chamberlains sing, father? Or did they read aloud?

HIALMAR: No, they only chattered. They wanted me to recite something for them; but I knew better than that.

EKDAL: Didn't you do it?

GINA: Oh, you might have done it.

HIALMAR: No; one mustn't be at everybody's beck and call. (*Walks about the room.*) I won't, at any rate.

EKDAL: No, no; Hialmar's not to be had for the asking.

HIALMAR: I don't see why I should bother myself to entertain people on the rare occasions when I go into society. Let the others exert themselves. These fellows go from one great dinner-table to the next and gorge and guzzle day out and day in. It's for them to bestir themselves and do something in return for all the good food they get.

GINA: But you didn't say that?

HIALMAR (*humming*): Ho-ho-ho – ; faith, I gave them a bit of my mind.

EKDAL: Not the Chamberlains!

HIALMAR: Oh, why not? (*Lightly.*) We got into a little dispute about Tokay afterwards.

EKDAL: Tokay! There's a fine wine for you?

HIALMAR (*comes to a standstill*): It may be a fine wine. But of course you know the vintages differ; it all depends on how much sunshine the grapes have got.

GINA: Why, you know everything, Ekdal.

EKDAL: And did they dispute that?

HIALMAR: They tried to; but they didn't much like being told that it was just the same with Chamberlains – that with them, too, different batches were of different qualities.

GINA: What things you think of !

EKDAL: Hee-hee! So they got that in their pipes too.

HIALMAR: Right to their faces.

EKDAL: Do you hear that, Gina? He said it right to the Chamberlain's faces.

GINA: Just think – ! Right to their faces!

HIALMAR: Yes, but I don't want it talked about. One doesn't speak of such things. The whole affair passed off in all friendliness, of course. They were nice, genial fellows; I didn't want to wound them – not I!

EKDAL: Right to their faces!

HEDVIG (*caressingly*): How nice it is to see you in a dresscoat! It suits you, father.

HIALMAR: Yes, doesn't it? And this one really sits to perfection. It fits almost as if it had been made for me; – a little tight in the arm-holes perhaps; – help me, Hedvig. (*Takes off the coat.*) I think I'll put on my jacket. Where's my jacket, Gina?

GINA: Here it is. (*Brings the jacket and helps him.*)

HIALMAR: That's it! Don't forget to send the coat back to Molvik first thing tomorrow morning.

GINA (*laying it away*): I'll be sure and see to it.

HIALMAR (*stretching himself*): After all, this is more comfortable. A free-and-easy indoor costume suits my whole personality better. Don't you think so, Hedvig?

HEDVIG: Yes, father.

HIALMAR: When I loosen my necktie into a pair of flowing ends – like this – eh?

HEDVIG: Yes, that goes so well with your moustache and the sweep of your curls.

HIALMAR: I shouldn't call them curls exactly; I'd rather say locks.

HEDVIG: Yes, but they're really big curls.

HIALMAR: No, locks

HEDVIG (*after a pause, twitching his jacket*): Father!

HIALMAR: Well, what is it?

HEDVIG: Oh, you know very well.

HIALMAR: No, really I don't –

HEDVIG (*half laughing, half whimpering*): Oh yes, father; now don't tease me any longer!

HIALMAR: Why, what do you mean?

HEDVIG (*shaking him*): Oh, nonsense; come, where are they, father? All the good things you promised me, you know?

HIALMAR: Oh – if I haven't forgotten all about them!

HEDVIG: Now you're only making game of me, father! Oh, it's a shame! Where have you put them?

HIALMAR: No, I positively forgot to get anything. But wait a little! I've got something else for you, Hedvig. (*Goes and searches in the coat pockets.*)

HEDVIG (*skipping and clapping her hands*): Oh mother, mother!

GINA: There, you see; if only you give him time –

HIALMAR (*with a paper*): Look, here it is.

HEDVIG: That? Why, that's only a paper.

HIALMAR: That's the bill of fare, the whole bill of fare. Here you see: 'Menu' – that means bill of fare.

HEDVIG: Haven't you anything else?

HIALMAR: I forgot the other things, I tell you. But you may take my word for it, these dainties are very unsatisfying. Sit down at the table and read the bill of fare, and then I'll describe to you how the dishes taste. Here you are, Hedvig.

HEDVIG (*gulping down her tears*): Thank you.

(*She seats herself, but does not read; Gina makes signs to her; Hialmar notices it.*)

HIALMAR (*walking up and down the room*): No one knows how much the father of a family has to think of; and if he forgets the slightest thing, he's treated to sour faces at once. Well, well, one gets used to that too. (*Stops near the stove, by the old man's chair.*) Have you peeped in there this evening, father?

EKDAL: Yes, to be sure I have. She's gone into the basket.

HIALMAR: Ah, she's gone into the basket! Then she's beginning to get used to it.

EKDAL: Yes; just as I prophesied. But you know there are still a few little things –

HIALMAR: A few improvements, yes.

EKDAL: They're quite necessary, you know.

HIALMAR: Yes. Let's have a talk about the improvements, father. Come, and we'll sit on the sofa.

EKDAL: All right. H'm,-let me fill my pipe first. Must just clean it too. H'm. (*He goes into this room.*)

GINA (*smiling at Hialmar*): His pipe!

HIALMAR: Oh yes, yes, Gina; let him alone –; the poor shipwrecked old man. – Yes, these improvements – we'd better get them out of hand tomorrow.

GINA: You'll hardly have time tomorrow, Ekdal.

HEDVIG (*interposing*): Oh yes he will, mother!

GINA: – for remember those copies that have to be retouched; they've sent for them time after time.

HIALMAR: Oh, bother the copies. I'll soon get them finished. Have any new orders come in?

GINA: No, worse luck; tomorrow I've nothing but those two sittings, you know.

HIALMAR: Nothing else? Oh no, when one doesn't set about things with a will –

GINA: But what more can I do? Don't I advertise in the papers as much as we can afford?

HIALMAR: Yes, the papers, the papers; you see how much good *that* does. And I suppose no one has been to see the room either?

GINA: No, not yet.

HIALMAR: That was only to be expected. Unless one's on the alert – The thing is to make a real effort, Gina.

HEDVIG (*going towards him*): Shall I fetch you the flute, father?

HIALMAR: No; no flute for me; *I* want no pleasures in this world. (*Walking about.*) Yes, I'll work tomorrow; you'll see if I don't. You may be sure I'll work as long as my strength holds out.

GINA: But my dear good Ekdal, I didn't mean it in that way.

HEDVIG: Father, shall I bring in a bottle of beer?

HIALMAR: No, certainly not. I require nothing, nothing – (*comes to a standstill*). Beer? Were you talking about beer?

HEDVIG (*cheerfully*): Yes, father; beautiful fresh beer.

HIALMAR: Well – since you insist upon it, you may bring in a bottle.

GINA: Yes, do; and we'll be nice and cosy.

(*Hedvig runs towards the kitchen door.*)

HIALMAR (*by the stove, stops her, looks at her, puts his arm round her neck, and presses her to him*): Hedvig, Hedvig!

HEDVIG (*joyfully and in tears*): My dear, kind father!

HIALMAR: No, don't call me that. Here have I been revelling at the rich man's table, – been sitting and gorging myself at the groaning board – ! And I couldn't even – !

GINA (*sitting at the table*): Oh nonsense, nonsense, Ekdal.

HIALMAR: Oh, but you mustn't be too hard upon me. You know that I love you for all that.

HEDVIG (*throwing her arms round him*): And we love you, oh so dearly, father!

HIALMAR: And if I'm unreasonable sometimes – why then – you must remember that I'm a man beset by a host of cares. There there! (*Dries her eyes.*) No beer at such a moment as this. Give me the flute. (*Hedvig runs to the bookcase and fetches it.*) Thanks! That's right. With my flute in my hand and you two at my side – ah – !

(*Hedvig seats herself at the table near Gina; Hialmar wanders up and down, then sets energetically to work and plays a Bohemian peasant dance, but in a slow plaintive tempo, and with sentimental expression.*)

HIALMAR (*breaking off the melody, holds out his left hand to Gina, and says with emotion*): Our roof may be poor and humble, Gina; but it is home. And with all my heart I say: here dwells my happiness.

(*He begins to play again; almost immediately after, a knocking is heard at the entrance door.*)

GINA (*rising*): Hush, Ekdal, – I think there's somebody coming.

HIALMAR (*laying the flute in the bookcase*): There! Again!

(*Gina goes and opens the door.*)

GREGERS WERLE (*in the passage*): Excuse me –

GINA (*starting back slightly*): Oh!

GREGERS: – Doesn't Mr. Ekdal, the photographer, live here?

GINA: Yes, he does.

HIALMAR (*going towards the door*): Gregers! You here after all? Well, come in, then.

GREGERS (*coming in*): I told you I would come and look you up.

HIALMAR: But this evening – ? Have you left the party?

GREGERS: I've left both the party and my father's house – Good evening, Mrs. Ekdal. I don't know whether you recognise me?

GINA: Oh yes; it's not difficult to know young Mr. Werle again.

GREGERS: No, I'm like my mother; and of course you remember her.

HIALMAR: Have you left the house, do you say?

GREGERS: Yes, I've gone to a hotel.

HIALMAR: Indeed. Well, since you've come, take off your coat and sit down.

GREGERS: Thanks.

(*He draws off his overcoat. He is now dressed in a plain grey suit of a countrified cut.*)

HIALMAR: Here, on the sofa. Make yourself comfortable.

(*Gregers seats himself on the sofa; Hialmar takes a chair at the table.*)

GREGERS (*looking around him*): So these are your quarters, Hialmar – this is your home.

HIALMAR: This is the studio, as you see –

GINA: But it's the largest of our rooms, so we generally sit here.

HIALMAR: We used to live in a better place; but this flat has one great advantage: there are such capital outer rooms –

GINA: And we have a room on the other side of the passage, that we can let.

GREGERS (*to Hialmar*): Ah, so you have lodgers too?

HIALMAR: No, not yet. They're not so easy to find, you see; you've got to keep your eyes about you. (*To Hedvig.*) What about that beer?

(*Hedvig nods and goes out into the kitchen.*)

GREGERS: Your daughter, I suppose?

HIALMAR: Yes, that's Hedvig.

GREGERS: And she's your only child?

HIALMAR: Yes, the only one. She's the joy of our lives, and – (*lowering his voice*) – at the same time our deepest sorrow, Gregers.

GREGERS: What do you mean?

HIALMAR: She's in danger of losing her eyesight.

GREGERS: Becoming blind?

HIALMAR: Yes. Only the first symptoms have appeared as yet,

and she may not feel it much for some time. But the doctor has warned us. It's coming, inexorably.

GREGERS: What an awful misfortune! How do you account for it?

HIALMAR (*sighs*): Hereditary, no doubt.

GREGERS (*starting*): Hereditary?

GINA: Ekdal's mother had weak eyes.

HIALMAR: Yes, so my father says; I can't remember her.

GREGERS: Poor child! And how does she take it?

HIALMAR: Oh, you can imagine we haven't the heart to tell her of it. She suspects no danger. Gay and careless and chirping like a little bird, she's fluttering into the eternal night of her life. (*Overcome.*) Oh, it's cruelly hard for me, Gregers.

(*Hedvig brings a tray with her and beer glasses, which she sets upon the table.*)

HIALMAR (*stroking her hair*): Thanks, thanks, Hedvig.

(*Hedvig puts her arm round his neck and whispers in his ear.*)

HIALMAR: No, no bread and butter just now. (*Looks up.*) But perhaps you'd like some, Gregers.

GREGERS (*with a gesture of refusal*): No, no thank you.

HIALMAR (*still melancholy*): Well, you can bring in a little all the same. If you have a crust, that's all I want. And put plenty of butter on it, mind.

(*Hedvig nods gaily and goes out into the kitchen again.*)

GREGERS (*who has been following her with his eyes*): She seems quite strong and healthy otherwise.

GINA: Yes. In other ways there's nothing amiss with her, thank goodness.

GREGERS: She promises to be very like you, Mrs. Ekdal. How old is she now?

GINA: Hedvig will soon be exactly fourteen; her birthday is the day after tomorrow.

GREGERS: She's pretty tall for her age.

GINA: Yes, she's shot up wonderfully this last year.

GREGERS: It makes one realise one's own age to see these young people growing up. – How long is it now since you were married?

GINA: We've been married – let me see – nearly fifteen years.

GREGERS: Is it so long as that?

GINA (*becomes attentive; looks at him*): Yes, it is indeed.

HIALMAR: Yes, so it is. Fifteen years all but a few months. (*Changing his tone.*) They must have been long years for you, up at the works, Gregers.

GREGERS: They seemed long while I was living them; now they're over, I hardly know how the time has gone.

(*Old Ekdal comes from his room without his pipe, but with his old-fashioned uniform cap on his head; his gait is somewhat unsteady.*)

EKDAL: There, Hialmar, now we can have a good talk about this – h'm – what was it again?

HIALMAR (*going towards him*): Father, we've a visitor here – Gregers Werle. – I don't know if you remember him.

EKDAL (*looking at Gregers, who has risen*): Werle? Is that the son? What does he want with me?

HIALMAR: Nothing; it's me he's come to see.

EKDAL: Oh! Then there's nothing wrong?

HIALMAR: No, of course not.

EKDAL (*swinging his arms*): Not that I'm afraid, you know; but –

GREGERS (*goes over to him*): Let me give you a greeting from your old hunting-grounds, Lieutenant Ekdal.

EKDAL: Hunting-grounds?

GREGERS: Yes, up in Höidal, about the works, you know.

EKDAL: Oh, up there. Yes, I knew all those places well in the old times.

GREGERS: You were a great sportsman then.

EKDAL: So I was, I don't deny it. You're looking at my uniform cap. I don't ask anybody's leave to wear it in the house. So long as I don't go out in the streets with it –

(*Hedvig brings a plate of bread and butter, which she puts upon the table.*)

HIALMAR: Sit down, father, and have a glass of beer. Help yourself, Gregers.

(*Ekdal mutters and stumbles over to the sofa. Gregers seats himself on the chair nearest to him, Hialmar on the other side of Gregers. Gina sits a little way from the table, sewing; Hedvig stands beside her father.*)

GREGERS: Can you remember, Lieutenant Ekdal, how Hialmar and I used to come up and visit you in the summer and at Christmas?

EKDAL: Did you? No, no, no; I don't remember it. But sure enough I've been a great sportsman. I've shot bears too. I've shot nine of them.

GREGERS (*looking sympathetically at him*): And now you never get any shooting?

EKDAL: Can't say that, sir. Get a shot now and then perhaps. Of course not in the old way. For the woods, you see – the woods, the woods – ! (*Drinks.*) Are the woods fine up there now?

GREGERS: Not so fine as in your time. They've been thinned a good deal.

EKDAL: Thinned? (*More softly, and as if afraid.*) It's dangerous work that. Bad things come of it. The woods avenge themselves.

HIALMAR (*filling up his glass*): Come – a little more, father.

GREGERS: How can a man like you – such a man for the open air – live in the midst of a stuffy town, boxed within four walls?

EKDAL (*laughs quietly and glances at Hialmar*): Oh, it's not so bad here. Not at all so bad.

GREGERS: But don't you miss all that you used to be so fond of – the cool sweeping breezes, the free life in the woods and on the uplands, amongst beasts and birds – ?

EKDAL (*smiling*): Hialmar, shall we let him see it?

HIALMAR (*hastily and a little embarrassed*): Oh no, no, father; not this evening.

GREGERS: What does he want to show me?

HIALMAR: Oh, it's only something – you can see it another time.

GREGERS (*continues, to the old man*): You see, I've been thinking, Lieutenant Ekdal, that you should come up with me to the works; I'm sure to be going back soon. You could probably get some copying there too. And here, you have nothing on earth to interest you – nothing to liven you up.

EKDAL (*stares in astonishment at him*): Have *I* nothing on earth to – !

GREGERS: Of course you have Hialmar; but then he has his own family. And a man like you, who has always had such a passion for what is free and wild –

EKDAL (*thumps the table*): Hialmar, he *shall* see it!

HIALMAR: Oh but, father, is it worthwhile? It's all dark.

EKDAL: Nonsense; it's moonlight. (*Rises.*) He *shall* see it, I tell you. Let me pass! Come and help me, Hialmar!

HEDVIG: Oh yes, do, father!

HIALMAR (*rising*): Very well, then.

GREGERS (*to Gina*): What is it?

GINA: Oh, you mustn't think it's anything so very wonderful.

(*Ekdal and Hialmar have gone to the back wall and are each pushing back a side of the sliding-door; Hedvig helps the old man; Gregers remains standing by the sofa; Gina sits still and sews.*

Through the open doorway a large, deep, irregular garret is seen with odd nooks and corners; a couple of stove-pipes running through it, from rooms below. There are skylights through which clear moonlight shines in on some parts of the great room; others lie in deep shadow.)

EKDAL (*to Gregers*): You may come right in if you like.

GREGERS (*going over to them*): But what is it?

EKDAL: Come and see. H'm.

HIALMAR (*somewhat embarrassed*): This belongs to father, you understand.

GREGERS (*at the door, looks into the garret*): Why, you keep poultry, Lieutenant Ekdal!

EKDAL: Should think we did keep poultry. They've gone to roost now. But you should just see our fowls by daylight!

HEDVIG: And there's a –

EKDAL: Hush – hush; don't say anything about it yet.

GREGERS: And you've got pigeons too, I see.

EKDAL: Oh yes, haven't we got pigeons! They have their nests up there under the roof-tree; for pigeons like to roost high, you see.

HIALMAR: They aren't all common pigeons.

EKDAL: Common! Should think not indeed! We have tumblers, and a pair of pouters too. But come here! Can you see that hutch down there by the wall?

GREGERS: Yes; what do you use it for?

EKDAL: That's where the rabbits sleep, sir.

GREGERS: Dear me, so you've rabbits too?

EKDAL: Yes, I believe you, we have rabbits! He's asking if we have rabbits, Hialmar! H'm. But now comes *the* thing, you must know; here we have it; move away, Hedvig. Stand here; that's right, – and now look down there. Don't you see a basket with straw in it?

GREGERS: Yes. And I see there's a fowl in the basket.

EKDAL: H'm – 'a fowl' –

GREGERS: Isn't it a duck?

EKDAL (*hurt*): Yes, of course it's a duck.

HIALMAR: But what *kind* of duck, do you think?

HEDVIG: It's not just a common duck.

EKDAL: Hush!

GREGERS: And it's not a Turkish duck either.

EKDAL: No, Mr. – Werle; it's not a Turkish duck; for it's a wild duck!

GREGERS: No, is it really? A wild duck?

EKDAL: Yes, it is. That 'fowl' as you call it – is the wild duck. It's our wild duck, sir.

HEDVIG: *My* wild duck. She belongs to me.

GREGRES: And can it live up here in the garret? Does it thrive?

EKDAL: Of course it has a trough of water to splash about in, you know.

HIALMAR: Fresh water every other day.

GINA (*turning towards Hialmar*): But my dear Ekdal, it's getting icy cold here.

EKDAL: H'm, let's shut up, then. It's as well not to disturb their night's rest, too. Close up, Hedvig.

(*Hialmar and Hedvig push the garret doors together.*)

EKDAL: Another time you shall see her properly. (*Seats himself in the armchair by the stove.*) Oh, they're curious things, these wild ducks, I can tell you.

GREGERS: How did you manage to catch it, Lieutenant Ekdal?

EKDAL: I didn't catch it. There's a certain man in this town whom we have to thank for it.

GREGERS (*starts slightly*): That man wasn't my father, was he?

EKDAL: You've hit it. Your father and no one else. H'm.

HIALMAR: It was odd that you should guess that, Gregers.

GREGERS: You were telling me that you owed such a lot of things to my father; and so I thought perhaps –

GINA: But we didn't get the duck from Mr. Werle himself –

EKDAL: It's Håkon Werle we have to thank for her, all the same, Gina. (*To Gregers.*) He was out in a boat, you see, and he shot her. But your father's sight is pretty bad now. H'm; he only wounded her.

GREGERS: Ah! She got a couple of shot in her body, I suppose.

HIALMAR: Yes, two or three.

HEDVIG: She was hit under the wing, so that she couldn't fly.

GREGERS: And so she dived to the bottom, eh?

EKDAL (*sleepily, in a thick voice*): Of course. Wild ducks always do that. They shoot to the bottom as deep as they can get, sir, and bite themselves fast in the tangle and seaweed and all the confounded stuff that grows down there. And they never come up again.

GREGERS: But your wild duck came up again, Lieutenant Ekdal.

EKDAL: Your father had such an extraordinarily clever dog. And that dog – he dived in after the duck and fished her up again.

GREGERS (*who has turned to Hialmar*): And then you took her in here!

HIALMAR: Not at once; at first she was taken home to your father's house; but she wouldn't thrive there; so Pettersen was told to put an end to her.

EKDAL (*half asleep*): H'm, yes, Pettersen – that ass –

HIALMAR (*speaking more softly*): That's how we got her, you see; for father knows Pettersen a little; and when he heard about the wild duck he got him to hand her over to us.

GREGERS: And she thrives all right in the garret there?

HIALMAR: Yes, wonderfully well. She's got fat. You see she's been in there so long now that she's forgotten her natural wild life; and it all depends on that.

GREGERS: You're right there, Hialmar. Only never let her get a glimpse of the sky and the sea – But I mustn't stop any longer; I think your father's asleep.

HIALMAR: Oh, as for that –

GREGERS: But, by-the-by – you said you had a room to let – a spare room?

HIALMAR: Yes; what then? Do you know of anybody –

GREGERS: Can I have that room?

HIALMAR: You?

GINA: Oh no, Mr. Werle, *you* –

GREGERS: May I have the room? If so, I'll take possession first thing tomorrow morning.

HIALMAR: Yes, with the greatest pleasure –

GINA: But, Mr. Werle, it's not at all the sort of room for *you.*

HIALMAR: Gina! how can you say that?

GINA: Well, the room's neither large enough nor light enough, and –

GREGERS: That doesn't matter, Mrs. Ekdal.

HIALMAR: I call it quite a nice room, and not badly furnished either.

GINA: But remember the two that live underneath.

GREGERS: What two?

GINA: Oh, one of them has been a tutor –

HIALMAR: He's a Mr. Molvik.

GINA: And then there's a doctor called Relling.

GREGERS: Relling? I know him a little; he practised for a time up in Höidal.

GINA: They're a pair of regular ne'er-do-wells. They're often out on the loose in the evenings, and then they come home very late, and they're not always quite –

GREGERS: One soon gets accustomed to that sort of thing. I hope I'll be like the wild duck –

GINA: H'm; I think you ought to sleep upon it first, all the same.

GREGERS: You seem very unwilling to have me in the house, Mrs. Ekdal.

GINA: Oh no! how can you think so?

HIALMAR: Well, you really behave strangely about it, Gina. (*To Gregers.*) Then you're thinking of staying in the town for the present?

GREGERS (*putting on his overcoat*): Yes, now I'm thinking of remaining here.

HIALMAR: And yet not at your father's? What do you propose to do?

GREGERS: Ah, if I only knew that, I shouldn't be so badly off! But when one has the misfortune to be called Gregers – ! 'Gregèrs' – and then 'Werle' after it; did you ever hear anything so hideous?

HIALMAR: Oh, I don't think so at all.

GREGERS: Ugh! Bah! I feel as if I should like to spit upon the fellow that answers to such a name. When one has the misfortune to be Gregers – Werle in this world, as I am –

HIALMAR (*laughs*): Ha ha! If you weren't Gregers Werle, what would you like to be?

GREGERS: If I could choose, I should like best to be a clever dog.

GINA: A dog!

HEDVIG (*involuntarily*): Oh no!

GREGERS: Yes, an extraordinarily clever dog; one that goes to the bottom after wild ducks when they dive and bite themselves fast in tangle and seaweed, down among the ooze.

HIALMAR: Look here now, Gregers – I don't understand a word of all this.

GREGERS: Oh well, I daresay it's not worth understanding. Then I'll move in early tomorrow morning. (*To Gina.*) I won't give you any trouble, for I do everything for myself. (*To Hialmar.*) We'll leave the rest till tomorrow. Goodnight, Mrs. Ekdal. (*Nods to Hedvig.*) Goodnight.

GINA: Goodnight, Mr. Werle.

HEDVIG: Goodnight.

HIALMAR (*who has lighted a candle*): Stop a minute, I must show you a light; it's sure to be dark on the stairs.

(*Gregers and Hialmar go out through the passage door.*)

GINA (*looking straight before her, with her sewing in her lap*): Wasn't that strange talk about his wanting to be a dog!

HEDVIG: Do you know, mother, I believe he meant something quite different by that.

GINA: What should he mean?

HEDVIG: Oh, I don't know; but it seemed to me he meant something different from what he said, all the time.

GINA: Do you think so? Yes, it was strange.

HIALMAR (*comes back*): The lamp was still burning. (*Puts out the candle and sets it down.*) Ah, now one can get a mouthful of food at last. (*Begins to eat the bread and butter.*) Well, you see, Gina – if you just keep your eyes open –

GINA: How, keep your eyes open?

HIALMAR: Why, aren't we lucky to have got the room let at last? And just think – to a person like Gregers – a good old friend.

GINA: I don't know what to say about it.

HEDVIG: Oh, mother, you'll see; it'll be such fun!

HIALMAR: You're very strange. You were so bent upon letting the room before, and now you don't like it.

GINA: Yes, I do, Ekdal; if it had only been to someone else – But what do you suppose Mr. Werle will say?

HIALMAR: Old Werle? It doesn't concern him.

GINA: But surely you can see that something's gone wrong between them again, as the young man's leaving home. You know very well how matters stand between those two.

HIALMAR: Yes, that's very likely, but –

GINA: And now Mr. Werle may think that it's you who have egged him on –

HIALMAR: Let him think so, then! Mr. Werle has done a great deal for me; far be it from me to deny it. But that doesn't make me everlastingly dependent upon him.

GINA: But, my dear Ekdal, mayn't grandfather suffer for it? Perhaps he'll lose the little bit of work he gets from Gråberg now.

HIALMAR: I'm inclined to say: so much the better! Isn't it humiliating for a man like me to see his grey-haired father going about as a pariah? But the fullness of time will soon come now, I trust. (*Takes a fresh piece of bread and butter.*) As sure as I've a mission in life, I mean to fulfil it now.

HEDVIG: Oh yes, father, do!

GINA: Hush, don't wake him!

HIALMAR (*more softly*): I *will* fulfil it, I say. The day will come when – And therefore it's a good thing that we've let the room, for that makes me more independent. The man who has a mission in life must be independent. (*By the armchair, with emotion.*) Poor old white-haired father! Rely on your Hialmar. He has broad shoulders – strong shoulders, at any rate. You shall yet wake up some fine day and – (*To Gina.*) Don't you believe it?

GINA (*rising*): Yes, of course I do; but in the meantime let's see about getting him to bed.

HIALMAR: Yes, come.

(*They take hold of the old man carefully.*)

Act Three

Hialmar Ekdal's studio. It is morning; the daylight shines through the large window in the slanting roof; the curtain is drawn back.

Hialmar is sitting at the table, busy retouching a photograph; several others lie before him. Presently Gina, in her hat and cloak, enters by the passage door; she has a covered basket on her arm.

HIALMAR: Back already, Gina?

GINA: Oh yes, one has to look sharp. (*Sets her basket on a chair, and takes off her things.*)

HIALMAR: Did you look in at Gregers' room?

GINA: Yes, I did. It's a rare sight, I can tell you; he's begun by making a pretty mess of it.

HIALMAR: Indeed?

GINA: He was determined to do everything for himself, he said; so when he set to work to light the stove, he must needs screw the damper round until the whole room was full of smoke. Ugh! It smelt like –

HIALMAR: Well, really!

GINA: But that's not the worst of it; for then he wanted to put out the fire, and poured all the water from his ewer into the stove, so that the floor was swimming like a pig-sty.

HIALMAR: How annoying!

GINA: I've got the porter's wife to clear up after him, pig that he is! But the room won't be habitable till the afternoon.

HIALMAR: What's he doing with himself in the meantime?

GINA: He said he was going out for a little while.

HIALMAR: I looked in upon him too, for a moment – after you had gone.

GINA: So I heard. You've asked him to lunch.

HIALMAR: Just to a little bit of early lunch, you know. It's his first day – we can hardly do less. You've got something in the house, I suppose?

GINA: I'll have to find something or other.

HIALMAR: And don't be too sparing, for I think Relling and Molvik are coming up too. I just met Relling on the stairs, you see; so I had to –

GINA: Oh, are we have those two as well?

HIALMAR: Good Lord – a couple more or less can't make any difference.

OLD EKDAL (*opens his door and looks in*): I say, Hialmar – (*sees Gina*). Oh!

GINA: Do you want anything, grandfather?

EKDAL: Oh no, it doesn't matter. H'm! (*Retires again.*)

GINA (*takes up the basket*): Be sure you see that he doesn't go out.

HIALMAR: All right, all right. – And, Gina, it wouldn't be amiss if you had a little herring-salad; Relling and Molvik were out on the loose again last night.

GINA: If only they don't come up too soon for me –

HIALMAR: No, of course they won't; take your own time.

GINA: Very well; and meanwhile you can be working a bit.

HIALMAR: Well, I *am* working! I'm working as hard as I can!

GINA: Then you'll have that job off your hands, you see. (*She goes out to the kitchen wth her basket.*)

(*Hialmar sits for a time working at the photograph; he does it lazily and listlessly.*)

EKDAL (*peeps in, looks round the studio and says softly*): Are you busy?

HIALMAR: Yes, I'm toiling away at these pictures –

EKDAL: Well, well, of course – since you're so busy – h'm! (*He goes out again; the door stands open.*)

HIALMAR (*continues for some time in silence; then he lays down his brush and goes over to the door*): Are *you* busy, father?

EKDAL (*in a grumbling tone, inside*): If you're busy, I'm busy too. H'm!

HIALMAR: Oh, all right. (*Goes to his work again.*)

EKDAL (*presently, coming to the door again*): H'm; I say, Hialmar, I'm not so very busy, you know.

HIALMAR: I thought you were writing.

EKDAL: Oh, devil take it! Can't Gråberg wait a day or two? It's not a matter of life and death, I should think.

HIALMAR: No; and you're not his slave either.

EKDAL: And about that other business in there –

HIALMAR: Just what I was thinking of. Do you want to go in? Shall I open the door for you?

EKDAL: Well, it wouldn't do any harm.

HIALMAR (*rises*): Then we'd have that off our hands.

EKDAL: Yes, exactly. It's got to be ready first thing tomorrow. It is tomorrow, isn't it? H'm?

HIALMAR: Yes, of course it's tomorrow.

(*Hialmar and Ekdal push aside the sliding door. The morning sun is shining in through the skylights; some doves are flying about; others are perched, cooing, upon the rafters; the hens cackle now and then, farther back in the garret.*)

HIALMAR: There, now you can get to work, father.

EKDAL (*goes in*): Aren't you coming too?

HIALMAR: Well, really, do you know –; I almost think – (*Sees Gina at the kitchen door.*) I? No; I haven't time; I must work. – But now for our new dodge –

(*He pulls a cord; a curtain slips down inside, the lower part consisting *of a piece of sailcloth, the upper part of a stretched net. The floor of the garret is thus no longer visible.*)

HIALMAR (*goes to the table*): There! Now I can sit in peace for a little while.

GINA: Is he rampaging in there again?

HIALMAR: Would you have preferred him to slip down to Madam Eriksen's? (*Seats himself.*) Do you want anything? You were saying –

GINA: I was only going to ask if you think we can lay the lunch-table here?

HIALMAR: Yes; nobody has made any early appointment, I suppose?

GINA: No, we've no one today except those two sweethearts that are to be taken together.

HIALMAR: Why the deuce couldn't they be taken together another day!

GINA: But my dear Ekdal, I told them to come in the afternoon, when you're having your nap.

HIALMAR: Oh, that's capital. Very well, we'll have lunch here, then.

GINA: All right; but there's no hurry about laying the cloth; you can have the table for an hour yet.

HIALMAR: Do you think I'm not sticking at my work? I'm at it as hard as I can!

GINA: Then you'll be free later, you know. (*Goes out into the kitchen again. Short pause.*)

EKDAL (*in the garret doorway, behind the net*): Hialmar!

HIALMAR: Well?

EKDAL: Afraid we'll have to move the water-trough, after all.

HIALMAR: That's what I've been saying all along.

EKDAL: H'm – h'm – h'm. (*Goes away from the door again.*

(Hialmar goes on working a little; glances towards the garret and half rises. Hedvig comes in from the kitchen.)

HIALMAR (*sits down again hurriedly*): What do you want?

HEDVIG: I only wanted to come in beside you, father.

HIALMAR (*after a pause*): It seems to me you go poking your nose everywhere. Are you set to watch me?

HEDVIG: No, not at all.

HIALMAR: What's mother doing out there?

HEDVIG: Oh, mother's in the middle of making the herring-salad. (*Goes to the table.*) Isn't there any little thing I could help you with, father?

HIALMAR: Oh no. I must bear the whole burden – so long as my strength holds out. You needn't trouble, Hedvig; if only your father keeps his health –

HEDVIG: Oh no, father! You shan't talk in that horrible way.

(*She wanders about a little, stops by the doorway, and looks into the garret.*)

HIALMAR: What's he doing?

HEDVIG: I think he's making a new path to the water-trough.

HIALMAR: He'll never manage it by himself! And I'm doomed to sit here – !

HEDVIG (*goes to him*): Let me take the brush, father; I know how to do it.

HIALMAR: Oh, nonsense; you'll only hurt your eyes.

HEDVIG: Not a bit. Give me the brush.

HIALMAR (*rising*): Well, it'll only take a minute or two.

HEDVIG: Pooh, what harm can it do, then? (*Takes the brush.*) There! (*Seats herself.*) And here's one I can begin upon.

HIALMAR: But mind you don't hurt your eyes! Do you hear? *I* won't be answerable; you must take the responsibility upon yourself – so I tell you!

HEDVIG (*retouching*): Yes, yes, all right.

HIALMAR: You're quite clever at it, Hedvig. Only a minute or two, you know. (*He slips through by the edge of the curtain into the garret. Hedvig sits at her work. Hialmar and Ekdal are heard disputing inside.*)

HIALMAR (*appears behind the net*): I say, Hedvig – give me those pincers that are lying on the shelf. And the chisel. (*Turns away inside.*) Now you shall see, father. Just let me show you what I mean.

(*Hedvig has fetched the required tools from the shelf, and hands them in to him.*)

HIALMAR: Ah, thanks. He couldn't have got on without me.

(*Goes in again; they are heard carpentering and talking inside. Hedvig stands looking in at them. A moment later there is a knock at the passage door; she does not notice it.*)

GREGERS WERLE (*bareheaded, in indoor dress, enters and stops near the door*): H'm – !

HEDVIG (*turns and goes towards him*): Good morning. Please come in.

GREGERS: Thank you. (*Looks towards the garret.*) You seem to have workpeople in the house.

HEDVIG: No, it's only father and grandfather. I'll tell them you are here.

GREGERS: No, no don't do that; I'd rather wait a little. (*Seats himself on the sofa.*)

HEDVIG: It's so untidy here. (*Begins to clear away the photographs.*)

GREGERS: Oh, don't move them. Are those pictures that have to be finished?

HEDVIG: Yes, they're a few I was helping father with.

GREGERS: Don't let me disturb you at all.

HEDVIG: Oh no.

(*She gathers the things to her and sits down to work; Gregers looks at her, meanwhile, in silence.*)

GREGERS: Did the wild duck sleep well last night?

HEDVIG: Yes, I think so, thanks.

GREGERS (*turning towards the garret*): It looks quite different by day from what it did last night in the moonlight.

HEDVIG: Yes, it varies so much. It looks different in the morning and in the afternoon; and it's different on rainy days from what it is in fine weather.

GREGERS: Have you noticed that?

HEDVIG: Yes, how could I help it?

GREGERS: Are *you* fond of being in there with the wild duck?

HEDVIG: Yes, when I can manage it –

GREGERS: Perhaps you haven't much leisure; you go to school, I daresay?

HEDVIG: No, not now; father's afraid of me hurting my eyes.

GREGERS: Oh; then he reads with you himself?

HEDVIG: Father has promised to read with me; but he hasn't had time yet.

GREGERS: Then is there nobody else that helps you a little?

HEDVIG: Yes, Mr. Molvik; but he's not always exactly – quite –

GREGERS: Sober?

HEDVIG: Yes, I suppose that's it!

GREGERS: Ah, then you've time for anything you please. And in there I suppose it's a sort of world by itself?

HEDVIG: Oh yes, quite. And there are such lots of wonderful things.

GREGERS: Indeed?

HEDVIG: Yes, there are big cupboards full of books, and a great many of the books have pictures in them.

GREGERS: Aha!

HEDVIG: And there's an old bureau with drawers and flaps, and a big clock with figures that come out. But it doesn't go now.

GREGERS: So time has come to a standstill in there – in the wild duck's domain.

HEDVIG: Yes. And there's an old paint-box and things of that sort; and all the books.

GREGERS: And you read the books, I suppose?

HEDVIG: Oh yes, when I get the chance. Most of them are English, though, and I don't understand English. But then I look at the pictures. – There's one great big book called 'Harrison's History of London'. It must be a hundred years old; and there are such heaps of pictures in it. At the beginning there's Death with an hour-glass, and a girl. I think that's horrid. But then there are all the other pictures of churches, and castles, and streets, and big ships sailing on the sea.

GREGERS: But tell me, where did all these wonderful things come from?

HEDVIG: Oh, an old sea captain once lived here, and he brought them home. They used to call him 'The Flying Dutchman', That was curious, because he wasn't a Dutchman.

GREGERS: Wasn't he?

HEDVIG: No. But he disappeared at last; and so he left all these things behind him.

GREGERS: Tell me, now, when you're sitting in there looking at the pictures, don't you wish you could travel and see the great world itself?

HEDVIG: Oh no! I mean always to stay at home and help father and mother.

GREGERS: To finish photographs?

HEDVIG: No, not only that. I should love above everything to learn to engrave pictures like those in the English books.

GREGERS: H'm. What does your father say to that?

HEDVIG: I don't think father likes it; he's so strange about that. Only think, he talks of my learning basket-making, and straw-plaiting! But I don't think *that* would lead to much.

GREGERS: Oh no, I don't think so either.

HEDVIG: But father was right in saying that if I had learnt basket-making I could have made the new basket for the wild duck.

GREGERS: So you could; and it was, strictly speaking, your business, wasn't it?

HEDVIG: Yes, for it's my wild duck.

GREGERS: Of course it is.

HEDVIG: Yes, it belongs to me. But I lend it to father and grandfather as often as they please.

GREGERS: Indeed? What do they do with it?

HEDVIG: Oh, they look after it, and build places for it, and so on.

GREGERS: No doubt; for the wild duck is by far the most distinguished inhabitant of the garret, I suppose.

HEDVIG: Yes, indeed she is; for she's a real wild fowl, you know. And she's so much to be pitied; she has no one to care for, poor thing.

GREGERS: She has no family, as the rabbits have –

HEDVIG: No. The hens too, many of them, were chickens together; but she's been taken right away from all her belongings. And then there's such a lot that's strange about the wild duck. Nobody knows her, and nobody knows where she came from either.

GREGERS: And she has been down in the depths of the sea.

HEDVIG (*with a quick glance at him, represses a smile and asks*): Why do you say, 'the depths of the sea'?

GREGERS: What else should I say?

HEDVIG: You could you, 'the bottom of the sea'.

GREGERS: Oh, mayn't I just as well say the depths of the sea?

HEDVIG: Yes; but it sounds so strange to me when other people speak of the depths of the sea.

GREGERS: Why so? Tell me why?

HEDVIG: No, I won't; because it's so stupid.

GREGERS: Oh no, I'm sure it's not. Do tell me why you smiled.

HEDVIG: Well, this is the reason: whenever I come to realise suddenly – in a flash – what's in there, it always seems to me that the whole room and everything in it should be called 'the depths of the sea'. – But that's so stupid.

GREGERS: You mustn't say that.

HEDVIG: Yes, because it's only a garret.

GREGERS (*looks fixedly at her*): Are you so sure of that?

HEDVIG (*astonished*): That it's a garret?

GREGERS: Are you quite certain of it?

(*Hedvig is silent, and looks at him open-mouthed. Gina comes in from the kitchen with the table things.*)

GREGERS (*rising*): I've come in upon you too early.

GINA: Oh, you must be somewhere; and we're nearly ready now, any way. Clear the table, Hedvig.

(*Hedvig clears away her things; she and Gina lay the cloth during the following. Gregers seats himself in the armchair, and turns over an album.*)

GREGERS: I hear you can retouch, Mrs. Ekdal.

GINA (*with a side glance*): Yes, I can.

GREGERS: That was exceedingly lucky.

GINA: How lucky?

GREGERS: Since Ekdal was to be a photographer, I mean.

HEDVIG: Mother can take photographs too.

GINA: Oh, yes. I've had to teach myself that too.

GREGERS: So it's you that really carry on the business, I suppose?

GINA: Yes, when Ekdal hasn't time himself.

GREGERS: He's a great deal taken up with his old father, no doubt.

GINA: Yes; and Ekdal isn't the sort of man to do nothing but take portraits of everyday people.

GREGERS: I quite agree with you; but having once gone in for the thing –

GINA: You know, Mr. Werle, Ekdal's not like one of your common photographers.

GREGERS: Of course not; but still –

(*A shot is fired within the garret.*)

GREGERS (*starting up*): What's that?

GINA: Ugh! Now they're firing again!

GREGERS: Have they firearms in there?

HEDVIG: They're out shooting.

GREGERS: What! (*At the door of the garret.*) Are you shooting, Hialmar?

HIALMAR (*inside the net*): Are you there? I didn't know; I was so taken up – (*To Hedvig.*) Why didn't you let us know? (*Comes into the studio.*)

GREGERS: Do you go shooting in the garret?

HIALMAR (*showing a double-barrelled pistol*): Oh, only with this.

GINA: Yes, you and grandfather will do yourselves an injury some day with that pigstol.

HIALMAR (*with irritation*): I believe I've told you that this kind of firearm is called a *pistol.*

GINA: Oh, that's not much better, that I can see.

GREGERS: So you've become a sportsman too, Hialmar?

HIALMAR: Only a little rabbit-shooting now and then. It's mostly to please father, you understand.

GINA: Men are so strange; they must always have something to pervert themselves with.

HIALMAR (*snappishly*): Just so; we must always have something to *divert* ourselves with.

GINA: Yes, that's exactly what I say.

HIALMAR: H'm (*To Gregers.*) You see the garret's luckily so situated that no one can hear us shooting. (*Lays the pistol on the top shelf of the bookcase.*) Don't touch the pistol, Hedvig! One of the barrels is loaded, remember that.

GREGERS (*looking through the net*): You have a fowling-piece too, I see.

HIALMAR: That's father's old gun. It's no use now; there's something gone wrong with the lock. But it's fun to have it all the same, for we can take it to pieces now and then, and grease it and screw it together again. – Of course it's mostly father that fiddle-faddles with all that sort of thing.

HEDVIG (*beside Gregers*): Now you can see the wild duck properly.

GREGERS: I'm just looking at her. She droops one wing rather, I think.

HEDVIG: Well, no wonder; she was wounded, you know.

GREGERS: And she trails one foot a little. Isn't that so?

HIALMAR: Perhaps a very little bit.

HEDVIG: Yes, it was by that foot the dog seized her.

HIALMAR: But otherwise she hasn't the least thing the matter with her, and that's really wonderful for a creature that's got a charge of shot in her body, and has been between a dog's teeth –

GREGERS (*with a glance at Hedvig*): – And that's been in the depths of the sea – so long.

HEDVIG (*smiling*): Yes.

GINA (*laying the table*): That blessed wild duck! What a lot of fuss you make over her.

HIALMAR: H'm – is lunch nearly ready?

GINA: Yes, directly. Hedvig, you must come and help me now. (*Gina and Hedvig go out into the kitchen.*)

HIALMAR (*in a low voice*): I think you'd better not stand there looking in at father; he doesn't like it. (*Gregers moves away from the garret door.*) I may as well shut up before the others come. (*Claps his hands to send the fowls back.*) Ssh – ssh, in with you! (*Draws up the curtain and pulls the doors together.*) All these appliances are my own invention. It's really amusing to have things of this sort to potter about, and to put to rights when they get out of order. And it's quite necessary, you see; for Gina objects to having rabbits and fowls in the studio.

GREGERS: Of course. I suppose it's your wife that's the ruling spirit here?

HIALMAR: I generally leave the details of business to her; for then I can take refuge in the parlour and think of more important things.

GREGERS: What things may they be, Hialmar?

HIALMAR: I wonder you haven't asked about that sooner. But perhaps you haven't heard of the invention?

GREGERS: The invention? No.

HIALMAR: Really? Haven't you? Oh no, out there in the wilderness –

GREGERS: So you've invented something, have you?

HIALMAR: I haven't quite completed it yet; but I'm working at it. You can imagine that when I resolved to give myself up to photography, it wasn't with the idea of doing nothing but take portraits of all sorts of everyday people.

GREGERS: No; your wife was saying the same thing just now.

HIALMAR: I swore that if I consecrated my powers to this handicraft I would so exalt it that it should become both an art and a science. And therefore I resolved to devote myself to this great invention.

GREGERS: And what's the nature of the invention? What is it to do?

HIALMAR: Oh, my dear fellow, you mustn't ask for details yet. It takes time, you see. And you mustn't think that my motive is vanity. It's not for my own sake that I'm working. Oh no; it's my life's mission that stands before me night and day.

GREGERS: What is your life's mission?

HIALMAR: Do you forget the old man with the silver hair?

GREGERS: Your poor father? Well, but what can you do for him?

HIALMAR: I can awaken his self-respect from the dead, by raising the name of Ekdal to honour and dignity again.

GREGERS: Then that's your life's mission?

HIALMAR: Yes. I want to save the shipwrecked man. For shipwrecked he was by the very first blast of the storm. Even while those terrible investigations were going on, he was no longer himself. That pistol there – the one we use to shoot rabbits with – has played its part in the tragedy of the house of Ekdal.

GREGERS: The pistol? Indeed?

HIALMAR: When the sentence of imprisonment was passed – he had the pistol in his hand –

GREGERS: Had he – ?

HIALMAR: Yes; but he dared not use it. His courage failed him. So broken, so demoralised was he even then! Oh, can you understand it? He, a soldier; he, who had shot nine bears, and who was descended from two lieutenant-colonels – one after the other, of course. – Can you understand it, Gregers?

GREGERS: Yes, I understand it well enough.

HIALMAR: I don't. And once more the pistol played a part in our family history. When he had put on the grey clothes and was under lock and key – oh, that was a terrible time for me, I can tell you. I had the blinds drawn down over both my windows. When I peeped out I saw the sun shining as usual. I couldn't understand it. I saw the people going along the street, laughing and talking about indifferent things. I couldn't understand it. It seemed to me that the whole of existence must be at a standstill – as if under an eclipse.

GREGERS: I felt like that too, when my mother died.

HIALMAR: In that hour Hialmar Ekdal pointed the pistol at his own breast.

GREGERS: You too thought of – !

HIALMAR: Yes.

GREGERS: But you didn't fire?

HIALMAR: No. At the decisive moment I won the victory over myself. I remained in life. But I can assure you it takes some courage to choose life under those circumstances.

GREGERS: Well, that depends on how one takes it.

HIALMAR: Yes, entirely. But it was all for the best, for now I shall soon perfect my invention; and Dr. Relling thinks, as I do myself, that father will be allowed to wear his uniform again. I will ask for that as my only reward.

GREGERS: So that's what he meant about his uniform?

HIALMAR: Yes, that's what he most yearns for. You can't imagine how my heart bleeds for him. Every time we celebrate any little family festival – for example, Gina's and my wedding-day, or whatever it may be – in comes the old man in the lieutenant's uniform of happier days. But if he only hears a knock at the door – for he daren't show himself to strangers, you know – he hurries back to his room again as fast as his legs can carry him. Oh, it's heartrending for a son to see such things!

GREGERS: How long do you think it will be before your invention is completed?

HIALMAR: Come now, you mustn't expect me to enter into particulars like that. An invention is a thing one hasn't entire control over. It depends largely on intuition – on inspiration – and it's almost impossible to predict when the inspiration may come.

GREGERS: But it's advancing?

HIALMAR: Yes, certainly, it's advancing. I turn it over in my mind every day: I'm full of it. Every afternoon, when I've had my dinner, I shut myself up in the parlour where I can ponder undisturbed. But I can't be goaded to it; it's not a bit of good; Relling says so too.

GREGERS: And don't you think that all that business in the garret draws you off and distracts you too much?

HIALMAR: No, no, no, quite the contrary. You mustn't say that. I can't be everlastingly absorbed in the same laborious train of thought. I must have something outside of it to fill up the pauses. The inspiration, the intuition, you see – when it comes, it comes, and there's an end of it.

GREGERS: My dear Hialmar, I almost think you have something of the wild duck in you.

HIALMAR: Something of the wild duck? How do you mean?

GREGERS: You've dived down and bitten yourself fast in the undergrowth.

HIALMAR: Are you alluding to the almost fatal shot that has broken father's wing – and mine too?

GREGERS: Not mainly to that. I don't say that you've been wounded; but you've strayed into a poisonous marsh, Hialmar; you have an insidious disease within you, and you've sunk down to die in the dark.

HIALMAR: I? To die in the dark? Look here, Gregers, you must really leave off talking such nonsense.

GREGERS: Don't be afraid; I will try to help you up again. I, too, have a mission in life now; I found it yesterday.

HIALMAR: That's all very well; but you'll please leave *me* out of it. I can assure you that – apart from my easily explained melancholy, of course – I am as contented as any one can wish to be.

GREGERS: Your contentment is an effect of the marsh vapours.

HIALMAR: Now, my dear Gregers, pray don't go on about disease and poison; I'm not used to that sort of talk. In my house, nobody ever speaks to me about unpleasant things.

GREGERS: Ah, I can easily believe that.

HIALMAR: It's not good for me, you see. And there aren't any marsh vapours here, as you express it. The poor photographer's roof is lowly, I know – and my circumstances are narrow. But I'm an inventor, and I'm the breadwinner of a family. That exalts me above my mean surroundings. – Ah, here comes lunch!

(*Gina and Hedvig bring bottles of ale, a decanter of brandy, glasses, etc. At the same time, Relling and Molvik enter from the passage; they are both without hat or overcoat. Molvik is dressed in black.*)

GINA (*setting things upon the table*): Oh, you two have come in the nick of time.

RELLING: Molvik got it into his head that he could smell herring-salad, and then there was no holding him. Good morning again, Ekdal.

HIALMAR: Gregers, may I introduce Mr. Molvik. Doctor – Oh, you know Relling, don't you?

GREGERS: Yes, slightly.

RELLING: Oh, Mr. Werle, junior! Yes, we two have been on each other's tracks up at the Höidal works. You've just moved in?

GREGERS: I moved in this morning.

RELLING: Molvik and I live right underneath you; so you haven't far to go for the doctor and the clergyman, if you should need them.

GREGERS: Thanks, it's not unlikely; for yesterday we were thirteen at table.

HIALMAR: Oh, come now, don't let's get upon unpleasant subjects again!

RELLING: You can make your mind easy, Ekdal; I'll be hanged if the finger of fate points to you.

HIALMAR: I hope not, for the sake of my family. But let us sit down and eat and drink and be merry.

GREGERS: Shan't we wait for your father?

HIALMAR: No, he'll have his taken in to him later. Come along!

(*The men seat themselves at table, and eat and drink. Gina and Hedvig go in and out and wait upon them.*)

RELLING: Molvik was frightfully screwed yesterday, Mrs. Ekdal.

GINA: Really? Yesterday again?

RELLING: Didn't you hear him when I brought him home last night?

GINA: No, I can't say I did.

RELLING: That was a good thing, for Molvik was disgusting last night.

GINA: Is that true, Molvik?

MOLVIK: Let us blot out last night's proceedings. That sort of thing is totally apart from my better self.

RELLING (*to Gregers*): It comes over him like a sort of possession, and then I have to go out on the loose with him. Mr. Molvik is dæmonic, you see.

GREGERS: Dæmonic?

RELLING: Molvik's dæmonic, yes.

GREGERS: H'm.

RELLING: And daemonic natures are not made to walk straight through the world; they must meander a little now and then. – Well, so you still stick up there at those horrible grimy works?

GREGERS: I have stuck there until now.

RELLING: And did you manage to enforce that claim you went about asserting?

GREGERS: Claims? (*Understands him.*) Ah, I see.

HIALMAR: Have you been enforcing claims, Gregers?

GREGERS: Oh, nonsense.

RELLING: Faith, but he has, though! He went round to all the cotters' cabins, presenting something he called the claim of the ideal.

GREGERS: I was young then.

RELLING: You're right; you were very young. And as for the claim of the ideal – you never got it honoured while I was up there.

GREGERS: Nor since either.

RELLING: Ah, then you've learnt to knock a little discount off, I expect.

GREGERS: Never, when I stand before a true man.

HIALMAR: Well, that's reasonable, I should say. A little butter, Gina.

RELLING: And a slice of bacon for Molvik.

MOLVIK: Ugh! not bacon! (*A knock at the garret door.*)

HIALMAR: Open the door, Hedvig; father wants to come out.

(*Hedvig goes over and opens the door a little way; Ekdal comes in with a fresh rabbit skin; she closes the door after him.*)

EKDAL: Good morning, gentlemen! Good sport today. Shot a big one.

HIALMAR: And you've skinned it before I came!

EKDAL: Salted it too. It's good tender meat, is rabbit; it's sweet; it tastes like sugar. Good appetite to you, gentlemen! (*Goes into his room.*)

MOLVIK (*rising*): Excuse me – ; I can't – ; I must go downstairs as quickly as –

RELLING: Drink some soda water, man!

MOLVIK (*hurrying away*): Ugh-ugh! (*Goes through the passage door.*)

RELLING (*to Hialmar*): Let's drain a glass to the old hunter.

HIALMAR (*clinks glasses with him*): To the man of daring deeds that has looked death in the face!

RELLING: To the grey-haired – (*drinks*). I say, is his hair grey or white?

HIALMAR: Something between the two, I think; for that matter, he hasn't very many hairs left on his head.

RELLING: Well, one can get through the world with a wig. After all, you're a happy man, Ekdal; you have this noble mission to strive for –

HIALMAR: And I do strive, I can tell you.

RELLING: And you have your excellent wife, waddling quietly in and out in her felt slippers, and making everything cosy and comfortable about you.

HIALMAR: Yes, Gina (*nods to her*), you're a good companion on the path of life.

GINA: Oh, don't sit there criticising me.

RELLING: And your Hedvig too, Ekdal!

HIALMAR (*affected*): The child, yes! The child before everything! Hedvig, come here to me. (*Strokes her hair.*) What day is it tomorrow, eh?

HEDVIG (*shaking him*): Oh no, you're not to say anything, father!

HIALMAR: It cuts me to the heart when I think how poor an affair it'll be; only a little festivity in the garret –

HEDVIG: Oh, but that's just what I like!

RELLING: Just you wait till the wonderful invention sees the light, Hedvig!

HIALMAR: Yes, indeed! then you shall see – ! Hedvig, I've resolved to make your future secure. You shall live in comfort all your days. I will demand something or other for you. That shall be the poor inventor's sole reward.

HEDVIG (*whispering, with her arms round his neck*): Oh, you dear, kind father!

RELLING (*to Gregers*): Don't you find it delightful, for once in a way, to sit at a well-spread table in a happy family circle?

HIALMAR: Yes, I really prize these social hours.

GREGERS: For my part, I don't thrive in marsh vapours.

RELLING: Marsh vapours?

HIALMAR: Oh, don't begin with that talk again!

GINA: Heaven knows there's no bad smell here, Mr. Werle; I give the place a good airing every blessed day.

GREGERS (*leaves the table*): No airing will drive out the taint I mean.

HIALMAR: Taint!

GINA: Yes, what do you say to that, Ekdal!

RELLING: Excuse me, but haven't you yourself brought the taint from those mines up there?

GREGERS: It's like you to call what I bring into this house a taint.

RELLING (*goes up to him*): I tell you what it is, Mr. Werle, junior: I have a strong suspicion that you're still carrying about that claim of the ideal, large as life, in your coat-tail pocket.

GREGERS: I carry it in my breast.

RELLING: Well, wherever you've got it, I advise you not to come dunning us with it here, so long as I'm on the premises.

GREGERS: And if I do it all the same?

RELLING: Then you'll go head-foremost downstairs; now I've warned you.

HIALMAR (*rising*): Oh, but Mr. Relling – !

GREGERS: Yes, just you turn me out –

GINA (*steps between them*): You mustn't do that, Relling. But I must say, Mr. Werle, that it ill becomes you to talk about swamps and taints, after all the mess you made with your stove.

(*A knock at the passage door.*)

HEDVIG: Mother, there's somebody knocking.

HIALMAR: There now, we're going to have a whole lot of people!

GINA: Let me go – (*Goes over and opens the door, starts, and draws back.*) Oh – oh dear!

(*Werle, in a fur coat, advances one step into the room.*)

WERLE: Excuse me; but I think my son is staying here.

GINA (*with a gulp*): Yes.

HIALMAR (*approaching him*): Won't you do us the honour to – ?

WERLE: Thank you, I merely wish to speak to my son.

GREGERS: What is it? Here I am.

WERLE: I wish to speak with you in your room.

GREGERS: In my room? – well – (*is going*).

GINA: No, your room's not in a fit state to –

WERLE: Well then, out in the passage there; I want to have a few words with you alone.

HIALMAR: You can do that here, sir. Come into the parlour, Relling.

(*Hialmar and Relling go off to the right. Gina takes Hedvig with her into the kitchen.*)

GREGERS (*after a short pause*): Well, now we're alone.

WERLE: From something you let fall last evening, and from your coming to lodge with the Ekdals, I can't help inferring that you have some hostile intention towards me.

GREGERS: I intend to open Hialmar Ekdal's eyes. He shall see his position as it really is – that is all.

WERLE: Is that the mission in life you spoke of yesterday?

GREGERS: Yes. You have left me no other.

WERLE: Is it I that have crippled your mind, Gregers?

GREGERS: You have crippled my whole life. I'm not thinking of all that about mother – but it's thanks to you that I have a guilty conscience continually pursuing and gnawing at me.

WERLE: Aha, it's your conscience that's ill at ease, is it?

GREGERS: I ought to have taken a stand against you when the trap was set for Lieutenant Ekdal. I should have cautioned him, for I had a misgiving as to what was in the wind.

WERLE: Yes, that was the time to have spoken.

GREGERS: I did not dare to, I was so cowed and spiritless. I was mortally afraid of you, not only then, but long afterwards.

WERLE: You've got over that fear now, it appears.

GREGERS: Yes, fortunately. The wrong done to old Ekdal, both by me and by – others, can never be remedied; but Hialmar I can rescue from all the falsehood and deception that are bringing him to ruin.

WERLE: Do you think that'll be doing him a kindness?

GREGERS: I firmly believe so.

WERLE: You think our friend the photographer is the sort of man to appreciate such friendly offices?

GREGERS: Yes, I do.

WERLE: H'm, we shall see.

GREGERS: Besides, if I'm to go on living, I must try and find some cure for my sick conscience.

WERLE: It will never be well. Your conscience has been sickly from childhood. That's an inheritance from your mother, Gregers – the only inheritance she left you.

GREGERS (*with a scornful half-smile*): Haven't you yet digested your resentment at your own miscalculation as to the fortune she would bring you?

WERLE: Don't let us get upon irrelevant subjects. – Then you keep to your purpose of setting young Ekdal upon what you imagine to be the right scent?

GREGERS: Yes, that's my fixed resolve.

WERLE: Well, in that case I might have spared myself this visit; for of course it's useless to ask you to return home with me?

GREGERS: Quite useless.

WERLE: And I suppose you won't enter the firm either?

GREGERS: No.

WERLE: Very good. But as I'm thinking of marrying again, your share in the property will fall to you at once.

GREGERS (*quickly*): No, I don't wish that.

WERLE: You don't wish it?

GREGERS: No, I daren't take it, for conscience' sake.

WERLE (*after a pause*): Are you going up to the works again?

GREGERS: No; I consider myself released from your service.

WERLE: But what are you going to do?

GREGERS: Only to fulfil my mission, nothing more.

WERLE: Well, but afterwards? What are you going to live upon?

GREGERS: I have laid by a little out of my salary.

WERLE: How long will *that* last?

GREGERS: I think it will last out my time.

WERLE: What do you mean?

GREGERS: I shall answer no more questions.

WERLE: Goodbye, then, Gregers.

GREGERS: Goodbye.

HIALMAR (*peeping in*): He's gone, isn't he?

GREGERS: Yes.

(*Hialmar and Relling enter; also Gina and Hedvig from the kitchen.*)

RELLING: That lunch was a failure.

GREGERS: Put on your coat, Hialmar; I want you to come for a long walk with me.

HIALMAR: With pleasure. What was it your father wanted? Anything about me?.

GREGERS: Come along. We must have a talk. I'll go and put on my overcoat. (*Goes out by the passage door.*)

GINA: You shouldn't go out with him, Ekdal.

RELLING: No, don't you do it. Stay where you are.

HIALMAR (*gets his hat and overcoat*): Oh, nonsense! When a friend of my youth feels impelled to open his mind to me in private –

RELLING: But deuce take it – don't you see the fellow's mad, cracked, demented!

GINA: There, you hear! His mother before him had mad fits like that sometimes.

HIALMAR: The more need for a friend's watchful eye. (*To Gina.*) Be sure you have dinner ready in good time. Goodbye for the present. (*Goes out by the passage door.*)

RELLING: It's a pity the fellow didn't go to hell through one of the Höidal mines.

GINA: Good Lord! what makes you say that?

RELLING (*muttering*): Oh, I have my reasons.

GINA: Do you think young Werle is really mad?

RELLING: No, worse luck; he's no madder than people in general. But one disease he's certainly suffering from.

GINA: What is it that's wrong with him?

RELLING: Well, I'll tell you, Mrs. Ekdal. He's suffering from chronic integrity in an acute form.

GINA: Integrity?

HEDVIG: Is that a kind of disease?

RELLING: Yes, it's a national disease; but it only appears sporadically. (*Nods to Gina.*) Thanks for your hospitality. (*He goes out by the passage door.*)

GINA (*walking to and fro*): Ugh, that Gregers Werle – he's always been a horrible creature.

HEDVIG (*standing by the table, and looking searchingly at her*): I think all this is very strange.

Act Four

Hialmar Ekdal's studio. A photograph has just been taken; a camera with the cloth over it, a pedestal, two chairs, folding table, etc., are standing out in the room. Afternoon light; the sun is going down; a little later it begins to grow dusk.

Gina stands in the passage doorway, with a little box and a wet glass plate in her hand, and is speaking to somebody outside.

GINA: Yes, certainly. When I make a promise I keep it. The first dozen shall be ready on Monday. Good afternoon. (*Some one is heard going downstairs. Gina shuts the door, slips the plate into the box, and puts it into the covered camera.*)

HEDVIG (*comes in from the kitchen*): Are they gone?

GINA (*tidying up*): Yes, thank goodness, I've got rid of them at last.

HEDVIG: But can you imagine why father hasn't come home yet?

GINA: Are you sure he's not down in Relling's room?

HEDVIG: No, he's not; I ran down the kitchen stair and asked just now.

GINA: And I suppose his dinner's getting cold.

HEDVIG: Yes, I can't understand it. Father's always so careful to be home to dinner!

GINA: Oh, he'll be here directly, you'll see.

HEDVIG: I wish he would come; everything seems so queer today.

GINA (*calls out*): There he is!

(*Hialmar Ekdal comes in at the passage door.*)

HEDVIG (*going to him*): Father! Oh, what a time we've been waiting for you!

GINA (*glances at him*): You've been a long time away, Ekdal.

HIALMAR (*without looking at her*): Rather long, yes.

(*He takes off his overcoat; Gina and Hedvig go to help him; he motions them away.*)

GINA: Perhaps you've had dinner with Werle?

HIALMAR (*hanging up his coat*): No.

GINA (*going towards the kitchen door*): Then I'll bring some in for you.

HIALMAR: No; let the dinner be. I don't want anything to eat.

HEDVIG (*going nearer to him*): Aren't you well, father?

HIALMAR: Well? Oh yes, tolerably. Gregers and I had a tiring walk.

GINA: You oughtn't to have gone so far, Ekdal; you're not used to it.

HIALMAR: H'm; there's many a thing a man must get used to in this world. (*Wanders about the room.*) Has any one been here whilst I was out?

GINA: Nobody but the two sweethearts.

HIALMAR: No new orders?

GINA: No, no today.

HEDVIG: There'll be some tomorrow, father, you'll see.

HIALMAR: I hope there will; for tomorrow I'm going to set to work in earnest.

HEDVIG: Tomorrow! Don't you remember what day it is tomorrow?

HIALMAR: Oh yes, by-the-by – Well, the day after, then. Henceforth I mean to do everything myself; I'll do all the work alone.

GINA: What's the good of that, Ekdal? It'll only make life a burden to you. I can manage the photography; and you can go on working at your invention.

HEDVIG: And think of the wild duck, father – and all the hens and rabbits and – !

HIALMAR: Don't talk to me of all that trash! From tomorrow I'll never set foot in the garret again.

HEDVIG: Oh but, father, you promised that we should have a little entertainment –

HIALMAR: H'm, true. Well then, from the day after tomorrow. I'm almost inclined to wring that cursed wild duck's neck!

HEDVIG (*shrieks*): The wild duck!

GINA: Well I never!

HEDVIG (*shaking him*): Oh no, father; you know it's my wild duck!

HIALMAR: That's why I don't do it. I haven't the heart to – for your sake, Hedvig. But in my inmost soul I feel that I ought to do it. I ought not to suffer a creature that has been in those hands under my roof.

GINA: Why, good gracious, because grandfather got it from that wretched Pettersen –

HIALMAR (*wandering about*): There are certain claims – what shall I call them? – let me say claims of the ideal – certain obligations, which a man cannot set aside without injury to his soul.

HEDVIG (*going after him*): But think of the wild duck – the poor wild duck!

HIALMAR (*stops*): I tell you I'll spare it – for your sake. Not a hair of its head shall be touched – I mean, I'll spare it. There are greater problems than that to be dealt with. But you should go out a little now, Hedvig, as usual; it's getting dusk enough for you now.

HEDVIG: No, I don't care about going out now.

HIALMAR: Yes, do; it seems to me you peer about so with your eyes; all these vapours in here are bad for you. The air is heavy under this roof.

HEDVIG: Very well then, I shall run down the kitchen stair and take a little walk. My cloak and hat? – oh, they're in my own room. Father – be sure you don't do the wild duck any harm whilst I'm out.

HIALMAR: Not a feather of its head shall be touched. (*Draws her to him.*) You and I, Hedvig – we two – ! Well, go along.

(*Hedvig nods to her parents and goes out through the kitchen.*)

HIALMAR (*walks about without looking up*): Gina.

GINA: Yes?

HIALMAR: From tomorrow, or say from the day after tomorrow, I should like to keep the household account-book myself.

GINA: Do you want to keep the accounts too, now?

HIALMAR: Yes; or to put down the receipts at any rate.

GINA: Lord help us! that's soon done.

HIALMAR: One would hardly think so; at any rate you seem to make the money go a very long way. (*Stops and looks at her.*) How do you manage it?

GINA: It's because Hedvig and I need so little.

HIALMAR: Is it the case that father is very liberally paid for the copying he does for Mr. Werle?

GINA: I don't know whether the pay is so liberal. I don't know the prices for such work.

HIALMAR: Well, what does he get, about? Let me hear!

GINA: Oh, it varies; it comes to about as much as he costs us, with a little pocket-money over.

HIALMAR: As much as he costs us! And you've never told me this before!

GINA: No, I couldn't; it pleased you so much to think he got everything from you.

HIALMAR: And he gets it from Mr. Werle!

GINA: Oh yes; he has plenty and to spare, he has.

HIALMAR: Light the lamp for me, please!

GINA (*lighting the lamp*): And of course we don't know that it's Mr. Werle himself; it may be Gråberg –

HIALMAR: Why attempt such an evasion?

GINA: I don't know; I only thought –

HIALMAR: H'm!

GINA: It wasn't I that got grandfather that writing. It was Bertha, when she used to come about us.

HIALMAR: It seems to me your voice is trembling.

GINA (*putting the lamp-shade on*): Is it?

HIALMAR: And your hands are shaking, aren't they?

GINA (*firmly*): Speak straight out, Ekdal. What has he been saying about me?

HIALMAR: Is it true – can it be true that – that there was an – an understanding between you and Mr. Werle, while you were in service there?

GINA: That's not true. Not at that time. Mr. Werle did come after me, I own it. And his wife thought there was something in it, and then she made such a hocus-pocus and hurly-burly, and she knocked and drove me about so, that I left her service.

HIALMAR: But afterwards, then?

GINA: Well, then I went home. And mother – well, she wasn't the woman you took her for, Ekdal; she kept on worrying and worrying at me about one thing and another – for Mr. Werle was a widower by that time.

HIALMAR: Well, and then?

GINA: I suppose you must know it. He didn't give it up until he'd had his way.

HIALMAR (*striking his hands together*): And this is the mother of my child! How could you hide this from me?

GINA: It was wrong of me; I ought certainly to have told you long ago.

HIALMAR: You should have told me at the very first; then I should have known what you were.

GINA: But would you have married me all the same?

HIALMAR: How can you suppose so?

GINA: That's just why I didn't dare to tell you anything then. I'd come to care for you so much, you know; and I couldn't go and make myself utterly miserable –

HIALMAR (*walks about*): And this is my Hedvig's mother! And to know that all I see before me – (*kicks at a chair*) – all that I call my home – I owe to a favoured predecessor! Oh, that scoundrel Werle!

GINA: Do you repent the fifteen years we've lived together?

HIALMAR: Haven't you every day, every hour, repented of the spider's-web of deceit you had spun around me? Answer me that! How could you help writhing with penitence and remorse?

GINA: My dear Ekdal, I've had plenty to do looking after the house and all the daily business –

HIALMAR: Then you never think of reviewing your past?

GINA: No; heaven knows I'd almost forgotten those old stories.

HIALMAR: Oh, that blank, callous contentment! To me there is something revolting about it. Think of it – never so much as a twinge of remorse!

GINA: But tell me, Ekdal, what would have become of you if you hadn't had a wife like me?

HIALMAR: Like you – !

GINA: Yes; for you know I've always been a little more practical and wide-awake than you. Of course I'm a year or two older.

HIALMAR: What would have become of me!

GINA: You'd got into all sorts of bad ways when first you met me; you can't deny that.

HIALMAR: So that's what you call bad ways? Oh, you don't understand what a man goes through when he's in grief and despair – especially a man of my fiery temperament.

GINA: Well, that may be so. And I don't say I've anything to boast of; for you became a moral of a husband directly you'd a house and home of your own. And now we'd got everything so nice and cosy about us; and Hedvig and I were just thinking we'd soon be able to give ourselves a little rein, in the way of both food and clothes.

HIALMAR: In the swamp of deceit, yes.

GINA: Oh, that that wretched creature had never set his foot inside our doors!

HIALMAR: And I, too, thought my home such a pleasant one. That was a delusion. Where shall I now find the elasticity of spirit to bring my invention into the world of reality? Perhaps it will die with me; and then it will be your past, Gina, that will have killed it.

GINA (*nearly crying*): You mustn't say such things, Ekdal. I've only wanted to do what was best for you all my days!

HIALMAR: I ask you, what becomes of the breadwinner's dream? When I used to lie in there on the sofa and ponder over the invention, I had a clear enough presentiment that it would sap my vitality to the last drop. I felt even then that the day when I held the patent in my hand would be the day – of my release. And then it was my dream that you should live on and be known as the deceased inventor's well-to-do widow!

GINA (*drying her tears*): No, you mustn't talk like that, Ekdal. May the Lord never let me see the day I am left a widow!

HIALMAR: Oh, the whole dream has vanished. It's all over now. All over!

(*Gregers Werle opens the passage door cautiously and looks in.*)

GREGERS: May I come in?

HIALMAR: Yes, come in.

GREGERS (*comes forward, his face beaming with satisfaction, and holds out both his hands to them*): Well, dear friends – ! (*Looks from one to the other, and whispers to Hialmar.*) Haven't you done it yet?

HIALMAR (*aloud*): It *is* done.

GREGERS: It *is*?

HIALMAR: I have passed through the bitterest moments of my life.

GREGERS: But also the most ennobling, I should think.

HIALMAR: Well, we've got through it for the present.

GINA: God forgive you, Mr. Werle.

GREGERS (*in great surprise*): But I don't understand this.

HIALMAR: What don't you understand?

GREGERS: After so great a crisis – a crisis that's to be the starting-point of an entirely new life – of a communion founded on truth and free from falsehood of any kind –

HIALMAR: Yes, yes, I know; I know that quite well.

GREGERS: I confidently expected, when I entered the room, to find the light of transfiguration beaming upon me from both man and wife. And now I see nothing but dullness, oppression, gloom –

GINA: Oh, is that it? (*Takes off the lamp-shade.*)

GREGERS: You will not understand me, Mrs. Ekdal. Ah well, *you*, I suppose, need time too – But you, Hialmar? Surely you feel a new consecration after the great crisis?

HIALMAR: Yes, of course I do. That is, – in a sort of way.

GREGERS: For I'm sure there's nothing in the world to compare with the joy of forgiving one who has erred, and raising her up to one's self in love.

HIALMAR: Do you think a man can so easily throw off the effects of the bitter cup I have drained?

GREGERS: No, perhaps not a common man. But a man like you!

HIALMAR: Good God! I know that well enough. But you must keep me up to it, Gregers. It takes time, you know.

GREGERS: You have a great deal of the wild duck in you, Hialmar.

(*Relling has come in at the passage door.*)

RELLING: Oho! is the wild duck to the fore again?

HIALMAR: Yes; Mr. Werle's wing-broken prey.

RELLING: Mr. Werle's – ? So you're discussing him?

HIALMAR: Him and – ourselves.

RELLING (*in an undertone to Gregers*): May the devil take you!

HIALMAR: What's that you're saying?

RELLING: I was uttering a heartfelt wish that this quack-salver would take himself off. If he stops here he's sure to get you both into a mess.

GREGERS: These two won't make a mess of it, Mr. Relling. Of course I won't speak of Hialmar – him we know. But she too, in her innermost heart, has certainly something loyal and sincere –

GINA (*almost crying*): You might have let me pass for what I was, then.

RELLING (*to Gregers*): Is it rude to ask what you really want in this house.

GREGERS: To lay the foundations of a true marriage.

RELLING: So you don't think Ekdal's marriage is good enough as it is?

GREGERS: No doubt it's as good a marriage as most others, worse luck. But a *true* marriage it has never been.

HIALMAR: You have never had eyes for the claims of the ideal, Relling.

RELLING: All rubbish, my boy! But excuse me, Mr. Werle: how

many – in round numbers – how many true marriages have you seen in the course of your life?

GREGERS: Scarcely a single one.

RELLING: Nor I either.

GREGERS: But I've seen innumerable marriages of the opposite kind. And it has been my fate to see at close quarters what ruin such a marriage can work.

HIALMAR: A man's whole moral basis may give way under his feet; that's the terrible part of it.

RELLING: Well, I can't say I've ever been exactly married, so I don't pretend to speak with authority. But this I know, that the child enters into the marriage problem. And you must leave the child in peace.

HIALMAR: Oh – Hedvig! my poor Hedvig!

RELLING: Yes, you must be good enough to keep Hedvig outside of all this. You two are grown-up people; you can, in God's name, mess and muddle with your relations as you please. But you must deal circumspectly with Hedvig, I tell you; or else you may do her a great injury.

HIALMAR: An injury!

RELLING: Yes, or she may do herself an injury – and perhaps others too.

GINA: How can you know that, Relling?

HIALMAR: Her sight is in no immediate danger, is it?

RELLING: I'm not talking about her sight. Hedvig is at a critical age. She'll be taking all sorts of mischief into her head.

GINA: That's true – I've noticed it already! She's taken to carrying on with the fire, out in the kitchen. She calls it playing at house-on-fire. I'm often afraid she'll really set fire to the house.

RELLING: You see; I thought as much.

GREGERS (*to Relling*): But how do you account for that?

RELLING (*low*): Her constitution's changing, sir.

HIALMAR: So long as the child has me – ! So long as I'm above ground – !

(*A knock at the door.*)

GINA: Hush, Ekdal; there's some one in the passage. (*Calls out.*) Come in!

(*Mrs. Sörby, in walking dress, comes in.*)

MRS. SÖRBY: Good evening.

GINA (*going towards her*): Is that really you, Bertha?

MRS. SÖRBY: Yes, of course it is. But I've come inopportunely, I'm afraid?

HIALMAR: No, not at all; an emissary from *that* house –

MRS. SÖRBY (*to Gina*): To tell the truth, I hoped your men-folk would be out at this time; I just ran up to have a little chat with you, and to say goodbye.

GINA: Indeed? Are you going away, then?

MRS. SÖRBY: Yes, tomorrow morning, – up to Höidal. Mr. Werle has started this afternoon. (*Lightly, to Gregers.*) He wished me to say goodbye for him.

GINA: Only fancy – !

HIALMAR: So Mr. Werle has gone? And now you're going after him?

MRS. SÖRBY: Yes, what do you say to that, Ekdal?

HIALMAR: I say : beware!

GREGERS: I must explain the situation. My father and Mrs. Sörby are going to be married.

HIALMAR: Going to be married!

GINA: Oh, Bertha, so it's come to that at last!

RELLING (*his voice quivering a little*): This is surely not true?

MRS. SÖRBY: Yes, my dear Relling, it's true enough.

RELLING: You're going to marry again?

MRS. SÖRBY: Yes, it looks like it. Werle has got a special licence, and we're going to be married quite quietly, up at the works.

GREGERS: Then I must wish you all happiness, like a dutiful stepson.

MRS. SÖRBY: Thank you very much – if you mean what you say. I hope it will lead to happiness, both for Werle and for me.

RELLING: You have every reason to hope that. Mr. Werle never gets drunk, so far as I know; and I don't suppose he's in the habit of thrashing his wives, like the late lamented horse-doctor.

MRS. SÖRBY: Oh now, let Sörby rest in peace. He had his good points too.

RELLING: Mr. Werle has better ones, I should think.

MRS. SÖRBY: He hasn't frittered away all that was good in him, at any rate. The man who does that must take the consequences.

RELLING: I shall go out with Molvik this evening.

MRS. SÖRBY: You mustn't do that, Relling. Don't do it – for my sake.

RELLING: There's nothing else for it. (*To Hialmar.*) If you're going with us, come along.

GINA: No, thank you. Ekdal doesn't go in for such dispensations.

HIALMAR (*half aloud, in vexation*): Oh, do hold your tongue!

RELLING: Goodbye, Mrs. – Werle. (*Goes out through the passage door.*)

GREGERS (*to Mrs. Sörby*): You seem to be pretty intimate with Dr. Relling.

MRS. SÖRBY: Yes, we've known each other for many years. At one time it seemed as if things might have gone further between us.

GREGERS: It was surely lucky for you that they didn't.

MRS. SÖRBY: You may well say that. But I've always been wary of acting on impulse. A woman can't afford absolutely to throw herself away.

GREGERS: Aren't you just the least bit afraid that I may let my father know about this old friendship?

MRS. SÖRBY: Why, of course I've told him all about it myself.

GREGERS: Indeed?

MRS. SÖRBY: Your father knows everything that could, with any truth, be said about me. I've told him all; it was the first thing I did when I became aware of his intentions.

GREGERS: Then you've been franker than most people, I think.

MRS. SÖRBY: I've always been frank. We women get on best that way.

HIALMAR: What do you say to that, Gina?

GINA: Oh, we women are very different. Some get on best one way, some another.

MRS. SÖRBY: Well, for my part, Gina, I believe it's wisest to act as I've done. And Werle has no secrets either, on his side. That's really the bond of union between us, you see. Now he can sit and talk with me as openly as a child. He's never had the chance to do that before. Fancy a man like him, full of health and vitality, passing his whole youth and the prime of his life in listening to nothing but moral homilies! And very often the homilies were called forth by the most imaginary offences – at least so I believe.

GINA: That's true enough.

GREGERS: If you ladies are going to indulge in mutual confidences, I had better retire.

MRS. SÖRBY: You can stay so far as that's concerned. I shan't say a word more. But I wanted you to know that I had done nothing secretly or in any underhand way. It may seem as if

I'd come in for a great piece of luck; and that's true in a sense. But after all, I don't think I'm getting any more than I'm giving. I shall stand by him always, and I can tend and care for him as no one else can, now that he's getting helpless.

HIALMAR: Getting helpless?

GREGERS (*to Mrs. Sörby*): Don't speak of that here.

MRS. SÖRBY: There's no disguising it any longer, however much he would like to. He's going blind.

HIALMAR (*starts*): Going blind? That's strange. He too becoming blind!

GINA: Lots of people do.

MRS. SÖRBY: And you can imagine what that means to a business man. Well, I shall try as well as I can to make my eyes replace his. But I mustn't stay any longer, I'm so busy just now. – Oh, by-the-by, Ekdal, I was to tell you that if there was anything Werle could do for you, you must just apply to Gråberg.

GREGERS: I'm sure Hialmar will decline that offer with thanks.

MRS. SÖRBY: Indeed? I don't think he used to be so –

GINA: No, Bertha, Ekdal doesn't need anything from Mr. Werle now.

HIALMAR (*slowly, and with emphasis*): Will you present my compliments to your future husband, and say that I intend very shortly to pay a visit to Mr. Gråberg –

GREGERS: What! You don't really mean that?

HIALMAR: To pay a visit to Mr. Gråberg, I say, and obtain an account of the sum I owe his principal. I will pay that debt of honour – ha, ha, ha! a debt of honour let us call it! In any case I will pay the whole, with five per cent interest.

GINA: But, my dear Ekdal, God knows we haven't got the money to do it.

HIALMAR: Please tell your future husband that I am working assiduously at my invention. Please tell him that what stimulates me in this laborious task is the wish to free myself from a torturing burden of debt. That is my reason for proceeding with the invention. The entire profits are to be devoted to repaying your future husband's pecuniary advances.

MRS. SÖRBY: Something has happened here.

HIALMAR: Yes, that is so.

MRS. SÖRBY: Well, goodbye. I had something else to speak to you about, Gina; but it must keep till another time. Goodbye.

(*Hialmar and Gregers bow silently. Gina follows Mrs. Sörby to the door.*)

HIALMAR: Not beyond the threshold, Gina!

(*Mrs. Sörby goes; Gina shuts the door after her.*)

HIALMAR: There now, Gregers; I've got that burden of debt off my mind.

GREGERS: You soon will, at all events.

HIALMAR: I think my attitude may be called correct.

GREGERS: You are the man I have always taken you for.

HIALMAR: In certain cases, it's impossible to disregard the claim of the ideal. Yet, as the breadwinner of a family, I cannot but writhe and groan under it. I can tell you it's no joke for a man without capital to attempt the repayment of a long-standing obligation, over which, so to speak, there lies the dust of oblivion. But it can't be helped: the Man in me demands his rights.

GREGERS (*putting his hand on Hialmar's shoulder*): My dear Hialmar, now wasn't it a good thing I came?

HIALMAR: Yes.

GREGERS: Aren't you glad to have had your true position made clear to you?

HIALMAR (*somewhat impatiently*): Yes, of course I am. But there's one thing that's exasperating to my sense of justice.

GREGERS: And what's that?

HIALMAR: It is that – but I don't know whether I ought to express myself so unreservedly about your father.

GREGERS: Say what you please, so far as I am concerned.

HIALMAR: Well then, isn't it exasperating to think that it's not I, but he, who will realise the true marriage?

GREGERS: How can you say such a thing?

HIALMAR: I say it because it's the case. Isn't the marriage between your father and Mrs. Sörby founded upon complete confidence, upon entire and unreserved candour on both sides? They hide nothing from each other, they keep no secrets in the background; their relation is based, if I may put it so, on mutual confession and absolution.

GREGERS: Well, what then?

HIALMAR: Well, isn't that the whole thing? Didn't you yourself say that these were just the difficulties that had to be overcome in order to found a true marriage?

GREGERS: But this is quite another matter, Hialmar. You surely don't compare either yourself or your wife with those two – ? Oh, you understand me well enough.

HIALMAR: Say what you like, there's something in all this that hurts and offends my sense of justice. It really looks as if there were no just providence to rule the world.

GINA: Oh no, Ekdal; you mustn't say such things.

GREGERS: H'm; don't let's get upon those questions.

HIALMAR: And yet, after all, I can't but recognise the guiding finger of fate. He's going blind.

GINA: Oh, you can't be sure of that.

HIALMAR: It's indubitable. At all events we oughtn't to doubt it;

for in that very fact lies the just retribution. He has blinded a confiding fellow-creaure in days gone by.

GREGERS: Unfortunately he has blinded many.

HIALMAR: And now comes inexorable, mysterious Fate, and demands Werle's own eyes.

GINA: Oh, how dare you say such dreadful things! I'm getting quite frightened.

HIALMAR: It is profitable to dive into the night side of existence now and then.

(*Hedvig, in her hat and cloak, comes in through the passage door. She is in high spirits, and out of breath.*)

GINA: Are you back already?

HEDVIG: Yes, I didn't care to go any farther. It was a good thing, too, for I met some one at the door.

HIALMAR: It must have been that Mrs. Sörby.

HEDVIG: Yes.

HIALMAR (*walks up and down*): I hope you've seen her for the last time.

(*Silence. Hedvig, discouraged, looks first at one and then at the other, as if to ascertain their frame of mind.*)

HEDVIG (*approaching, coaxingly*): Father.

HIALMAR: Well – what is it, Hedvig?

HEDVIG: Mrs. Sörby had got something for me.

HIALMAR (*stops*): For you?

HEDVIG: Yes. Something for tomorrow.

GINA: Bertha has always given you some little thing on your birthday.

HIALMAR: What is it?

HEDVIG: Oh, I mustn't tell you just now. Mother is to give it to me tomorrow morning before I'm up.

HIALMAR: What's all this nonsense that I'm to be kept in the dark about!

HEDVIG (*quickly*): No, you may see it if you like. It's a big letter. (*Takes the letter out of her cloak pocket.*)

HIALMAR: A letter, too?

HEDVIG: Yes, it is only a letter. The rest will come later, I suppose. But fancy – a letter! I've never had a letter before. And there's 'Miss' written upon it. (*Reads.*) 'Miss Hedvig Ekdal.' Only fancy – that's me!

HIALMAR: Let me see that letter.

HEDVIG (*hands it to him*): There it is.

HIALMAR: That's Mr. Werle's hand.

GINA: Are you sure of that, Ekdal?

HIALMAR: Look for yourself.

GINA: Oh, do you think I know about suchlike things?

HIALMAR: Hedvig, may I open the letter – and read it?

HEDVIG: Yes, of course you may, if you want to.

GINA: No, not tonight, Ekdal; it's to be kept till tomorrow.

HEDVIG (*softly*): Oh, can't you let him read it! It's sure to be something good; and then father'll be glad, and it'll all be pleasant again.

HIALMAR: I may open it, then?

HEDVIG: Yes, do, father. I'm so anxious to know what it is.

HIALMAR: All right. (*Opens the letter, takes out a paper, reads it through, and appears bewildered.*) What's this – ?

GINA: What does it say?

HEDVIG: Oh yes, father, tell us!

HIALMAR: Be quiet. (*Reads it through again; he has turned pale, but says with self-control.*) It's a deed of gift, Hedvig.

HEDVIG: Is it? What sort of gift am I to have?

HIALMAR: Read for yourself.

(*Hedvig goes over and reads for a time by the lamp.*)

HIALMAR (*half-aloud, clenching his hands*): The eyes! The eyes! – and then that letter!

HEDVIG (*leaves off reading*): Yes, but it seems to me that it's grandfather that's to have it.

HIALMAR (*takes the letter from her*): Gina – can you understand this?

GINA: I know nothing whatever about it; tell me what's the matter.

HIALMAR: Mr. Werle writes to Hedvig that her old grandfather needn't trouble himself any longer with the copying, but that he can henceforth draw on the office for a hundred crowns a month.

GREGERS: Aha!

HEDVIG: A hundred crowns, mother! I read that.

GINA: What a good thing for grandfather.

HIALMAR: A hundred crowns a month so long as he needs it – that means, of course, so long as he lives.

GINA: Well, so he's provided for, poor dear.

HIALMAR: But there's more to come. You didn't read that, Hedvig. Afterwards this gift is to pass on to you.

HEDVIG: To me! The whole of it?

HIALMAR: He writes that the same amount is assured to you for the whole of your life. Do you hear that, Gina?

GINA: Yes, I hear.

HEDVIG: Fancy – all that money I'm to get! (*Shakes him.*) Father, father, aren't you glad – ?

HIALMAR (*eluding her*): Glad! (*Walks about.*) Oh, what vistas – what perspectives open up before me! It's Hedvig, Hedvig that he showers these benefactions upon!

GINA: Yes, because it's Hedvig's birthday –

HEDVIG: And you'll get it all the same, father! You may be sure I shall give all the money to you and mother.

HIALMAR: To mother, yes! There we have it.

GREGERS: Hialmar, this is a trap he's setting for you.

HIALMAR: Do you think it's another trap?

GREGERS: When he was here this morning he said: Hialmar Ekdal is not the man you imagine him to be.

HIALMAR: Not the man – !

GREGERS: You will see that, he said.

HIALMAR: He wanted to show you that I would let myself be put off with money – !

HEDVIG: Oh, mother, what does all this mean?

GINA: Go and take off your things.

(*Hedvig goes out by the kitchen door, half-crying.*)

GREGERS: Yes, Hialmar – now we shall see who was right, he or I.

HIALMAR (*slowly tears the paper across, lays both pieces on the table, and says*): Here is my answer.

GREGERS: Just what I expected.

HIALMAR (*goes over to Gina, who stands by the stove, and says in a low voice*): Now please make a clean breast of it. If the connection between you and him was quite over when you – came to care for me, as you call it, why did he put us in a position to marry?

GINA: I suppose he thought our house would be open to him.

HIALMAR: Only that? Wasn't he afraid of a possible contingency?

GINA: I don't know what you mean.

HIALMAR: I want to know whether – your child has the right to live under my roof.

GINA (*draws herself up; her eyes flash*): You ask that!

HIALMAR: You shall answer me this one question: Does Hedvig belong to me – or – ? Well!

GINA (*looking at him with cold defiance*): I don't know.

HIALMAR (*quivering a little*): You don't know!

GINA: How should *I* know? A creature like *me* –

HIALMAR (*quietly, turning away from her*): Then I have nothing more to do in this house.

GREGERS: Take care, Hialmar! Think what you're doing!

HIALMAR (*puts on his overcoat*): In this case, there's nothing for a man like me to think twice about.

GREGERS: Yes, indeed, there are endless things to be considered. You three must be together if you're to attain the true frame of mind for self-sacrificing forgiveness.

HIALMAR: I don't want to attain it. Never, never! My hat! (*Takes his hat.*) My home has fallen in ruins about me. (*Bursts into tears.*) Gregers, I have no child!

HEDVIG (*who has opened the kitchen door*): What is that you're saying? (*Coming to him.*) Father, father!

GINA: There, you see!

HIALMAR: Don't come near me, Hedvig! Keep far away. I can't bear to see you. Oh! those eyes! – Goodbye. (*Makes for the door.*)

HEDVIG (*clinging tight to him and screaming loudly*): No, no! Don't leave me!

GINA (*cries out*): Look at the child, Ekdal! Look at the child!

HIALMAR: I won't! I cannot! I must get out – away from all this!

(*He tears himself away from Hedvig, and goes out through the passage door.*)

HEDVIG (*with despairing eyes*): He's going away from us, mother! He's going away from us! He'll never come back again!

GINA: Don't cry, Hedvig. Father's sure to come back again.

HEDVIG (*throws herself sobbing on the sofa*): No, no, he'll never come home to us any more.

GREGERS: Do you believe I meant all for the best, Mrs. Ekdal?

GINA: Yes, I suppose so; but God forgive you, all the same.

HEDVIG (*lying on the sofa*): Oh, this will kill me! What have I done to him? Mother, you must fetch him home again!

GINA: Yes, yes, yes; only calm yourself, and I'll go out and look for him. (*Puts on her outdoor things.*) Perhaps he's gone in to Relling's. But you mustn't lie there and cry. Promise me!

HEDVIG (*weeping convulsively*): Yes, I'll leave off; if only father comes back!

GREGERS (*to Gina, who is going*): After all, hadn't you better leave him to fight out his bitter fight to the end?

GINA: Oh, he can do that afterwards. First and foremost we must pacify the child. (*Goes out by the passage door.*)

HEDVIG (*sits up and dries her tears*): Now you must tell me what all this means. Why doesn't father want me any more?

GREGERS: You mustn't ask that until you're a big girl – quite grown-up.

HEDVIG (*sobs*): But I can't go on bearing all this misery till I'm grown-up. – I think I know what it is. – Perhaps I'm not really father's child.

GREGERS (*uneasily*): How could that be?

HEDVIG: Mother might have found me. And perhaps father has just got to know it; I've read of such things.

GREGERS: Well, but if it were so –

HEDVIG: I think he might love me just as well for all that. Yes, even more. We got the wild duck as a present, and I love it so dearly all the same.

GREGERS (*diverting the conversation*): Ah, the wild duck, by-the-by! Let's talk about the wild duck a little, Hedvig.

HEDVIG: The poor wild duck! He doesn't want to see it any more either. Only think, he wanted to wring its neck!

GREGERS: Oh, he won't do that.

HEDVIG: No; but he said he wanted to. And I think it was horrid of father to say it; for I pray for the wild duck every night, and ask that it may be preserved from death and all that is evil.

GREGERS (*looking at her*): Do you say your prayers every night?

HEDVIG: Yes.

GREGERS: Who taught you to do that?

HEDVIG: I myself; once when father was very ill, and had leeches on his neck, and said that death was staring him in the face.

GREGERS: Well?

HEDVIG: Then I prayed for him as I lay in bed; and since then I've always kept it up.

GREGERS: And now you pray for the wild duck too?

HEDVIG: I thought it was best to bring in the wild duck; for she was so weakly at first.

GREGERS: Do you pray in the morning, too?

HEDVIG: No, of course not.

GREGERS: Why not in the morning?

HEDVIG: In the morning it's light, and there's nothing in particular to be afraid of.

GREGERS: And your father was going to wring the neck of the wild duck that you love so dearly?

HEDVIG: No; he said he would like to wring its neck; but he would spare it for my sake; and that was kind of father.

GREGERS (*coming a little nearer*): But suppose you were to sacrifice the wild duck, of your own free will, for his sake?

HEDVIG (*rising*): The wild duck!

GREGERS: Suppose you were to sacrifice, for his sake, the dearest treasure you have in the world?

HEDVIG: Do you think that would do any good?

GREGERS: Try it, Hedvig.

HEDVIG (*softly, with flashing eyes*): Yes, I will try it.

GREGERS: Have you really the courage for it, do you think?

HEDVIG: I'll ask grandfather to shoot the wild duck for me.

GREGERS: Yes, do. But not a word to your mother about it!

HEDVIG: Why not?

GREGERS: She doesn't understand us.

HEDVIG: The wild duck! I'll try it tomorrow morning!

(*Gina comes in by the passage door.*)

HEDVIG (*going towards her*): Did you find him, mother?

GINA: No, but I heard he had called and taken Relling with him.

GREGERS: Are you sure of that?

GINA: Yes, the porter's wife said so. Molvik went with them too, she said.

GREGERS: This evening, when his mind so sorely needs to wrestle in solitude – !

GINA (*takes off her things*): Yes, men are never to be depended on. The Lord only knows where Relling has dragged him to! I ran over to Madam Eriksen's, but they weren't there.

HEDVIG (*struggling to keep back her tears*): Oh, if he should never come home any more!

GREGERS: He will come home again. I shall have news to give him tomorrow; and then you'll see how he'll come. You may rely upon that, Hedvig, and sleep in peace. Good-night.

(*He goes out through the passage door.*)

HEDVIG (*throws herself sobbing on Gina's neck*): Mother, mother!

GINA (*pats her shoulder and sighs*): Ah, yes; Relling was right, he was. That's what happens when crazy people go about presenting the claims of the what-do-you-call-it.

Act Five

Hialmar Ekdal's studio. Cold grey, morning light. Wet snow lies upon the large panes of the sloping roof-window.

Gina comes from the kitchen with an apron and bib on, and carrying a dusting-brush and a duster; she goes towards the sitting-room door. At the same moment Hedvig comes hurriedly in from the passage.

GINA (*stops*): Well?

HEDVIG: Oh, mother! I almost think he's down at Relling's –

GINA: There, you see!

HEDVIG: – because the porter's wife says she could hear that Relling had two people with him when he came home last night.

GINA: That's just what I thought.

HEDVIG: But he might just as well have gone right away, if he won't come up to us.

GINA: I'll go down and speak to him, at all events.

(*Old Ekdal, in dressing-gown and slippers, and with a lighted pipe, appears at the door of his room.*)

EKDAL: Hialmar – Isn't Hialmar at home?

GINA: No, he's gone out.

EKDAL: So early? And in such a furious snowstorm? Well, well; don't mind me; I can take my morning walk alone. (*He slides the garret door aside; Hedvig helps him; he goes in; she closes it after him.*)

HEDVIG (*in an undertone*): Only think, mother, when grandfather hears that father's going to leave us.

GINA: Oh, nonsense; grandfather mustn't hear anything about

it. It was a heaven's mercy that he wasn't at home yesterday in all that hurly-burly.

HEDVIG: Yes, but –

(*Gregers comes in by the passage door.*)

GREGERS: Well, have you any news of him?

GINA: They say he's down at Relling's.

GREGERS: At Relling's! Has he really been out with those creatures?

GINA: Yes, like enough.

GREGERS: When he should have been yearning for solitude, for earnest self-examination –

GINA: Yes, you may well say so.

(*Relling enters from the passage.*)

HEDVIG (*going to him*): Is father in your room?

GINA (*at the same time*): Is he there?

RELLING: Yes, of course he is.

HEDVIG: And you never let us know!

RELLING: Yes; I'm a brute. But in the first place I had to look after the other brute; I mean our dæmonic friend, of course; and then I fell asleep, so sound asleep that –

GINA: What does Ekdal say today?

RELLING: He says nothing whatever.

HEDVIG: Doesn't he speak?

RELLING: Not a blessed word.

GREGERS: No, no; I can understand that very well.

GINA: But what's he doing, then?

RELLING: He's lying on the sofa, snoring.

GINA: Oh, is he? Yes, Ekdal's a rare one to snore.

HEDVIG: Asleep? Can he sleep?

RELLING: Well, it certainly looks like it.

GREGERS: Very natural, after the spiritual conflict that has rent him –

GINA: And then he's not accustomed to roving about out of doors at night.

HEDVIG: It's perhaps a good thing that he's getting some sleep, mother.

GINA: Of course it is; and we must take care not to rouse him too early. Thank you, Relling. I must get the house cleaned up a bit now, and then – Come and help me, Hedvig.

(*Gina and Hedvig go into the sitting-room.*)

GREGERS (*turning to Relling*): What's your theory as to the spiritual tumult that's now going on in Hialmar Ekdal?

RELLING: Upon my word I haven't noticed any spiritual tumult about him.

GREGERS: What! not at such a crisis, when his whole life has been placed on a new foundation –? How can you think that such an individuality as Hialmar's –?

RELLING: Oh, individuality – he! If he ever had any tendency to the abnormal developments you call individuality, it was extirpated, root and fibre, before he was out of his teens.

GREGERS: It would be strange if that were so, considering the loving care with which he was brought up.

RELLING: By those two affected, hysterical maiden aunts, you mean?

GREGERS: Let me tell you that they were women who never forgot the claim of the ideal – but of course, you'll simply make game of me again.

RELLING: No, I'm in no humour for that. I know all about these ladies; for he has favoured me with floods of rhetoric on the subject of his 'two soul-mothers'. But I don't think he has much to thank them for. Ekdal's misfortune is that in his own circle he has always been looked upon as a shining light –

GREGERS: Not without reason, surely. Look at the depth of his mind!

RELLING: I've never discovered it. That his father believed in it I don't so much wonder; the old lieutenant has been an ass all his days.

GREGERS: He has had a childlike mind all his days; that's what you don't understand.

RELLING: Well, so be it. But then, when our dear, sweet Hialmar went to college, he immediately passed for the great light of the future amongst his comrades too. He was handsome, the rascal – red and white – a shop-girl's ideal of manly beauty; and with his superficially emotional temperament, and his sympathetic voice, and his talent for declaiming other people's verses and other people's thoughts –

GREGERS (*indignantly*): Is it Hialmar Ekdal you're talking about in that strain?

RELLING: Yes, with your permission; I'm simply showing you the other side of the idol you're grovelling before.

GREGERS: I shouldn't have thought I was so utterly blind.

RELLING: Oh, there's nothing strange in that. You're a sick man, too, you see.

GREGERS: You're right there.

RELLING: Yes. Yours is a complicated case. First of all there's that troublesome integrity-fever; and then – what's worse – you're always in a delirium of hero-worship; you must always have something to adore, outside yourself.

GREGERS: Yes, I must certainly seek it outside myself.

RELLING: But you make such shocking mistakes about every new phœnix you think you have discovered. Here again you've come to a cotter's cabin with your claim of the ideal; the people of the house are insolvent.

GREGERS: If you don't think better than that of Hialmar

Ekdal, what pleasure can you find in being everlastingly with him?

RELLING: Well, you see, I'm supposed to be a sort of a doctor – save the mark! I can't but give a hand to the poor sick people who live under the same roof with me.

GREGERS: Oh, indeed! Ekdal is sick too, is he?

RELLING: Most people are, worse luck.

GREGERS: And what remedy are you applying in Hialmar's case?

RELLING: My usual one. I'm fostering the life-illusion in him.

GREGERS: Life – illusion? Is that what you said?

RELLING: Yes, I said illusion. For illusion, you know, is the stimulating principle.

GREGERS: May I ask with what illusion Hialmar is inoculated?

RELLING: No, thanks; I don't betray professional secrets to quacksalvers. You would probably go and make a still worse muddle of him. But my method is infallible. I've applied it to Molvik as well. I've made him 'dæmonic'. That's the blister I have to put on *his* neck.

GREGERS: Isn't he really dæmonic, then?

RELLING: What the devil do you mean by dæmonic? It's only a piece of hocus-pocus I've invented to keep up a spark of life in him. But for that, the poor harmless creature would have succumbed to self-contempt and despair many a long year ago. And then the old lieutenant! But he has hit upon his own cure, you see.

GREGERS: Lieutenant Ekdal? What of him?

RELLING: Just think of the old bear-hunter shutting himself up in that dark garret to shoot rabbits! I tell you there isn't a happier sportsman in the world than that old man pottering about in there among all that rubbish. The four or five withered Christmas-trees he has saved up are the same to him as the whole great fresh Höidal forest; the cock and the hens are big game-birds in the fir-tops; and the rabbits that flop about the garret floor are the bears he has to battle with – the mighty hunter of the mountains!

GREGERS: Poor unfortunate old man! Yes; he has had to narrow the ideals of his youth, indeed!

RELLING: While I think of it, Mr. Werle, junior, don't use that foreign word: ideals. We've got the excellent native word: lies.

GREGERS: Do you think the two things are related?

RELLING: Yes, just about as closely as typhus and putrid fever.

GREGERS: Dr. Relling, I shall not give in until I have rescued Hialmar from your clutches.

RELLING: So much the worse for him. Rob the average man of his life-illusion, and you rob him of his happiness at the same time. (*To Hedvig, who comes in from the sitting room.*) Well, little wild duck-mother, I'm just going down to see whether papa is still lying meditating upon that wonderful invention of his. (*Goes out by the passage door.*)

GREGERS (*approaches Hedvig*): I can see by your face that you haven't done it.

HEDVIG: What? Oh, that about the wild duck. No.

GREGERS: Your courage failed when the time for action came, I suppose.

HEDVIG: No, that wasn't it. But when I awoke this morning, and remembered what we had been talking about, it seemed so strange.

GREGERS: Strange?

HEDVIG: Yes, I don't know – Yesterday evening, at the moment, I thought there was something so delightful about it; but since I've slept and thought of it again, it somehow doesn't seem worth while.

GREGERS: Ah, I thought you couldn't have grown up quite unharmed in this house.

HEDVIG: I don't care about that, if only father would come up –

GREGERS: Oh, if only your eyes had been opened to that which gives life its value – if you possessed the true, joyous, fearless spirit of sacrifice, you would soon see how he would come up to you. – But I believe in you still, Hedvig. (*He goes out by the passage door.*)

(*Hedvig wanders about the room for a time; she is on the point of going into the kitchen when a knock is heard at the garret door. Hedvig goes over and opens it a little; old Ekdal comes out; she pushes the door to again.*)

EKDAL: H'm, it's not much fun to take one's morning walk alone.

HEDVIG: Wouldn't you like to go shooting, grandfather?

EKDAL: It's not the weather for it today. It's so dark there, you can scarcely see where you're going.

HEDVIG: Do you never want to shoot anything besides the rabbits?

EKDAL: Do you think the rabbits aren't good enough?

HEDVIG: Yes, but what about the wild duck?

EKDAL: Ho-ho! are you afraid I shall shoot your wild duck? Never in the world. Never.

HEDVIG: No, I suppose you couldn't; they say it's very difficult to shoot wild ducks.

EKDAL: Couldn't! Should rather think I could.

HEDVIG: How would you set about it, grandfather? – I don't mean with *my* wild duck, but with others?

EKDAL: I should take care to shoot them in the breast, you know; that's the surest place. And then you must shoot against the feathers, you see – not the way of the feathers.

HEDVIG: Do they die then, grandfather?

EKDAL: Yes, they die right enough – when you shoot properly. Well, I must go in and have a wash. H'm – understand – h'm. (*Goes into his room.*)

(*Hedvig waits a little, glances towards the sitting-room door, goes over to the bookcase, stands on tiptoe, takes the double-barrelled pistol down from the shelf, and looks at it. Gina, with brush and duster, comes from the sitting-room. Hedvig hastily lays down the pistol, unobserved.*)

GINA: Don't stand raking amongst father's things, Hedvig.

HEDVIG (*goes away from the bookcase*): I was only going to tidy up a bit.

GINA: Go into the kitchen, and see if the coffee's keeping hot; I'll take his breakfast on a tray, when I go down to him.

(*Hedvig goes out. Gina begins to sweep and clean up the studio. Presently the passage door is opened with hesitation, and Hialmar Ekdal looks in. He has on his overcoat, but not his hat; he is unwashed, and his hair is dishevelled and unkempt. His eyes are dull and heavy.*)

GINA (*standing with the brush in her hand, and looking at him*): Oh, there now, Ekdal – so you've come after all?

HIALMAR (*comes in and answers in a toneless voice*): I come – only to depart again immediately.

GINA: Yes, yes, I suppose so. But, Lord help us! what a sight you are!

HIALMAR: A sight?

GINA: And your nice winter-coat too! Well, that's done for.

HEDVIG (*at the kitchen door*): Mother, hadn't I better – ? (*Sees Hialmar, gives a loud scream of joy, and runs to him.*) Oh father, father!

HIALMAR (*turns away and makes a gesture of repulsion*): Away, away, away! (*To Gina.*) Keep her away from me, I say!

GINA (*in a low tone*): Go into the sitting-room, Hedvig.

(*Hedvig goes silently in.*)

HIALMAR (*fussily pulls out the table-drawer*): I must have my books with me. Where are my books?

GINA: Which books?

HIALMAR: My scientific books, of course; the technical magazines I use for my invention.

GINA (*searches in the bookcase*): Is it these with paper covers?

HIALMAR: Yes, of course.

GINA (*lays a heap of magazines on the table*): Shan't I get Hedvig to cut them for you?

HIALMAR: I don't require to have them cut for me.

(*Short silence.*)

GINA: Then you're still bent on leaving us, Ekdal?

HIALMAR (*rummaging amongst the books*): Yes, that's a matter of course, I should think.

GINA: Well, well.

HIALMAR (*vehemently*): How can I live here, to be stabbed to the heart every hour of the day?

GINA: God forgive you for thinking so vilely of me.

HIALMAR: Prove – !

GINA: I think it's you that have got to prove.

HIALMAR: After a past like yours? There are certain claims – I may almost call them claims of the ideal –

GINA: But what about grandfather? What's to become of him, poor dear?

HIALMAR: I know my duty; my helpless father will come with me. I'm going out into the town to make arrangements – H'm – (*hesitatingly*) has any one found my hat on the stairs?

GINA: No. Have you lost your hat?

HIALMAR: Of course I had it on when I came in last night;

there's no doubt about that; but I couldn't find it this morning.

GINA: Lord help us! where have you been to with those two ne'er-do-wells?

HIALMAR: Oh, don't bother me about trivial things. Do you suppose I'm in the humour to remember details?

GINA: If only you haven't caught cold, Ekdal. (*Goes out into the kitchen.*)

HIALMAR (*talks to himself in a low tone of irritation, whilst he empties the table-drawer*): You're a scoundrel, Relling! – You're a low fellow! – Ah, you shameless tempter! – I wish I could get some one to murder you!

(*He lays some old letters on one side, finds the torn paper of yesterday, takes it up and looks at the pieces; puts it down hurriedly as Gina enters.*)

GINA (*sets a tray with coffee, etc., on the table*): Here's a drop of something warm, if you'd like it. And there's some bread and butter and a snack of salt meat.

HIALMAR (*glancing at the tray*): Salt meat? Never under this roof! It's true I haven't had a mouthful of solid food for nearly twenty-four hours; but no matter. – My memoranda! The commencement of my autobiography! What's become of my diary, and all my important papers? (*Opens the sitting-room door, but draws back.*) She's there, too!

GINA: Good Lord! the child must be *somewhere!*

HIALMAR: Come out.

(*He makes room, Hedvig comes, scared, into the studio.*)

HIALMAR (*with his hand upon the door-handle, says to Gina*): In these, the last moments I spend in my former home, I wish to be spared from interlopers. (*Goes into the room.*)

HEDVIG (*with a bound towards her mother, asks softly, trembling*): Does that mean me?

GINA: Stay out in the kitchen, Hedvig; or, no – you'd better go into your own room. (*Speaks to Hialmar as she goes in to him.*) Wait a bit, Ekdal; don't rummage so in the drawers; I know where everything is.

HEDVIG (*stands a moment immovable, in terror and perplexity, biting her lips to keep back the tears; then she clenches her hands convulsively, and says softly*): The wild duck! (*She steals over and takes the pistol from the shelf, opens the garret door a little way, creeps in, and draws the door to after her.*)

(*Hialmar and Gina can be heard disputing in the sitting-room.*)

HIALMAR (*comes in with some manuscript books and old loose papers, which he lays upon the table*): That portmanteau's no good! There are a thousand and one things I must drag with me.

GINA (*following with the portmanteau*): Why not leave all the rest for the present, and only take a shirt and a pair of woollen drawers with you.

HIALMAR: Whew – all these wearisome preparations – !

(*Pulls off his overcoat and throws it upon the sofa.*)

GINA: And there's the coffee getting cold.

HIALMAR: H'm.

(*Drinks a mouthful without thinking of it, and then another.*)

GINA (*dusting the backs of the chairs*): Your great difficulty will be to find such a big garret for the rabbits.

HIALMAR: What! Am I to drag all those rabbits with me too?

GINA: I'm sure grandfather can't get on without his rabbits.

HIALMAR: He must just get used to doing without them. Haven't *I* got to sacrifice very much greater things than rabbits!

GINA (*dusting the bookcase*): Shall I put the flute in the portmanteau for you?

HIALMAR: No. No flute for me. But give me the pistol!

GINA: Do you want to take the pistol with you?

HIALMAR: Yes. My loaded pistol.

GINA (*searching for it*): It's gone. He must have taken it in with him.

HIALMAR: Is he in the garret?

GINA: Yes, of course he's in the garret.

HIALMAR: H'm – poor lonely old man.

(*He takes a piece of bread and butter, eats it, and finishes his cup of coffee.*)

GINA: If we hadn't let that room, you could have moved in there.

HIALMAR: And continued to live under the same roof with – ! Never – never!

GINA: But couldn't you put up with the sitting-room for a day or two? You could have it all to yourself.

HIALMAR: Never within these walls!

GINA: Well then, down with Relling and Molvik.

HIALMAR: Don't mention those creatures' names to me! It takes away my appetite only to think of them – Oh no, I must go out into the storm and the snow-blast – go from house to house and seek shelter for my father and myself.

GINA: But you've got no hat, Ekdal! You've lost your hat, you know.

HIALMAR: Oh, those two brutes, those slaves of all the vices! A hat must be got for me. (*Takes another piece of bread and butter.*) Something must be done. For I have no mind to throw away my life, either. (*Looks for something on the tray.*)

GINA: What are you looking for?

HIALMAR: Butter.

GINA: I'll get you some at once. (*Goes out into the kitchen.*)

HIALMAR (*calls after her*): Oh, it doesn't matter; dry bread is all I require.

GINA (*brings a dish of butter*): Look here; this is fresh churned.

(*She pours out another cup of coffee for him; he seats himself on the sofa, spreads more butter on the already buttered bread, and eats and drinks a while in silence.*)

HIALMAR: Could I, without being intruded on by any one – by any one at all – could I live in the sitting-room for a day or two?

GINA: Yes, you could quite well, if you only would.

HIALMAR: For I see no possibility of getting all father's things out in such a hurry.

GINA: And besides, you'll have to tell him first that you don't mean to live with us others any longer.

HIALMAR (*pushes away his coffee cup*): Yes, there's that too; I'll have to lay bare the whole complicated history to him – I must turn matters over; I must have breathing-time; I can't take the whole burden upon my shoulders in a single day.

GINA: No, especially in such horrible weather as it is outside.

HIALMAR (*touching Werle's letter*): I see that paper is still lying about here.

GINA: Yes, *I* haven't touched it.

HIALMAR: So far as I'm concerned it's mere waste paper –

GINA: Well, I'm certainly not thinking of making any use of it.

HIALMAR: – but we'd better not let it get lost all the same – in all the upset when I move, it might easily –

GINA: I'll take care of it, Ekdal.

HIALMAR: The donation is really made to father, and it rests with him to accept or decline it.

GINA (*sighs*): Yes, poor old father –

HIALMAR: To make quite safe – Where shall I find some gum?

GINA (*goes to the bookcase*): Here's the gum-pot.

HIALMAR: And a brush?

GINA: Here's the brush too. (*Brings him the things.*)

HIALMAR (*takes a pair of scissors*): Just a strip of paper at the back – (*clips and gums*). Far be it from me to lay hands upon what is not my own – and least of all upon what belongs to a destitute old man – and to – the other as well. – There now. Let it lie there for a time; and when it's dry, take it away. I wish never to see that document again. Never!

(*Gregers Werle enters from the passage.*)

GREGERS (*somewhat surprised*): What – are you sitting here, Hialmar?

HIALMAR (*rises hurriedly*): I had sunk down from fatigue.

GREGERS: You've been having breakfast, I see.

HIALMAR: The body sometimes makes its claims felt too.

GREGERS: What have you decided to do?

HIALMAR: For a man like me, there's only one way to go. I'm just putting my most important things together. But it takes time, you know.

GINA (*rather impatiently*): Am I to get the room ready for you, or shall I pack your portmanteau?

HIALMAR (*after a glance of annoyance at Gregers*): Pack – and get the room ready!

GINA (*takes the portmanteau*): Very well; then I'll put in the shirt and the other things. (*Goes into the sitting-room and draws the door to after her.*)

GREGERS (*after a short silence*): I never thought this would be the end of it. Do you really feel it a necessity to leave house and home?

HIALMAR (*wanders about restlessly*): What would you have me do? – I am not fitted to bear unhappiness, Gregers. I must feel secure and at peace in my surroundings.

GREGERS: But can't you feel that here? Just try it. It seems to me you have firm ground to build upon now – if only you start afresh. And remember, you have your invention to live for.

HIALMAR: Oh, don't talk about my invention. It's perhaps still in the dim distance.

GREGERS: Indeed!

HIALMAR: Why, great heavens, what would you have me invent? Other people have invented almost everything already. It's more and more difficult every day –

GREGERS: And you've devoted so much work to it.

HIALMAR: It was that blackguard Relling that urged me to it.

GREGERS: Relling?

HIALMAR: Yes, it was he that first led me to notice my aptitude for making some notable discovery in photography.

GREGERS: Aha – it was Relling!

HIALMAR: Oh, I've been so truly happy over it! Not so much for the sake of the invention itself, but because Hedvig believed in it – believed in it with a child's whole earnestness of faith. At least, I've been fool enough to go and imagine that she believed in it.

GREGERS: Can you really think that Hedvig has been false towards you?

HIALMAR: I can think anything now. It's Hedvig that stands in my way. She will blot out the sunlight from my whole life.

GREGERS: Hedvig! Is it Hedvig you're talking of? How should she blot out your sunlight?

HIALMAR (*without answering*): I have loved that child so unspeakably. I have felt so unspeakably happy every time I came home to my poor room, and she flew to meet me, with her sweet little short-sighted eyes. Oh, confiding fool that I have been! I loved her unspeakably; and I yielded myself up to the dream, the delusion, that she loved me unspeakably in return.

GREGERS: Do you call that a delusion?

HIALMAR: How should I know? I can't get anything out of Gina; and besides, she's totally blind to the ideal side of these complications. But to you I feel impelled to open my mind, Gregers. I can't shake off this frightful doubt – perhaps Hedvig has never really and honestly loved me.

GREGERS: What would you say if she were to give you a proof of her love? (*Listens.*) What's that? I thought I heard the wild duck – ?

HIALMAR: It's the wild duck quacking. Father's in the garret.

GREGERS: Is he? (*His face lights up with joy.*) I say you may yet have proof that your poor misunderstood Hedvig loves you!

HIALMAR: Oh, what proof can she give me? I dare not believe in any assurances from that quarter.

GREGERS: Hedvig does not know what deceit means.

HIALMAR: Oh, Gregers, that's just what I can't be certain about. Who knows what Gina and that Mrs. Sörby may many a time have sat here whispering and tattling about? And Hedvig usually has her ears open, I can tell you. Perhaps the deed of gift didn't come so unexpectedly after all. In fact, I'm not sure but that I gathered something of the sort.

GREGERS: What spirit is this that has come over you?

HIALMAR: I've had my eyes opened. Just you notice; – you'll see, the deed of gift is only a beginning. Mrs. Sörby has always been a good deal taken up with Hedvig; and now she has the power to do whatever she likes for the child. They can take her from me whenever they please.

GREGERS: Hedvig will never leave you.

HIALMAR: Don't be so sure of that. If only they beckon to her and throw out a golden bait – ! Oh, and I have loved her so unspeakably! I would have counted it my highest happiness to take her tenderly by the hand and lead her, as one leads a timid child through a great dark empty room! – I am cruelly certain now that the poor photographer in his humble attic has never really and truly been anything to her. She has only cunningly contrived to keep on a good footing with him until the time came.

GREGERS: You don't believe that yourself, Hialmar.

HIALMAR: That's just the terrible part of it – I don't know what to believe – I never can know it. But can you really doubt that it must be as I say? Ho-ho, you rely too much upon the claim of the ideal, my good Gregers! If those others came, with the glory of wealth about them, and called to the child: 'Leave him: come to us: here life awaits you' – !

GREGERS (*quickly*): Well, what then?

HIALMAR: If I then asked her: Hedvig, are you willing to renounce that life for me? (*Laughs scornfully.*) No, thank you! You'd soon hear what answer I should get.

(*A pistol shot is heard from within the garret.*)

GREGERS (*loudly and joyfully*): Hialmar!

HIALMAR: There now; he must needs go shooting too.

GINA (*comes in*): Oh, Ekdal, I can hear grandfather blazing away in the garret by himself.

HIALMAR: I'll look in.

GREGERS (*eagerly, with emotion*): Wait a bit! Do you know what that was?

HIALMAR: Yes, of course I know.

GREGERS: No, you don't know. But *I* do. That was the proof!

HIALMAR: What proof?

GREGERS: It was a child's act of sacrifice. She has got your father to shoot the wild duck.

HIALMAR: To shoot the wild duck!

GINA: Oh, think of that – !

HIALMAR: What was that for?

GREGERS: She wanted to sacrifice to you her most cherished possession; for then she thought you would surely come to love her again.

HIALMAR (*tenderly, with emotion*): Oh, poor child!

GINA: What things she thinks of!

GREGERS: She only wanted your love again, Hialmar. She couldn't live without it.

GINA (*struggling with her tears*): There, you can see for yourself, Ekdal.

HIALMAR: Gina, where is she?

GINA (*sniffs*): Poor dear, she's sitting out in the kitchen, I daresay.

HIALMAR (*goes over, tears open the kitchen door, and says*): Hedvig, come, come in to me! (*Looks round.*) No, she's not here.

GINA: Then she must be in her own little room.

HIALMAR (*without*): No, she's not here either. (*Comes in.*) She must have gone out.

GINA: Yes, you wouldn't have her anywhere in the house.

HIALMAR: Oh, if she would only come home quickly, so that I can tell her – Everything will come right now, Gregers; now I believe we can begin life afresh.

GREGERS (*quietly*): I knew it; I knew the child would make amends.

(*Old Ekdal appears at the door of his room; he is in full uniform, and is busy buckling on his sword.*)

HIALMAR (*astonished*): Father! Are you there?

GINA: Have you been firing in your room?

EKDAL (*resentfully, approaching*): So you go shooting alone, Hialmar?

HIALMAR (*excited and confused*): Then it wasn't you that fired that shot in the garret?

EKDAL: *Me* that fired? H'm.

GREGERS (*calls out to Hialmar*): She has shot the wild duck herself!

HIALMAR: What can it mean? (*Hastens to the garret door, tears it aside, looks in and calls loudly.*) Hedvig!

GINA (*runs to the door*): Good God, what's that!

HIALMAR (*goes in*): She's lying on the floor!

GREGERS: Hedvig! lying on the floor. (*Goes in to Hialmar.*)

GINA (*at the same time*): Hedvig! (*Inside the garret.*) No, no, no!

EKDAL: Ho-ho! does she go shooting too, now?

(*Hialmar, Gina, and Gregers carry Hedvig into the studio; in her dangling right hand she holds the pistol fast clasped in her fingers.*)

HIALMAR (*distracted*): The pistol has gone off. She has wounded herself. Call for help! Help!

GINA (*runs into the passage and calls down*): Relling! Relling! Doctor Relling; come up as quick as you can!

(*Hialmar and Gregers lay Hedvig down on the sofa.*)

EKDAL (*quietly*): The woods avenge themselves.

HIALMAR (*on his knees beside Hedvig*): She'll soon come to now. She's coming to – ; yes, yes, yes.

GINA (*who has come in again*): Where has she hurt herself? I can't see anything –

(*Relling comes hurriedly, and immediately after him Molvik; the latter without his waistcoat and necktie, and with his coat open.*)

RELLING: What's the matter here?

GINA: They say Hedvig has shot herself.

HIALMAR: Come and help us!

RELLING: Shot herself! (*He pushes the table aside and begins to examine her.*)

HIALMAR (*kneeling and looking anxiously up at him*): It can't be dangerous? Speak, Relling! She's scarcely bleeding at all. It can't be dangerous?

RELLING: How did it happen?

HIALMAR: Oh, we don't know – !

GINA: She wanted to shoot the wild duck.

RELLING: The wild duck?

HIALMAR: The pistol must have gone off.

RELLING: H'm. Indeed.

EKDAL: The woods avenge themselves. But I'm not afraid, all the same. (*Goes into the garret and closes the door after him.*)

HIALMAR: Well, Relling – why do you say nothing?

RELLING: The ball has entered the breast.

HIALMAR: Yes, but she's coming to!

RELLING: Surely you can see that Hedvig is dead.

GINA (*bursts into tears*): Oh, my child, my child!

GREGERS (*huskily*): In the depths of the sea –

HIALMAR (*jumps up*): No, no, she must live! Oh, for God's sake, Relling – only a moment – only just till I can tell her how unspeakably I loved her all the time!

RELLING: The bullet has gone through her heart. Internal haemorrhage. Death must have been instantaneous.

HIALMAR: And I! I hunted her from me like an animal! And she crept terrified into the garret and died for love of me! (*Sobbing.*) I can never atone to her! I can never tell her – ! (*Clenches his hands and cries, upwards.*) O thou above – ! If thou *art* there! Why hast thou done this thing to me!

GINA: Hush, hush, you mustn't speak so wildly. We had no right to keep her, I suppose.

MOLVIK: The child is not dead, but sleepeth.

RELLING: Bosh!

HIALMAR (*becomes calm, goes over to the sofa, folds his arms, and looks at Hedvig*): There she lies so stiff and still.

RELLING (*tries to loosen the pistol*): It's so tight, so tight.

GINA: No, no, Relling, don't break her fingers; let the pigstol be.

HIALMAR: She shall take it with her.

GINA: Yes, let her. But the child mustn't lie here for a show. She shall go into her own little room. Help me in with her, Ekdal. (*Hialmar and Gina take Hedvig between them.*)

HIALMAR (*as they are carrying her*): Oh, Gina, Gina, can you survive this!

GINA: We must help each other to bear it. For now, at least, she belongs to both of us.

MOLVIK (*stretches out his arms and mumbles*): Blessed be the Lord; to earth thou shalt return; to earth thou shalt return –

RELLING (*whispers*): Hold your tongue, you fool; you're drunk.

(*Hialmar and Gina carry the corpse out through the kitchen door. Relling shuts it after them. Molvik slinks out into the passage.*)

RELLING (*goes over to Gregers and says*): No one shall ever convince me that the pistol went off by accident.

GREGERS (*who has stood terrified, with convulsive twitchings*): Who can say how the dreadful thing happened?

RELLING: The powder has burnt the body of her dress. She must have pressed the pistol right against her breast and fired.

GREGERS: Hedvig has not died in vain. Did you not see how sorrow set free what is noble in him?

RELLING: Most people are ennobled by the actual presence of death. But how long do you suppose this nobility will last?

GREGERS: Will it not endure and increase throughout his life?

RELLING: Before a year is over, little Hedvig will be nothing to him but a pretty theme for declamation.

GREGERS: How dare you say that of Hialmar Ekdal?

RELLING: We shall talk of this again, when the grass has first withered on her grave. Then you'll hear him spout about 'the child too early torn from her father's heart'; then you'll see him steep himself in a syrup of sentiment and self-admiration and self-pity. Just you see!

GREGERS: If you're right and I'm wrong, then life is not worth living.

RELLING: Oh, life would be quite tolerable, after all, if only we could be rid of the confounded duns that keep on pestering us, in our poverty, with the claim of the ideal.

GREGERS (*looking straight before him*): In that case, I'm glad that my destiny is what it is.

RELLING: Excuse me – what *is* your destiny?

GREGERS (*going*): To be the thirteenth at table.

RELLING: The devil it is.

Curtain

Ghosts

A Family Drama in Three Acts

Oswald (Simon Russell Beale) and Helen (Jane Lapotaire): Royal Shakespeare Company, 1993

Characters

MRS. ALVING (HELEN), *widow of Captain Alving, late Chamberlain to the King*

OSWALD ALVING, *her son, a painter*

PASTOR MANDERS

JACOB ENGSTRAND, *a carpenter*

REGINA ENGSTRAND, *Mrs. Alving's maid*

The action takes place at Mrs. Alving's country house, beside one of the large fjords in Western Norway.

Act One

A spacious garden room, with one door to the left, and two doors to the right. In the middle of the room a round table, with chairs about it. On the table lie books, periodicals, and newspapers. In the foreground to the left a window, and by it a small sofa, with a work table in front of it. In the background, the room is continued into a somewhat narrower conservatory, which is shut in by glass walls with large panes. In the right-hand wall of the conservatory is a door leading down into the garden. Through the glass wall one catches a glimpse of a gloomy fjord-landscape, veiled by steady rain.

Engstrand, the carpenter, stands by the garden door. His left leg is somewhat bent; he has a clump of wood under the sole of his boot. Regina, with an empty garden syringe in her hand, hinders him from advancing.

REGINA (*in a low voice*): What do you want? Stop where you are. You're positively dripping.

ENGSTRAND: It's the Lord's own rain, my girl.

REGINA: It's the devil's rain, *I* say.

ENGSTRAND: Lord! how you talk, Regina. (*Limps a few steps forward into the room.*) What I wanted to say was this –

REGINA: Don't clatter so with that foot of yours, I tell you! The young master's asleep upstairs.

ENGSTRAND: Asleep? In the middle of the day?

REGINA: It's no business of yours.

ENGSTRAND: I was out on the loose last night –

REGINA: I can quite believe that.

ENGSTRAND: Yes, we're weak vessels, we poor mortals, my girl –

REGINA: So it seems.

ENGSTRAND: – and temptations are manifold in this world, you see; but all the same, I was hard at work, God knows, at half-past five this morning.

REGINA: Very well; only be off now. I won't stop here and have *rendezvous* with you.

ENGSTRAND: What is it you won't have?

REGINA: I won't have any one find you here; so just you go about your business.

ENGSTRAND (*advances a step or two*): Blest if I go before I've had a talk with you. This afternoon I shall have finished my work at the school-house, and then I shall take tonight's boat and be off home to the town.

REGINA (*mutters*): A pleasant journey to you.

ENGSTRAND: Thank you, my child. Tomorrow the Asylum's to be opened, and then there'll be fine doings, no doubt, and plenty of intoxicating drink going, you know. And nobody shall say of Jacob Engstrand that he can't keep out of temptation's way.

REGINA: Oh!

ENGSTRAND: You see, there are to be any number of swells here tomorrow. Pastor Manders is expected from town, too.

REGINA: He's coming today.

ENGSTRAND: There you see! And I should be cursedly sorry if he found out anything to my disadvantage, don't you understand?

REGINA: Oh! is that your game?

ENGSTRAND: Is what my game?

REGINA (*looking hard at him*): What trick are you going to play on Pastor Manders?

ENGSTRAND: Hush! hush! Are you crazy? Do *I* want to play my trick on Pastor Manders? Oh no! Pastor Manders has been far too kind to me for that. But I just wanted to say, you know – that I mean to set off home again tonight.

REGINA: The sooner the better, say I.

ENGSTRAND: Yes, but I want to take you with me, Regina.

REGINA (*open-mouthed*): You want me – ? What are you talking about?

ENGSTRAND: I want to take you home, I say.

REGINA (*scornfully*): Never in this world shall you get me home with you.

ENGSTRAND: We'll see about that.

REGINA: Yes, you may be sure we'll see about it! I, who have been brought up by a lady like Mrs. Alving! I, who am treated almost as a daughter here! Is it me you want to go home with you? – to a house like yours? For shame!

ENGSTRAND: What the devil do you mean? Do you set yourself up against your father, girl?

REGINA (*mutters without looking at him*): You've said often enough I was no child of yours.

ENGSTRAND: Stuff! Why should you trouble about that?

REGINA: Haven't you many a time sworn at me and called me a – ? *Fi donc!*

ENGSTRAND: Curse me, now, if ever I used such an ugly word.

REGINA: Oh! I know quite well what word you used.

ENGSTRAND: Well, but that was only when I was a bit on, don't you know? H'm! Temptations are manifold in this world, Regina.

REGINA: Ugh!

ENGSTRAND: And besides, it was when your mother rode her high horse. I had to find something to twit her with, my child. She was always setting up for a fine lady. (*Mimics.*) 'Let me go, Engstrand; let me be. Remember I've been three years in Chamberlain Alving's family at Rosenvold.'

(*Laughs.*) Mercy on us! She could never forget that the Captain was made a Chamberlain while she was in service here.

REGINA: Poor mother! You very soon worried her into her grave.

ENGSTRAND (*turns on his heel*): Oh, of course! I'm to be blamed for everything.

REGINA (*turns away; half aloud*): Ugh! And that leg too!

ENGSTRAND: What do you say, girl?

REGINA: *Pied de mouton.*

ENGSTRAND: Is that English, eh?

REGINA: Yes.

ENGSTRAND: Oh, ah; you've picked up some learning out here; and that may come in useful now, Regina.

REGINA (*after a short silence*): What do you want with me in town?

ENGSTRAND: Can you ask what a father wants with his only child? Am I not a lonely and forsaken widower?

REGINA: Oh! don't try on any nonsense like that! Why do you want me?

ENGSTRAND: Well, let me tell you, I've been thinking of starting a new line of business.

REGINA (*contemptuously*): You've tried that often enough, and never done any good.

ENGSTRAND: Yes, but this time you shall see, Regina! Devil take me –

REGINA (*stamps*): Don't swear!

ENGSTRAND: Hush, hush; you're right enough there, my girl. What I wanted to say was just this – I've laid by a very tidy pile from this Orphanage job.

REGINA: Have you? That's a good thing for you.

ENGSTRAND: What can a man spend his ha'pence on here in the country?

REGINA: Well, what then?

ENGSTRAND: Why, you see, I thought of putting the money into some pay speculation. I thought of a sort of sailors' tavern –

REGINA: Horrid!

ENGSTRAND: A regular high-class affair, of course; not a mere pigstye for common sailors. No! damn it! it would be for captains and mates, and – and – all those swells, you know.

REGINA: And I was to – ?

ENGSTRAND: You were to help, to be sure. Only for appearance' sake, you understand. Devil a bit of hard work shall you have, my girl. You shall do exactly what you like.

REGINA: Oh, indeed!

ENGSTRAND: But there must be a petticoat in the house; that's as clear as daylight. For I want to have it a little lively in the evenings, with singing and dancing, and so forth. You must remember they're weary wanderers on the ocean of life. (*Nearer.*) Now don't be stupid and stand in your own light, Regina. What can become of you out here? Your mistress has given you a lot of learning; but what good is it to you? You're to look after the children at the new Orphanage, I hear. Is that the sort of thing for you, eh? Are you so desperately bent upon wearing yourself out for the sake of the dirty brats?

REGINA: No; if things go as I want them to, then – well, there's no saying – there's no saying.

ENGSTRAND: What do you mean by 'there's no saying'?

REGINA: Never you mind. How much money have you saved up here?

ENGSTRAND: What with one thing and another, a matter of seven or eight hundred crowns.

REGINA: That's not so bad.

ENGSTRAND: It's enough to make a start with, my girl.

REGINA: Aren't you thinking of giving me any?

ENGSTRAND: No, I'm damned if I am!

REGINA: Not even of sending me a scrap of stuff for a new dress?

ENGSTRAND: If you'll come to town with me, you can get dresses enough.

REGINA: Pooh! I can do that on my own account if I want to.

ENGSTRAND: No, a father's guiding hand is what you want, Regina. Now, I've my eyes on a capital house in Little Harbour Street. It won't need much ready-money, and it could be a sort of sailor's home, you know.

REGINA: But I will *not* live with you. I have nothing whatever to do with you. Be off!

ENGSTRAND: You wouldn't remain long with me, my girl. No such luck! If you knew how to play your cards, such a fine girl as you've grown in the last year or two –

REGINA: Well?

ENGSTRAND: You'd soon get hold of some mate – or perhaps even a captain –

REGINA: I won't marry any one of that sort. Sailors have no *savoir vivre.*

ENGSTRAND: What haven't they got?

REGINA: I know what sailors are, I tell you. They're not the sort of people to marry.

ENGSTRAND: Then never mind about marrying them. You can make it pay all the same. (*More confidentially.*) He – the Englishman – the man with the yacht – he gave three hundred dollars, he did; and she wasn't a bit handsomer than you.

REGINA (*going towards him*): Out you go!

ENGSTRAND (*falling back*): Come, come! You're not going to strike me, I hope.

REGINA: Yes, if you begin to talk about mother I shall strike you. Get away with you, I say. (*Drives him back towards the garden door.*) And don't bang the doors. Young Mr. Alving –

ENGSTRAND: He's asleep; I know. It's curious how you're taken up about young Mr. Alving – (*more softly*) Oho! it surely can't be he that – ?

REGINA: Be off at once! You're crazy, I tell you! No, not that way. There comes Pastor Manders. Down the kitchen stairs with you.

ENGSTRAND (*towards the right*): Yes, yes, I'm going. But just you talk to him that's coming there. He's the man to tell you what a child owes its father. For I am your father all the same, you know. I can prove it from the church register.

(*He goes out through the second door to the right, which Regina has opened, and fastens again after him. Regina glances hastily at herself in the mirror, dusts herself with her pocket-handkerchief, and settles her collar; then she busies herself with the flowers. Pastor Manders, in an overcoat, with an umbrella, and with a small travelling bag on a strap over his shoulder, comes through the garden door into the conservatory.*)

MANDERS: Good morning, Miss Engstrand.

REGINA (*turning round, surprised and pleased*): No, really! Good morning, Pastor Manders. Is the steamer in already?

MANDERS: It's just in. (*Enters the sitting room.*) Terrible weather we've been having lately.

REGINA (*follows him*): It's such blessed weather for the country, sir.

MANDERS: Yes, you're quite right. We townspeople think too little about that. (*He begins to take off his overcoat.*)

REGINA: Oh, mayn't I help you? There! Why, how wet it is! I'll just hang it up in the hall. And your umbrella, too – I'll open it and let it dry.

(*She goes out with the things through the second door on the right. Pastor Manders takes off his travelling bag and lays it and his hat on a chair. Meanwhile Regina comes in again.*)

MANDERS: Ah! it's a comfort to get safe under cover. Everything going on well here?

REGINA: Yes, thank you, sir.

MANDERS: You have your hands full, I suppose, in preparation for tomorrow?

REGINA: Yes, there's plenty to do, of course.

MANDERS: And Mrs. Alving is at home, I trust?

REGINA: Oh dear, yes. She's just upstairs looking after the young master's chocolate.

MANDERS: Yes, by-the-by – I heard down at the pier that Oswald had arrived.

REGINA: Yes, he came the day before yesterday. We didn't expect him before today.

MANDERS: Quite strong and well, I hope?

REGINA: Yes, thank you, quite; but dreadfully tired with the journey. He has made one rush all the way from Paris. I believe he came the whole way in one train. He's sleeping a little now, I think; so perhaps we'd better talk a little quietly.

MANDERS: Hush! – as quietly as you please.

REGINA (*arranging an armchair beside the table*): Now, do sit down, Pastor Manders, and make yourself comfortable. (*He sits down; she puts a footstool under his feet.*) There ! are you comfortable now, sir?

MANDERS: Thanks, thanks, I'm most comfortable. (*Looks at her.*) Do you know, Miss Engstrand, I positively believe you've grown since I last saw you.

REGINA: Do you think so, sir? Mrs. Alving says my figure has developed too.

MANDERS: Developed? Well, perhaps a little; just enough.

(*Short pause.*)

REGINA: Shall I tell Mrs. Alving you are here?

MANDERS: Thanks, thanks, there's no hurry, my dear child. By-the-by, Regina, my good girl, just tell me: how is your father getting on out here?

REGINA: Oh, thank you, he's getting on well enough.

MANDERS: He called upon me last time he was in town.

REGINA: Did he, indeed? He's always so glad of a chance of talking to you, sir.

MANDERS: And you often look in upon him at his work, I daresay?

REGINA: I? Oh, of course, when I have time, I –

MANDERS: Your father is not a man of strong character, Miss Engstrand. He stands terribly in need of a guiding hand.

REGINA: Oh, yes; I daresay he does.

MANDERS: He needs to have some one near him whom he cares for, and whose judgment he respects. He frankly admitted that when he last came to see me.

REGINA: Yes, he mentioned something of the sort to me. But I don't know whether Mrs. Alving can spare me; especially now that we've got the new Orphanage to attend to. And then I should be so sorry to leave Mrs. Alving; she has always been so kind to me.

MANDERS: But a daughter's duty, my good girl – Of course we must first get your mistress's consent.

REGINA: But I don't know whether it would be quite proper for me, at my age, to keep house for a single man.

MANDERS: What! My dear Miss Engstrand! When the man is your own father!

REGINA: Yes, that may be; but all the same – Now if it were in a thoroughly respectable house, and with a real gentleman –

MANDERS: But, my dear Regina –

REGINA: – one I could love and respect, and be a daughter to –

MANDERS: Yes, but my dear, good child –

REGINA: Then I should be glad to go to town. It's very lonely out here; you know yourself, sir, what it is to be alone in the world. And I can assure you I'm both quick and willing. Don't you know of any such place for me, sir?

MANDERS: I? No, certainly not.

REGINA: But, dear, dear sir, do remember me if –

MANDERS (*rising*): Yes, yes, certainly, Miss Engstrand.

REGINA: For if I –

MANDERS: Will you be so good as to fetch your mistress?

REGINA: I will, at once, sir. (*She goes out to the left.*)

MANDERS (*paces the room two or three times, stands a moment in the background with his hands behind his back, and looks out over the garden. Then he returns to the table, takes up a book, and looks at the title-page; starts, and looks at several*): H'm – indeed!

(*Mrs. Alving enters by the door on the left; she is followed by Regina, who immediately goes out by the first door on the right.*)

MRS. ALVING (*holds out her hand*): Welcome, my dear Pastor.

MANDERS: How do you do, Mrs. Alving? Here I am as I promised.

MRS. ALVING: Always punctual to the minute.

MANDERS: You may believe it wasn't so easy for me to get away. With all the Boards and Committees I belong to –

MRS. ALVING: That makes it all the kinder of you to come so early. Now we can get through our business before dinner. But where's your luggage?

MANDERS (*quickly*): I left it down at the inn. I shall sleep there tonight.

MRS. ALVING (*suppressing a smile*): Are you really not to be persuaded, even now, to pass the night under my roof?

MANDERS: No, no, Mrs. Alving; many thanks. I shall stay down there as usual. It's so convenient for starting again.

MRS. ALVING: Well, you must have your own way. But I really should have thought we two old people –

MANDERS: Now you're making fun of me. Ah! you're naturally in great spirits today – what between tomorrow's festival and Oswald's return.

MRS. ALVING: Yes; you can think what a delight it is to me! It's more than two years since he was home last. And now he has promised to stay with me all winter.

MANDERS: Has he really? That's very nice and dutiful of him. For I can well believe that life in Rome and Paris has far more attractions.

MRS. ALVING: True. But here he has his mother, you see. My own darling boy, he hasn't forgotten his old mother!

MANDERS: It would be grievous indeed, if absence and absorption in art and that sort of thing were to blunt his natural feelings.

MRS. ALVING: Yes, you may well say so. But there's nothing of that sort to fear in him. I'm quite curious to see whether you'll know him again. He'll be down presently; he's upstairs just now, resting a little on the sofa. But do sit down, my dear Pastor.

MANDERS: Thank you. Are you quite at liberty – ?

MRS. ALVING: Certainly. (*She sits by the table.*)

MANDERS: Very well. Then you shall see – (*He goes to the chair where his travelling bag lies, takes out a packet of papers, sits down on the opposite side of the table, and tries to find a clear space for the papers.*) Now, to begin with, here is – (*breaking off*) – Tell me, Mrs. Alving, how do these books come here?

MRS. ALVING: These books? They are books I am reading.

MANDERS: Do you read this sort of literature?

MRS. ALVING: Certainly I do.

MANDERS: Do you feel better or happier for reading of this kind?

MRS. ALVING: I feel, so to speak, more secure.

MANDERS: That's strange. How do you mean?

MRS. ALVING: Well, I seem to find explanation and confirmation of all sorts of things I myself have been thinking. For that's the wonderful part of it, Pastor Manders; there's really nothing new in these books, nothing but what most people think and believe. Only most people either don't formulate it to themselves, or else keep quiet about it.

MANDERS: Great heavens! Do you really believe that most people – ?

MRS. ALVING: I do, indeed.

MANDERS: But surely not in this country? Not here, among us?

MRS. ALVING: Yes, certainly, among us too.

MANDERS: Well, I really must say – !

MRS. ALVING: For the rest, what do you object to in these books?

MANDERS: Object to in them? You surely don't suppose that I have nothing to do but study such productions as these?

MRS. ALVING: That is to say, you know nothing of what you are condemning.

MANDERS: I have read enough *about* these writings to disapprove of them.

MRS. ALVING: Yes; but your own opinion –

MANDERS: My dear Mrs. Alving, there are many occasions in life when one must rely upon others. Things are so ordered in this world; and it's well that they are. How could society get on otherwise?

MRS. ALVING: Well, I daresay you're right there.

MANDERS: Besides, I of course don't deny that there may be much that is interesting in such books. Nor can I blame you for wishing to keep up with the intellectual movements that are said to be going on in the great world, where you have let your son pass so much of his life. But –

MRS. ALVING: But?

MANDERS (*lowering his voice*): But one shouldn't talk about it, Mrs. Alving. One is certainly not bound to account to everybody for what one reads and thinks within one's own four walls.

MRS. ALVING: Of course not; I quite think so.

MANDERS: Only think, now, how you are bound to consider the interests of this Orphanage which you decided on founding at a time when you thought very differently on spiritual matters – so far as I can judge.

MRS. ALVING: Oh yes; I quite admit that. But it was about the Ophanage –

MANDERS: It was about the Orphanage we were to speak; yes. All I say is: prudence, my dear lady! And now we'll get to business. (*Opens the packet, and takes out a number of papers.*) Do you see these?

MRS. ALVING: The documents?

MANDERS: All – and in perfect order. I can tell you it was hard work to get them in time. I had to put on strong pressure. The authorities are almost painfully scrupulous when you want them to come to the point. But here they are at last. (*Looks through the bundle.*) See! here is the formal deed of gift of the parcel of ground known as Solvik in the Manor of Rosenvold, with all the newly constructed buildings, schoolrooms, master's house, and chapel. And here is the legal fiat for the endowment and for the Regulations of the Institution. Will you look at them? (*Reads.*) 'Regulations for the Children's Home to be known as "Captain Alving's Foundation".'

MRS. ALVING (*looks long at the paper*): So there it is.

MANDERS: I have chosen the designation 'Captain' rather than 'Chamberlain'. 'Captain' looks less pretentious.

MRS. ALVING: Oh, yes; just as you think best.

MANDERS: And here you have the Bank Account of the capital lying at interest to cover the current expenses of the Orphanage.

MRS. ALVING: Thank you; but please keep it – it will be more convenient.

MANDERS: With pleasure. I think we will leave the money in the Bank for the present. The interest is certainly not what we could wish – four per cent. and six months' notice of withdrawal. If a good mortgage could be found later on – of course it must be a first mortgage and an undoubted security – then we could consider the matter.

MRS. ALVING: Certainly, my dear Pastor Manders. You are the best judge in these things.

MANDERS: I will keep my eyes open at any rate. But now there's one thing more which I have several times been intending to ask you.

MRS. ALVING: And what's that?

MANDERS: Shall the Orphanage buildings be insured or not?

MRS. ALVING: Of course they must be insured.

MANDERS: Well, stop a minute, Mrs. Alving. Let us look into the matter a little more closely.

MRS. ALVING: I have everything insured; buildings and movables and stock and crops.

MANDERS: Of course you have – on your own estate. And so have I – of course. But here, you see, it's quite another matter. The Orphange is to be consecrated, as it were, to a higher purpose.

MRS. ALVING: Yes, but that's no reason –

MANDERS: For my own part, I should not see the smallest impropriety in guarding against all contingencies –

MRS. ALVING: No, I should think not.

MANDERS: But what is the general feeling in the neighbourhood? You, of course, know better than I.

MRS. ALVING: H'm – the general feeling –

MANDERS: Is there any considerable number of people – really responsible people – who might be scandalised?

MRS. ALVING: What do you mean by 'really responsible people'?

MANDERS: Well, I mean people in such independent and influential positions that one cannot help allowing some weight to their opinions.

MRS. ALVING: There are several people of that sort here, who would very likely be shocked if –

MANDERS: There, you see! In town we have many such people. Think of all my colleagues' adherents! People would be only too ready to interpret our action as a sign that neither you nor I had the right faith in a Higher Providence.

MRS. ALVING: But for your own part, my dear Pastor, you can at least tell yourself that –

MANDERS: Yes, I know – I know; my conscience would be quite easy, that is true enough. But nevertheless we should not escape grave misinterpretation; and that might very likely react unfavourably upon the Orphanage.

MRS. ALVING: Well, in that case, then –

MANDERS: Nor can I lose sight of the difficult – I may even say painful – position *I* might perhaps get into. In the leading circles of the town people are much taken up about this Orphanage. It is, of course, founded partly for the benefit of the town, as well; and it is to be hoped it will, to a considerable extent, result in lightening our Poor Rates. Now, as I have been your adviser, and have had the business matters in my hands, I cannot but fear that I may have to bear the brunt of fanaticism.

MRS. ALVING: Oh, you mustn't run the risk of that.

MANDERS: To say nothing of the attacks that would assuredly be made upon me in certain papers and periodicals, which –

MRS. ALVING: Enough, my dear Pastor Manders. That consideration is quite decisive.

MANDERS: Then you do not wish the Orphanage insured?

MRS. ALVING: No. We'll let it alone.

MANDERS (*leaning back in his chair*): But if a disaster were to happen? – one can never tell. Would you be able to make good the damage?

MRS. ALVING: No; I tell you plainly I should do nothing of the kind.

MANDERS: Then I must tell you, Mrs. Alving, we are taking no small responsibility upon ourselves.

MRS. ALVING: Do you think we can do otherwise?

MANDERS: No, that's just the thing; we really cannot do otherwise. We must not expose ourselves to misinterpretation; and we have no right whatever to give offence to our neighbours.

MRS. ALVING: You, as a clergyman, certainly should not.

MANDERS: I really think, too, we may trust that such an institution has fortune on its side; in fact, that it stands under a Special Providence.

MRS. ALVING: Let us hope so, Pastor Manders.

MANDERS: Then we'll let the matter alone.

MRS. ALVING: Yes, certainly.

MANDERS: Very well. Just as you think best. (*Makes a note.*) Then – no insurance.

MRS. ALVING: It's rather curious that you should just happen to mention the matter today.

MANDERS: I have often thought of asking you about it –

MRS. ALVING: – for we very nearly had a fire down there yesterday.

MANDERS: You don't say so!

MRS. ALVING: Oh, it was of no importance. A heap of shavings had caught fire in the carpenter's workshop.

MANDERS: Where Engstrand works?

MRS. ALVING: Yes. They say he's often very careless with matches.

MANDERS: He has so many things in his head, that man – so many temptations. Thank God, he's now striving to lead a decent life, I hear.

MRS. ALVING: Indeed! Who says so?

MANDERS: He himself assures me of it. And he's certainly a capital workman.

MRS. ALVING: Oh, yes; so long as he's sober.

MANDERS: Yes, that's a sad weakness. But he's often driven to it by his bad leg, he says. Last time he was in town I was really touched by him. He came and thanked me so warmly for having got him work here, so that he might be near Regina.

MRS. ALVING: He doesn't see much of *her*.

MANDERS: Oh, yes; he has a talk with her every day. He told me so himself.

MRS. ALVING: Well, it may be so.

MANDERS: He feels so acutely that he needs some one to hold him back when temptation comes. That's what I can't help liking about Jacob Engstrand; he comes to you helplessly, accusing himself and confessing his own weakness. The last time he was talking to me – Believe me, Mrs. Alving, supposing it were a real necessity for him to have Regina home again –

MRS. ALVING (*rising hastily*): Regina!

MANDERS: – you must not set yourself against it.

MRS. ALVING: Indeed I shall set myself against it! And besides – Regina is to have a position in the Orphanage.

MANDERS: But, after all, remember he's her father –

MRS. ALVING: Oh! I know best what sort of a father he has been to her. No! she shall never go to him with my goodwill.

MANDERS (*rising*): My dear lady, don't take the matter so warmly. You misjudge Engstrand sadly. You seem to be quite terrified –

MRS. ALVING (*more quietly*): It makes no difference. I have taken Regina into my house, and there she shall stay. (*Listens.*) Hush, my dear Mr. Manders; don't say any more about it. (*Her face lights up with gladness.*) Listen! there's Oswald coming downstairs. Now we'll think of no one but him.

(*Oswald Alving, in a light overcoat, hat in hand and smoking a large meerschaum, enters through the door on the left; he stops in the doorway.*)

OSWALD: Oh! I beg your pardon; I thought you were in the study. (*Comes forward.*) Good morning, Pastor Manders.

MANDERS (*staring*): Ah – ! How strange – !

MRS. ALVING: Well now, what do you think of him, Mr. Manders?

MANDERS: I – I – can it really be – ?

OSWALD: Yes, it's really the Prodigal Son, sir.

MANDERS (*protesting*): My dear young friend – !

OSWALD: Well, then, the Reclaimed Son.

MRS. ALVING: Oswald remembers how much you were opposed to his becoming a painter.

MANDERS: To our human eyes many a step seems dubious

which afterwards proves – (*wrings his hand*). Anyhow, welcome, welcome home. Why, my dear Oswald – I suppose I may call you by your Christian name?

OSWALD: What else should you call me?

MANDERS: Very good. What I wanted to say was this, my dear Oswald – you mustn't believe that I utterly condemn the artist's calling. I have no doubt there are many who can keep their inner self unharmed in that profession, as in any other.

OSWALD: Let us hope so.

MRS. ALVING (*beaming with delight*): I know one who has kept both his inner and outer self unharmed. Just look at him, Mr. Manders.

OSWALD (*moves restlessly about the room*): Yes, yes, my dear mother; let's say no more about it.

MANDERS: Why, certainly – that's undeniable. And you have begun to make a name for yourself already. The newspapers have often spoken of you, most favourably. By-the-by, just lately they haven't mentioned you so often, I fancy.

OSWALD (*up in the conservatory*): I haven't been able to paint so much lately.

MRS. ALVING: Even a painter needs a little rest now and then.

MANDERS: I can quite believe it. And meanwhile he can be gathering his forces for some great work.

OSWALD: Yes. – Mother, will dinner soon be ready?

MRS. ALVING: In less than half an hour. He has a capital appetite, thank God.

MANDERS: And a taste for tobacco, too.

OSWALD: I found my father's pipe in my room and so –

MANDERS: Aha! then that accounts for it.

MRS. ALVING: For what?

MANDERS: When Oswald stood there, in the doorway, with the

pipe in his mouth, I could have sworn I saw his father, large as life.

OSWALD: No, really?

MRS. ALVING: Oh! how can you say so? Oswald takes after me.

MANDERS: Yes, but there's an expression about the corners of the mouth – something about the lips that reminds one exactly of Alving; at any rate, now that he's smoking.

MRS. ALVING: Not in the least. Oswald has rather a clerical curve about his mouth, I think.

MANDERS: Yes, yes; some of my colleagues have much the same expression.

MRS. ALVING: But put your pipe away, my dear boy; I won't have smoking in here.

OSWALD (*does so*): By all means. I only wanted to try it; for I once smoked it when I was a child.

MRS. ALVING: You?

OSWALD: Yes. I was quite small at the time. I recollect I came up to father's room one evening when he was in great spirits.

MRS. ALVING: Oh, you can't recollect anything of those times.

OSWALD: Yes, I recollect distinctly. He took me up on his knees, and gave me the pipe. 'Smoke, boy,' he said; 'smoke away, boy.' And I smoked as hard as I could, until I felt I was growing quite pale, and the perspiration stood in great drops on my forehead. Then he burst out laughing heartily –

MANDERS: That was most extraordinary.

MRS. ALVING: My dear friend, it's only something Oswald has dreamt.

OSWALD: No, mother, I assure you I didn't dream it. For – don't you remember this? – you came and carried me out into the nursery. Then I was sick, and I saw that you were crying. – Did father often play such pranks?

MANDERS: In his youth he overflowed with the joy of life –

OSWALD: And yet he managed to do so much in the world; so much that was good and useful; and he died so young, too.

MANDERS: Yes, you have inherited the name of an active and worthy man, my dear Oswald Alving. No doubt it will be an incentive to you –

OSWALD: It ought to, indeed.

MANDERS: It was good of you to come home for the ceremony in his honour.

OSWALD: I could do no less for my father.

MRS. ALVING: And I am to keep him so long! That's the best of all.

MANDERS: You're going to pass the winter at home, I hear.

OSWALD: My stay is indefinite, sir. But, oh! how delightful it is to be at home again!

MRS. ALVING (*beaming*): Yes, isn't it?

MANDERS (*looking sympathetically at him*): You went out into the world early, my dear Oswald.

OSWALD: I did. I sometimes wonder whether it wasn't *too* early.

MRS. ALVING: Oh, not at all. A healthy lad is all the better for it; especially when he's an only child. He oughtn't to hang on at home with his mother and father and get spoilt.

MANDERS: It's a very difficult question, Mrs. Alving. A child's proper place is, and must be, the home of his fathers.

OSWALD: There I quite agree with you, Pastor Manders.

MANDERS: Only look at your own son – there's no reason why we shouldn't say it in his presence – what has the consequence been for him? He's six or seven and twenty, and has never had the opportunity of learning what home life really is.

OSWALD: I beg your pardon, Pastor; there you're quite mistaken.

MANDERS: Indeed? I thought you had lived almost exclusively in artistic circles.

OSWALD: So I have.

MANDERS: And chiefly among the younger artists.

OSWALD: Yes, certainly.

MANDERS: But I thought few of these young fellows could afford to set up house and support a family.

OSWALD: There are many who can't afford to marry, sir.

MANDERS: Yes, that's just what I say.

OSWALD: But they can have a home for all that. And several of them have, as a matter of fact; and very pleasant, comfortable homes they are, too.

(*Mrs. Alving follows with breathless interest; nods, but says nothing.*)

MANDERS: But I am not talking of bachelors' quarters. By a 'home' I understand the home of a family, where a man lives with his wife and children.

OSWALD: Yes; or with his children and his children's mother.

MANDERS (*starts; clasps his hands*): But, good heavens –

OSWALD: Well?

MANDERS: Lives with – his children's mother!

OSWALD: Yes. Would you have him turn his children's mother out of doors?

MANDERS: Then it's illicit relations you are talking of! Irregular marriages, as people call them!

OSWALD: I have never noticed anything particularly irregular about the life these people lead.

MANDERS: But how is it possible that a – a young man or young woman with any decent principles can endure to live in that way? – in the eyes of all the world!

OSWALD: What are they to do? A poor young artist – a poor girl – it costs a lot to get married. What are they to do?

MANDERS: What are they to do? Let me tell you, Mr. Alving, what they ought to do. They ought to exercise self-restraint from the first; that's what they ought to do.

OSWALD: Such talk won't go far with warm-blooded young people, over head and ears in love.

MRS. ALVING: No, it wouldn't go far.

MANDERS (*continuing*): How can the authorities tolerate such things? Allow them to go on in the light of day? (*To Mrs. Alving.*) Had I not cause to be deeply concerned about your son? In circles where open immorality prevails, and has even a sort of prestige – !

OSWALD: Let me tell you, sir, that I have been a constant Sunday-guest in one or two such irregular homes –

MANDERS: On Sunday of all days!

OSWALD: Isn't that the day to enjoy oneself? Well, never have I heard an offensive word, and still less have I witnessed anything that could be called immoral. No; do you know when and where I have come across immorality in artistic circles?

MANDERS: No, thank heaven, I don't!

OSWALD: Well, then, allow me to inform you. I have met with it when one or other of our pattern husbands and fathers has come to Paris to have a look round on his own account, and has done the artists the honour of visiting their humble haunts. *They* knew what was what. These gentlemen could tell us all about places and things we had never dreamt of.

MANDERS: What! Do you mean to say that respectable men from home here would – ?

OSWALD: Have you never heard these respectable men, when they got home again, talking about the way in which immorality was running rampant abroad?

MANDERS: Yes, of course.

MRS. ALVING: I have too.

OSWALD: Well, you may take their word for it. They know what they're talking about! (*Presses his hands to his head.*) Oh! that that great, free, glorious life out there should be defiled in such a way!

MRS. ALVING: You mustn't get excited, Oswald. You will do yourself harm.

OSWALD: Yes; you're quite right, mother. It's not good for me. You see, I'm wretchedly worn out. I'll go for a little turn before dinner. Excuse me, Pastor; I know you can't take my point of view; but I couldn't help speaking out. (*He goes out through the second door to the right.*)

MRS. ALVING: My poor boy!

MANDERS: You may well say so. Then that's what he has come to!

(*Mrs. Alving looks at him silently.*)

MANDERS (*walking up and down*): He called himself the Prodigal Son – alas! alas!

(*Mrs. Alving continues looking at him.*)

MANDERS: And what do you say to all this?

MRS. ALVING: I say that Oswald was right in every word.

MANDERS (*stands still*): Right! Right! In such principles?

MRS. ALVING: Here, in my loneliness, I have come to the same way of thinking, Pastor Manders. But I've never dared to say anything. Well! now my boy shall speak for me.

MANDERS: You are much to be pitied, Mrs. Alving. But now I must speak seriously to you. And now it is no longer your business manager and adviser, your own and your late husband's early friend, who stands before you. It is the priest – the priest who stood before you in the moment of your life when you had gone most astray.

MRS. ALVING: And what has the priest to say to me?

MANDERS: I will first stir up your memory a little. The time is well chosen. Tomorrow will be the tenth anniversary of your husband's death. Tomorrow I shall have to speak to the whole assembled multitude. But today I will speak to you alone.

MRS. ALVING: Very well, Pastor Manders. Speak.

MANDERS: Do you remember that after less than a year of married life you stood on the verge of an abyss? That you forsook your house and home? That you fled from your husband? Yes, Mrs. Alving – fled, fled, and refused to return to him, however much he begged and prayed you?

MRS. ALVING: Have you forgotten how infinitely miserable I was in that first year?

MANDERS: It is only the spirit of rebellion that craves for happiness in this life. What right have we human beings to happiness? No, we have to do our duty! And your duty was to hold firmly to the man you had once chosen and to whom you were bound by a holy tie.

MRS. ALVING: You know very well what sort of life Alving was leading – what excesses he was guilty of.

MANDERS: I know very well what rumours there were about him, and I am the last to approve the life he led in his young days, if report did not wrong him. But a wife is not to be her husband's judge. It was your duty to bear with humility the cross which a Higher Power had, for your own good, laid upon you. But instead of that you rebelliously throw away the cross, desert the backslider whom you should have supported, go and risk your good name and reputation, and – nearly succeed in ruining other people's reputation into the bargain.

MRS. ALVING: Other people's? One other person's, you mean.

MANDERS: It was incredibly reckless of you to seek refuge with me.

MRS. ALVING: With our clergyman? With our intimate friend?

MANDERS: Just on that account. Yes, you may thank God that I possessed the necessary firmness; that I dissuaded you from your wild designs; and that it was vouchsafed me to lead you back to the path of duty, and home to your lawful husband.

MRS. ALVING: Yes, Pastor Manders, it was certainly your work.

MANDERS: I was but a poor instrument in a Higher Hand. And what a blessing has it not been to you, all the days of your life, that I got you to resume the yoke of duty and obedience! Did not everything happen as I foretold? Did not Alving turn his back on his errors, as a man should? Did he not live with you from that time, lovingly and blamelessly, all his days? Did he not become a benefactor to the whole district? And did he not raise you up to him, so that you little by little became his assistant in all his undertakings? And a capital assistant, too – Oh! I know, Mrs. Alving, that praise is due to you. But now I come to the next great error in your life.

MRS. ALVING: What do you mean?

MANDERS: Just as you once disowned a wife's duty, so you have since disowned a mother's.

MRS. ALVING: Ah!

MANDERS: You have been all your life under the dominion of a pestilent spirit of self-will. All your efforts have been bent towards emancipation and lawlessness. You have never known how to endure any bond. Everything that has weighed upon you in life you have cast away without care or conscience, like a burden you could throw off at will. It did not please you to be a wife any longer, and you left your husband. You found it troublesome to be a mother, and you sent your child forth among strangers.

MRS. ALVING: Yes. That is true. I did so.

MANDERS: And thus you have become a stranger to him.

MRS. ALVING: No! no! I am not.

MANDERS: Yes, you are; you must be. And how have you got him back again? Bethink yourself well, Mrs. Alving. You have sinned greatly against your husband; – that you recognise by raising yonder memorial to him. Recognise now, also, how you have sinned against your son. There may be time to lead him back from the paths of error. Turn back yourself, and save what may yet be saved in him. For (*with uplifted forefinger*) verily, Mrs. Alving, you are a guilt-laden mother! – This I have thought it my duty to say to you.

(*Silence.*)

MRS. ALVING (*slowly and with self-control*): You have now spoken out, Pastor Manders; and tomorrow you are to speak publicly in memory of my husband. I shall not speak tomorrow. But now I will speak frankly to you, as you have spoken to me.

MANDERS: To be sure; you will plead excuses for your conduct –

MRS. ALVING: No. I will only narrate.

MANDERS: Well?

MRS. ALVING: All that you have just said about me and my husband and our life after you had brought me back to the path of duty – as you called it – about all that you know nothing from personal observation. From that moment you, who had been our intimate friend, never set foot in our house again.

MANDERS: You and your husband left the town immediately after.

MRS. ALVING: Yes; and in my husband's lifetime you never came to see us. It was business that forced you to visit me when you undertook the affairs of the Orphanage.

MANDERS (*softly and uncertainly*): Helen – if that is meant as a reproach, I would beg you to bear in mind –

MRS. ALVING: – the regard you owed to your position, yes; and that I was a runaway wife. One can never be too careful with such unprincipled creatures.

MANDERS: My dear – Mrs. Alving, you know that is an absurd exaggeration –

MRS. ALVING: Well, well, suppose it is. My point is that your judgement as to my married life is founded upon nothing but current gossip.

MANDERS: Well, I admit that. What then?

MRS. ALVING: Well, then, Mr. Manders – I will tell you the truth. I have sworn to myself that one day you should know it – you alone!

MANDERS: What is the truth, then!

MRS. ALVING: The truth is that my husband died just as dissolute as he had lived all his days.

MANDERS (*feeling after a chair*): What do you say?

MRS. ALVING: After nineteen years of marriage, as dissolute – in his desires at any rate – as he was before you married us.

MANDERS: And those – those wild oats, those irregularities, those excesses, if you like, you call 'a dissolute life'?

MRS. ALVING: Our doctor used the expression.

MANDERS: I don't understand you.

MRS. ALVING: You need not.

MANDERS: It almost makes me dizzy. Your whole married life, the seeming union of all these years, was nothing more than a hidden abyss!

MRS. ALVING: Nothing more. Now you know it.

MANDERS: This is – it will take me long to accustom myself to the thought. I can't grasp it! I can't realise it! But how was it possible to – ? How could such a state of things be kept dark?

MRS. ALVING: That has been my ceaseless struggle, day after day. After Oswald's birth, I thought Alving seemed to be a little better. But it didn't last long. And then I had to struggle twice as hard, fighting for life or death, so that nobody should know what sort of a man my child's father was. And you know what power Alving had of winning people's hearts. Nobody seemed able to believe anything but good of him. He was one of those people whose life does not bide upon their reputation. But at last, Mr. Manders – for you must know the whole story – the most repulsive thing of all happened.

MANDERS: More repulsive than the rest?

MRS. ALVING: I had gone on bearing with him, although I knew very well the secrets of his life out of doors. But when he brought the scandal within our own walls –

MANDERS: Impossible! Here!

MRS. ALVING: Yes; here in our own home. It was there (*pointing towards the first door on the right*), in the dining room, that I first got to know of it. I was busy with something in there, and the door was standing ajar. I heard our housemaid come up from the garden, with water for those flowers.

MANDERS: Well – ?

MRS. ALVING: Soon after I heard Alving come too. I heard him say something softly to her. And then I heard – (*with a short laugh*) – oh! it still sounds in my ears, so hateful and yet so ludicrous – I heard my own servant-maid whisper, 'Let me go, Mr. Alving! Let me be.'

MANDERS: What unseemly levity on his part! But it cannot have been more than levity, Mrs. Alving; believe me, it cannot.

MRS. ALVING: I soon knew what to believe. Mr. Alving had his way with the girl; and that connection had consequences, Mr. Manders.

MANDERS (*as though petrified*): Such things in this house! in this house!

MRS. ALVING: I had borne a great deal in this house. To keep him at home in the evenings – and at night – I had to make myself his boon companion in his secret orgies up in his room. There I have had to sit alone with him, to clink glasses and drink with him, and to listen to his ribald, silly talk. I have had to fight with him to get him dragged to bed –

MANDERS (*moved*): And you were able to bear all that?

MRS. ALVING: I had to bear it for my little boy's sake. But when the last insult was added; when my own servant-maid – Then I swore to myself: This shall come to an end. And so I took the reins into my own hand – the whole control over him and everything else. For now I had a weapon against him, you see; he dared not oppose me. It was then I sent Oswald from home. He was in his seventh year, and was beginning to observe and ask questions, as children do. That I could not bear. It seemed to me the child must be poisoned by merely breathing the air of this polluted home. That was why I sent him away. And now you can see, too, why he was never allowed to set foot inside his home so long as his father lived. No one knows what it has cost me.

MANDERS: You have indeed had a life of trial.

MRS. ALVING: I could never have borne it if I hadn't had my work. For I may truly say that I have worked! All those additions to the estate – all the improvements – all the useful appliances, that won Alving such general praise – do you suppose *he* had energy for anything of the sort? – he who lay all day on the sofa and read an old court guide! No; this I will tell you too: it was I who urged him on when he had his better intervals; it was I who had to drag the whole load when he relapsed into his evil ways, or sank into querulous wretchedness.

MANDERS: And to that man you raise a memorial?

MRS. ALVING: There you see the power of an evil conscience.

MANDERS: Evil – ? What do you mean?

MRS. ALVING: It always seemed to me impossible but that the

truth must come out and be believed. So the Asylum was to deaden all rumours and banish doubt.

MANDERS: In that you have certainly not missed your aim, Mrs. Alving.

MRS. ALVING: And besides, I had one other reason. I did not wish that Oswald, my own boy, should inherit anything whatever from his father.

MANDERS: Then it is Alving's fortune that – ?

MRS. ALVING: Yes. The sums I have spent upon the Orphanage, year by year, make up the amount – I have reckoned it up precisely – the amount which made Lieutenant Alving a good match in his day.

MANDERS: I don't quite understand –

MRS. ALVING: It was my purchase-money. I do not choose that that money should pass into Oswald's hands. My son shall have everything from me – everything. (*Oswald Alving enters through the second door to the right; he has taken off his hat and overcoat in the hall. Mrs. Alving goes towards him.*) Are you back again already? my dear, dear boy!

OSWALD: Yes. What can a fellow do out of doors in this eternal rain? But I hear dinner's ready. That's capital!

REGINA (*with a parcel, from the dining room*): A parcel has come for you, Mrs. Alving. (*Hands it to her.*)

MRS. ALVING (*with a glance at Mr. Manders*): No doubt copies of the ode for tomorrow's ceremony.

MANDERS: H'm –

REGINA: And dinner is ready.

MRS. ALVING: Very well. We'll come directly. I'll just – (*Begins to open the parcel.*)

REGINA (*to Oswald*): Would Mr. Alving like red or white wine?

OSWALD: Both, if you please.

REGINA: *Bien.* Very well, sir. (*She goes into the dining room.*)

OSWALD: I may as well help to uncork it.

(*He also goes into the dining room, the door of which swings half-open behind him.*)

MRS. ALVING (*who has opened the parcel*): Yes, as I thought. Here is the Ceremonial Ode, Pastor Manders.

MANDERS (*with folded hands*): With what countenance I'm to deliver my discourse tomorrow – !

MRS. ALVING: Oh! you'll get through it somehow.

MANDERS (*softly, so as not to be heard in the dining room*): Yes; it would not do to provoke scandal.

MRS. ALVING (*under her breath, but firmly*): No. But then this long, hateful comedy will be ended. From the day after tomorrow it shall be for me as though he who is dead had never lived in this house. No one shall be here but my boy and his mother.

(*From within the dining room comes the noise of a chair overturned, and at the same moment is heard.*)

REGINA (*sharply, but whispering*): Oswald! take care! are you mad? Let me go!

MRS. ALVING (*starts in terror*): Ah!

(*She stares wildly towards the half-opened door. Oswald is heard coughing and humming. A bottle is uncorked.*)

MANDERS (*excited*): What is the world is the matter? What is it, Mrs. Alving.

MRS. ALVING (*hoarsely*): Ghosts! The couple from the conservatory – risen again!

MANDERS: What! Is it possible! Regina – ? Is she – ?

MRS. ALVING: Yes. Come. Not another word!

(*She seizes Mr. Manders by the arm, and walks unsteadily towards the dining room.*)

Act Two

The same room. The mist still lies heavy over the landscape. Manders and Mrs. Alving enter from the dining room.

MRS. ALVING (*still in the doorway*): *Velbekomme,* Mr. Manders. (*Turns back towards the dining room.*) Aren't you coming too, Oswald?

OSWALD (*from within*): No, thank you. I think I shall go out a little.

MRS. ALVING: Yes, do. The weather seems brighter now. (*She shuts the dining room door, goes to the hall door, and calls*) Regina!

REGINA (*outside*): Yes, Mrs. Alving.

MRS. ALVING: Go down to the laundry, and help with the garlands.

REGINA: I'll go directly, Mrs. Alving.

(*Mrs. Alving assures herself that Regina goes; then shuts the door.*)

MANDERS: I suppose he can't overhear us in there?

MRS. ALVING: Not when the door is shut. Besides, he's just going out.

MANDERS: I'm still quite upset: I can't think how I could get down a morsel of dinner.

MRS. ALVING (*controlling her nervousness, walks up and down*): No more can I. But what's to be done now?

MANDERS: Yes; what's to be done? Upon my honour, I don't know. I'm so utterly without experience in matters of this sort.

MRS. ALVING: I'm quite convinced that, so far, no mischief has been done.

MANDERS: No; heaven forbid! But it's an unseemly state of things, nevertheless.

MRS. ALVING: The whole thing is an idle fancy of Oswald's; you may be sure of that.

MANDERS: Well, as I say, I'm not accustomed to affairs of the kind. But I should certainly think –

MRS. ALVING: Out of the house she must go, and that immediately. That's as clear as daylight.

MANDERS: Yes, of course she must.

MRS. ALVING: But where to? It would not be right to –

MANDERS: Where to? Home to her father, of course.

MRS. ALVING: To whom did you say?

MANDERS: To her – But then, Engstrand is not – ? Good God, Mrs. Alving, it's impossible! You must be mistaken after all.

MRS. ALVING: Alas! I'm mistaken in nothing. Johanna confessed all to me, and Alving could not deny it. So there was nothing to be done but to get the matter hushed up.

MANDERS: No, you could do nothing else.

MRS. ALVING: The girl left our service at once, and got a good sum of money to hold her tongue for the time. The rest she managed for herself when she got into the town. She renewed her old acquaintance with Engstrand, no doubt gave him to understand how much money she had received, and told him some tale about a foreigner who put in here with a yacht that summer. So she and Engstrand got married in hot haste. Why, you married them yourself.

MANDERS: But then, how to account for – ? I recollect distinctly Engstrand coming to give notice of the marriage. He was broken down with contrition, and reproached himself so bitterly for the misbehaviour he and his sweetheart had been guilty of.

MRS. ALVING: Yes; of course he had to take the blame upon himself.

MANDERS: But such a piece of duplicity on his part! And towards me too! I never could have believed it of Jacob Engstrand. I shan't fail to give him a serious talking to; he may be sure of that. And then the immorality of such a connection! For money! How much did the girl receive?

MRS. ALVING: Three hundred dollars.

MANDERS: There! think of that! for a miserable three hundred dollars to go and marry a fallen woman!

MRS. ALVING: Then what have you to say of me? I went and married a fallen man.

MANDERS: But – good heavens! – what are you talking about? A fallen man?

MRS. ALVING: Do you think Alving was any purer when I went with him to the altar than Johanna was when Engstrand married her?

MANDERS: Well, but there's a world of difference between the two cases –

MRS. ALVING: Not so much difference after all, except in the price – a wretched three hundred dollars and a whole fortune.

MANDERS: How can you compare the two cases? You had taken counsel with your own heart and with your friends.

MRS. ALVING (*without looking at him*): I thought you understood where what you call my heart had strayed to at the time.

MANDERS (*distantly*): Had I understood anything of the kind, I should not have continued a daily guest in your husband's house.

MRS. ALVING: Well, the fact remains that with myself I took no counsel whatever.

MANDERS: Well then, with your nearest relatives – as your duty bade you – with your mother and both your aunts.

MRS. ALVING: Yes, that's true. Those three cast up the account for me. Oh! it's marvellous how clearly they made out that it would be downright madness to refuse such an offer. If mother could only see me now, and know what all that grandeur has come to!

MANDERS: Nobody can be held responsible for the result. This, at least, remains clear: your marriage was in accordance with law and order.

MRS. ALVING (*at the window*): Oh! that perpetual law and order! I often think that's what does all the mischief here in the world.

MANDERS: Mrs. Alving, that is a sinful way of talking.

MRS. ALVING: Well, I can't help it; I can endure all this constraint and cowardice no longer. It's too much for me. I must work my way out to freedom.

MANDERS: What do you mean by that?

MRS. ALVING (*drumming on the windowsill*): I ought never to have concealed the facts of Alving's life. But at that time I was afraid to do anything else – afraid on my own account. I was such a coward.

MANDERS: A coward?

MRS. ALVING: If people had come to know anything, they would have said – 'Poor man! with a runaway wife, no wonder he kicks over the traces.'

MANDERS: Such remarks might have been made with a certain show of right.

MRS. ALVING (*looking steadily at him*): If I were what I ought to be, I should go to Oswald and say, 'Listen, my boy; your father was self-indulgent and vicious – '

MANDERS: Merciful heavens – !

MRS. ALVING: – and then I should tell him all I have told you – every word of it.

MANDERS: The idea is shocking, Mrs. Alving.

MRS. ALVING: Yes; I know that. I know that very well. I'm shocked at it myself. (*Goes away from the window.*) I'm such a coward.

MANDERS: You call it 'cowardice' to do your plain duty? Have you forgotten that a son should love and honour his father and mother?

MRS. ALVING: Don't let us talk in such general terms. Let us ask: should Oswald love and honour Chamberlain Alving?

MANDERS: Is there no voice in your mother's heart that forbids you to destroy your son's ideals?

MRS. ALVING: But what about the truth?

MANDERS: But what about the ideals?

MRS. ALVING: Oh! Ideals! Ideals! If only I weren't such a coward!

MANDERS: Do not despise ideals, Mrs. Alving; they will avenge themselves cruelly. Take Oswald's case; he, unfortunately, seems to have few enough ideals as it is; but I can see that his father stands before him as an ideal.

MRS. ALVING: You're right there.

MANDERS: And this habit of mind you have yourself implanted and fostered by your letters.

MRS. ALVING: Yes; in my superstitious awe for Duty and Decency I lied to my boy, year after year. Oh! what a coward, what a coward I've been!

MANDERS: You have established a happy illusion in your son's heart, Mrs. Alving, and assuredly you ought not to undervalue it.

MRS. ALVING: H'm; who knows whether it's so happy after all – ?

But, at any rate, I won't have any goings-on with Regina. He shan't go and ruin the poor girl.

MANDERS: No; good God! that would be dreadful!

MRS. ALVING: If I knew he was in earnest, and that it would be for his happiness –

MANDERS: What? What then?

MRS. ALVING: But it couldn't be; for I'm sorry to say Regina is not a girl to make him happy.

MANDERS: Well, what then? What do you mean?

MRS. ALVING: If I weren't such a pitiful coward I would say to him, 'Marry her, or make what arrangement you please, only let us have nothing underhand about it.'

MANDERS: Good heavens, would you let them *marry!* Anything so dreadful – ! so unheard-of – !

MRS. ALVING: Do you really mean 'unheard-of'? Frankly, Pastor Manders, do you suppose that throughout the country there aren't plenty of married couples as closely akin as they?

MANDERS: I don't in the least understand you.

MRS. ALVING: Oh yes, indeed you do.

MANDERS: Ah, you are thinking of the possibility that – Yes, alas! family life is certainly not always so pure as it ought to be. But in such a case as you point to, one can never know – at least with any certainty. Here, on the other hand – that you, a mother, can think of letting your son – !

MRS. ALVING: But I can't – I wouldn't for anything in the world; that's precisely what I am saying.

MANDERS: No, because you are a 'coward', as you put it. But if you were not a 'coward', then – ? Good God! a connection so shocking.

MRS. ALVING: So far as that goes, they say we're all sprung from connections of that sort. And who is it that arranged the world so, Pastor Manders?

MANDERS: Questions of that kind I must decline to discuss with you, Mrs. Alving; you are far from being in the right frame of mind for them. But that you dare to call your scruples 'cowardly' – !

MRS. ALVING: Let me tell you what I mean. I am timid and half-hearted because I cannot get rid of the Ghosts that haunt me.

MANDERS: What do you say haunts you?

MRS. ALVING: Ghosts! When I heard Regina and Oswald in there, I seemed to see Ghosts before me. I almost think we're all of us Ghosts, Pastor Manders. It's not only what we have inherited from our father and mother that 'walks' in us. It's all sorts of dead ideas, and lifeless old beliefs, and so forth. They have no vitality, but they cling to us all the same, and we can't get rid of them. Whenever I take up a newspaper, I seem to see Ghosts gliding between the lines. There must be Ghosts all the country over, as thick as the sand of the sea. And then we are, one and all, so pitifully afraid of the light.

MANDERS: Ah! here we have the fruits of your reading! And pretty fruits they are, upon my word! Oh! those horrible, revolutionary, free-thinking books!

MRS. ALVING: You are mistaken, my dear Pastor. It was you yourself who set me thinking; and I thank you for it with all my heart.

MANDERS: I?

MRS. ALVING: Yes – when you forced me under the yoke you called Duty and Obligation; when you praised as right and proper what my whole soul rebelled against as something loathsome. It was then that I began to look into the seams of your doctrine. I wanted only to pick at a single knot; but when I had got that undone, the whole thing ravelled out. And then I understood that it was all machine-sewn.

MANDERS (*softly, with emotion*): And was that the upshot of my life's hardest battle?

MRS. ALVING: Call it rather your most pitiful defeat.

MANDERS: It was my greatest victory, Helen – the victory over myself.

MRS. ALVING: It was a crime against us both.

MANDERS: When you went astray, and came to me crying, 'Here I am; take me!' I commanded you, saying, 'Woman, go home to your lawful husband.' Was that a crime?

MRS. ALVING: Yes, I think so.

MANDERS: We two do not understand each other.

MRS. ALVING: Not now, at any rate.

MANDERS: Never – never in my most secret thoughts have I regarded you otherwise than as another's wife.

MRS. ALVING: Oh! – indeed?

MANDERS: Helen – !

MRS. ALVING: People so easily forget their past selves.

MANDERS: I do not. I am what I always was.

MRS. ALVING (*changing the subject*): Well, well, well; don't let us talk of old times any longer. You are now over head and ears in Commissions and Boards of Direction, and I am fighting my battle with Ghosts both within me and without.

MANDERS: Those without I shall help you to lay. After all the shocking things I've heard from you today, I cannot in conscience permit an unprotected girl to remain in your house.

MRS. ALVING: Don't you think the best plan would be to get her provided for – I mean, by a good marriage.

MANDERS: No doubt. I think it would be desirable for her in every respect. Regina is now at the age when – Of course I don't know much about these things, but –

MRS. ALVING: Regina matured very early.

MANDERS: Yes, did she not? I have an impression that she was remarkably well developed, physically, when I prepared her for confirmation. But in the meantime, she must go home, under her father's eye. – Ah! but Engstrand is not – That he – that *he* – could so hide the truth from me!

(*A knock at the door into the hall.*)

MRS. ALVING: Who can that be? Come in!

ENGSTRAND (*in his Sunday clothes, in the doorway*): I beg your pardon humbly, but –

MANDERS: Ah! H'm –

MRS. ALVING: Is that you, Engstrand?

ENGSTRAND: – there was none of the servants about, so I took the great liberty of just knocking.

MRS. ALVING: Oh! very well. Come in. Do you want to speak to me?

ENGSTRAND (*comes in*): No, I'm greatly obliged to you; it was with his Reverence I wanted to have a word or two.

MANDERS (*walking up and down the room*): H'm, indeed. You want to speak to me, do you?

ENGSTRAND: Yes, I should like so much to –

MANDERS (*stops in front of him*): Well; may I ask what you want?

ENGSTRAND: Well, it was just this, your Reverence; we've been paid off down yonder – my grateful thanks to you, ma'am, – and now everything's finished, I've been thinking it would be but right and proper if we, that have been working so honestly together all this time – well, I was thinking we ought to end up with a little prayer-meeting tonight.

MANDERS: A prayer-meeting? Down at the Orphanage?

ENGSTRAND: Oh, if your Reverence doesn't think it proper –

MANDERS: Oh yes! I do; but – h'm –

ENGSTRAND: I've been in the habit of offering up a little prayer in the evenings, myself.

MRS. ALVING: Have you?

ENGSTRAND: Yes, every now and then – just a little exercise, you might call it. But I'm a poor, common man, and have little enough gift, God help me! and so I thought, as the Reverend Mr. Manders happened to be here, I'd –

MANDERS: Well, you see, Engstrand, I must first ask you a question. Are you in the right frame of mind for such a meeting? Do you feel your conscience clear and at ease?

ENGSTRAND: Oh! God help us, your Reverence! we'd better not talk about conscience.

MANDERS: Yes, that's just what we must talk about. What have you to answer?

ENGSTRAND: Why – one's conscience – it can be bad enough now and then.

MANDERS: Ah, you admit that. Then will you make a clean breast of it, and tell the truth about Regina?

MRS. ALVING (*quickly*): Mr. Manders!

MANDERS (*reassuringly*): Just let me –

ENGSTRAND: About Regina! Lord! how you frighten me! (*Looks at Mrs. Alving.*) There's nothing wrong about Regina, is there?

MANDERS: We'll hope not. But I mean, what is the truth about you and Regina? You pass for her father, eh!

ENGSTRAND (*uncertain*): Well – h'm – your Reverence knows all about me and poor Johanna.

MANDERS: Come, no more prevarication! Your wife told Mrs. Alving the whole story before quitting her service.

ENGSTRAND: Well, then, may – ! Now, did she really?

MANDERS: So you're found out, Engstrand.

ENGSTRAND: And she swore and took her Bible oath –

MANDERS: Did she take her Bible oath?

ENGSTRAND: No; she only swore; but she did it so earnestly.

MANDERS: And you have hidden the truth from me all these years? Hidden it from me! from me, who have trusted you without reserve, in everything.

ENGSTRAND: Well, I can't deny it.

MANDERS: Have I deserved this of you, Engstrand? Haven't I always been ready to help you in word and deed, so far as it stood in my power? Answer me. Have I not?

ENGSTRAND: It would have been a poor look-out for me many a time but for the Reverend Mr. Manders.

MANDERS: And you reward me thus! You cause me to enter falsehoods in the Church Register, and you withhold from me, year after year, the explanations you owed alike to me and to truth. Your conduct has been wholly inexcusable, Engstrand; and from this time forward all is over between us.

ENGSTRAND (*with a sigh*): Yes! I suppose it must be.

MANDERS: How can you possibly justify yourself?

ENGSTRAND: How could I think she'd gone and made bad worse by talking about it? Will your Reverence just fancy yourself in the same trouble as poor Johanna –

MANDERS: I!

ENGSTRAND: Lord bless you! I don't mean just exactly the same. But I mean, if your Reverence had anything to be ashamed of in the eyes of the world, as the saying is – We men oughtn't to judge a poor woman too hardly, your Reverence.

MANDERS: I am not doing so. It's you I am reproaching.

ENGSTRAND: Might I make so bold as to ask your Reverence a bit of question?

MANDERS: Yes, ask away.

ENGSTRAND: Isn't it right and proper for a man to raise up the fallen?

MANDERS: Most certainly it is.

ENGSTRAND: And isn't a man bound to keep his sacred word?

MANDERS: Why, of course he is; but –

ENGSTRAND: When Johanna had got into trouble through that Englishman – or it might have been an American or a Russian, as they call them – well, you see, she came down into the town. Poor thing! she'd sent me about my business once or twice before: for she couldn't bear the sight of anything but what was handsome; and I'd got this damaged leg. Your Reverence recollects how I ventured up into a dancing-saloon, where seafaring people carried on with drink and devilry, as the saying goes. And then, when I was for giving them a bit of an admonition to lead a new life –

MRS. ALVING (*at the window*): H'm –

MANDERS: I know all about that, Engstrand; the ruffians threw you downstairs. You've told me of the affair already.

ENGSTRAND: I'm not puffed up about it, your Reverence. But what I wanted to say was, that then she came and confessed all to me, with weeping and gnashing of teeth. I can tell your Reverence I was sore at heart to hear it.

MANDERS: Were you indeed, Engstrand? Well, go on.

ENGSTRAND: So I said to her, 'The American, he's sailing about on the boundless sea. And as for you, Johanna,' said I, 'you've committed a grievous sin and you're a fallen creature. But Jacob Engstrand,' said I, 'he's got two good legs to stand upon, *he* has –' You know, your Reverence, I was speaking figurative-like.

MANDERS: I understand quite well. Go on.

ENGSTRAND: Well, that was how I raised her up and made an honest woman of her, so that folks shouldn't get to know how she'd gone astray with foreigners.

MANDERS: All that was very good of you. Only I can't approve of your stooping to take money –

ENGSTRAND: Money? I? Not a farthing!

MANDERS (*inquiringly to Mrs. Alving*): But –

ENGSTRAND: Oh, wait a minute! – now I recollect. Johanna had a trifle of money. But I would have nothing to do with it. 'No,' said I, 'that's mammon; that's the wages of sin. This dirty gold – or notes, or whatever it was – we'll just fling that back to the American,' said I. But he was gone and away, over the stormy sea, your Reverence.

MANDERS: Was he really, my good fellow?

ENGSTRAND: Ay, sir. So Johanna and I, we agreed that the money should go to the child's education; and so it did, and I can account for every blessed farthing of it.

MANDERS: Why, this alters the case considerably.

ENGSTRAND: That's just how it stands, your Reverence. And I make so bold as to say I've been an honest father to Regina, so far as my poor strength went; for I'm but a poor creature, worse luck!

MANDERS: Well, well, my good fellow –

ENGSTRAND: But I may make bold to say that I've brought up the child, and lived kindly with poor Johanna, and ruled over my own house, as the Scripture has it. But I could never think of going up to your Reverence and puffing myself up and boasting because I too had done some good in the world. No, sir, when anything of that sort happens to Jacob Engstrand, he holds his tongue about it. It doesn't happen so very often, I daresay. And when I do come to see your Reverence, I find a mortal deal to say about what's wicked and weak. For I do say – as I was saying just now – one's conscience isn't always as clean as it might be.

MANDERS: Give me your hand, Jacob Engstrand.

ENGSTRAND: Oh, Lord! your Reverence –

MANDERS: Come, no nonsense (*wrings his hand*) There we are!

ENGSTRAND: And if I might humbly beg your Reverence's pardon –

MANDERS: You? On the contrary, it's I who ought to beg your pardon –

ENGSTRAND: Lord, no, sir!

MANDERS: Yes, certainly. And I do it with all my heart. Forgive me for misunderstanding you. And I wish I could give you some proof of my hearty regret, and of my good-will towards you –

ENGSTRAND: Would your Reverence?

MANDERS: With the greatest pleasure.

ENGSTRAND: Well then, there's the very opportunity now. With the money I've saved here, I was thinking I might set up a Sailors' Home down in the town.

MRS. ALVING: You?

ENGSTRAND: Yes; it too might be a sort of Orphanage, in a manner of speaking. There are many temptations for seafaring folk ashore. But in this Home of mine, a man might feel as under a father's eye, I was thinking.

MANDERS: What do you say to this, Mrs. Alving?

ENGSTRAND: It isn't much I've got to start with, the Lord help me! But if I could only find a helping hand, why –

MANDERS: Yes, yes; we'll look into the matter. I entirely approve of your plan. But now, go before me and make everything ready, and get the candles lighted, so as to give the place an air of festivity. And then we'll pass an edifying hour together, my good fellow; for now I quite believe you're in the right frame of mind.

ENGSTRAND: Yes, I trust I am. And so I'll say goodbye, ma'am, and thank you kindly; and take good care of Regina for me – (*wipes a tear from his eye*) – poor Johanna's child; h'm, it's an odd thing, now; but it's just as if she'd grown into the very apple of my eye. It is indeed. (*He bows and goes out through the hall.*)

MANDERS: Well, what do you say of that man now, Mrs. Alving? That threw a totally different light on matters, didn't it?

MRS. ALVING: Yes, it certainly did.

MANDERS: It only shows how excessively careful one must be in judging one's fellow-creatures. But it's a great joy to ascertain that one has been mistaken. Don't you think so?

MRS. ALVING: I think you are, and will always be, a great baby, Manders.

MANDERS: I?

MRS. ALVING (*laying her two hands upon his shoulders*): And I say that I've half a mind to put my arms round your neck, and kiss you.

MANDERS (*stepping hastily back*): No, no! God bless me! What an idea!

MRS. ALVING (*with a smile*): Oh! you needn't be afraid of me.

MANDERS (*by the table*): You have sometimes such an exaggerated way of expressing yourself. Now, I'll just collect all the documents, and put them in my bag. (*He does so.*) There now. And now, goodbye for the present. Keep your eyes open when Oswald comes back. I shall look in again later. (*He takes his hat and goes out through the hall door.*)

MRS. ALVING (*sighs, looks for a moment out of the window, sets the room in order a little, and is about to go into the dining room, but stops at the door with a half-suppressed cry*): Oswald, are you still at table?

OSWALD (*in the dining room*): I'm only finishing my cigar.

MRS. ALVING: I thought you'd gone for a little walk.

OSWALD: In such weather as this? (*A glass clinks. Mrs. Alving leaves the door open, and sits down with her knitting on the sofa by the window.*) Wasn't that Pastor Manders that went out just now?

MRS. ALVING: Yes; he went down to the Orphanage.

OSWALD: H'm.

(*The glass and decanter clink again.*)

MRS. ALVING (*with a troubled glance*): Dear Oswald, you should take care of that liqueur. It's strong.

OSWALD: It keeps out the damp.

MRS. ALVING: Wouldn't you rather come in to me?

OSWALD: I mayn't smoke in there.

MRS. ALVING: You know quite well you may smoke cigars.

OSWALD: Oh! all right, then; I'll come in. Just a tiny drop more first! There! (*He comes into the room with his cigar, and shuts the door after him. A short silence.*) Where's Manders gone to?

MRS. ALVING: I've just told you; he went down to the Orphanage.

OSWALD: Oh, ah; so you did.

MRS. ALVING: You shouldn't sit so long at table after dinner, Oswald.

OSWALD (*holding his cigar behind him*): But I find it so pleasant, mother. (*Strokes and pets her.*) Just think what it is for me to come home and sit at mother's own table, in mother's room, and eat mother's delicious dinners.

MRS. ALVING: My dear, dear boy!

OSWALD (*somewhat impatiently walks about and smokes*): And what else can I do with myself here? I can't set to work at anything.

MRS. ALVING: Why can't you?

OSWALD: In such weather as this? Without a single ray of sunlight the whole day? (*Walks up the room.*) Oh! not to be able to work!

MRS. ALVING: Perhaps it was not quite wise of you to come home?

OSWALD: Oh, yes, mother; I had to.

MRS. ALVING: Why? I would ten times rather forgo the joy of having you here than –

OSWALD (*stops beside the table*): Now just tell me, mother: does it really make you so very happy to have me home again?

MRS. ALVING: Does it make me happy!

OSWALD (*crumpling up a newspaper*): I should have thought it must be pretty much the same to you whether I was in existence or not.

MRS. ALVING: Have you the heart to say that to your mother, Oswald?

OSWALD: But you've got on very well without me all this time.

MRS. ALVING: Yes; I've got on without you. That's true. (*A silence. Twilight gradually falls. Oswald walks to and fro across the room. He has laid his cigar down.*)

OSWALD (*stops beside Mrs. Alving*): Mother, may I sit on the sofa beside you?

MRS. ALVING (*makes room for him*): Yes, do, my dear boy.

OSWALD (*sits down*): Now I'm going to tell you something, mother.

MRS. ALVING (*anxiously*): Well?

OSWALD (*looks fixedly before him*): For I can't go on hiding it any longer.

MRS. ALVING: Hiding what? What is it?

OSWALD (*as before*): I could never bring myself to write to you about it; and since I've come home –

MRS. ALVING (*seizes him by the arm*): Oswald, what *is* the matter?

OSWALD (*as before*): Both yesterday and today I've tried to put the thoughts away from me – to get free from them; but it won't do.

MRS. ALVING (*rising*): Now you must speak out, Oswald.

OSWALD (*draws her down to the sofa again*): Sit still; and then I'll try to tell you. I complained of fatigue after my journey –

MRS. ALVING: Well, what then?

OSWALD: But it isn't that that's the matter with me; it isn't any ordinary fatigue –

MRS. ALVING (*tries to jump up*): You're not ill, Oswald?

OSWALD (*draws her down again*): Do sit still, mother. Only take it quietly. I'm not downright ill, either; not what's commonly called 'ill'. (*Clasps his hands above his head.*) Mother, my mind is broken down – ruined – I shall never be able to work again.

(*With his hands before his face, he buries his head in her lap, and breaks into bitter sobbing.*)

MRS. ALVING (*white and trembling*): Oswald! Look at me! No, no; it isn't true.

OSWALD (*looks up with despair in his eyes*): Never to be able to work again! Never! never! It will be like living death! Mother, can you imagine anything so horrible?

MRS. ALVING: My poor boy! How has this horrible thing come over you?

OSWALD (*sits upright*): That's just what I can't possibly grasp or understand. I've never led a dissipated life – never, in any respect. You mustn't believe that of me, mother. I've never done that.

MRS. ALVING: I'm sure you haven't, Oswald.

OSWALD: And yet this has come over me just the same – this awful misfortune!

MRS. ALVING: Oh, but it will pass away, my dear, blessed boy. It's nothing but over-work. Trust me, I am right.

OSWALD (*sadly*): I thought so too at first; but it isn't so.

MRS. ALVING: Tell me the whole story from beginning to end.

OSWALD: Well, I will.

MRS. ALVING: When did you first notice it?

OSWALD: It was directly after I had been home last time, and had got back to Paris again. I began to feel the most violent pains in my head – chiefly in the back of my head, I thought. It was as though a tight iron ring was being screwed round my neck and upwards.

MRS. ALVING: Well, and then?

OSWALD: At first I thought it was nothing but the ordinary headache I had been so plagued with when I was growing up –

MRS. ALVING: Yes, yes –

OSWALD: But it wasn't that. I soon found that out. I couldn't work. I wanted to begin upon a big new picture, but my powers seemed to fail me; all my strength was crippled; I couldn't form any definite images; everything swam before me – whirling round and round. Oh! it was an awful state! At last I sent for a doctor, and from him I learned the truth.

MRS. ALVING: How do you mean?

OSWALD: He was one of the first doctors in Paris. I told him my symptoms, and then he set to work asking me a heap of questions which I thought had nothing to do with the matter. I couldn't imagine what the man was after –

MRS. ALVING: Well?

OSWALD: At last he said: 'You have been worm-eaten from your birth.' He used that very word – *vermoulu.*

MRS. ALVING (*breathlessly*): What did he mean by that?

OSWALD: I didn't understand either, and begged him to explain himself more clearly. And then the old cynic said – (*clenching his fist*) Oh – !

MRS. ALVING: What did he say?

OSWALD: He said, 'The sins of the fathers are visited upon the children.'

MRS. ALVING (*rising slowly*): The sins of the fathers – !

OSWALD: I very nearly struck him in the face –

MRS. ALVING (*walks away across the floor*): The sins of the fathers –

OSWALD (*smiles sadly*): Yes; what do you think of that? Of course I assured him that such a thing was out of the question. But do you think he gave in? No, he stuck to it; and it was only when I produced your letters and translated the passages relating to father –

MRS. ALVING: But then?

OSWALD: Then of course he was bound to admit that he was on the wrong track; and so I got to know the truth – the incomprehensible truth! I ought to have held aloof from my bright and happy life among my comrades. It had been too much for my strength. So I had brought it upon myself!

MRS. ALVING: Oswald! Oh, no, don't believe it!

OSWALD: No other explanation was possible, he said. That's the awful part of it. Incurably ruined for life – by my own heedlessness! All that I meant to have done in the world – I never dare think of again – I'm not *able* to think of it. Oh! if I could but live over again, and undo all I've done! (*He buries his face in the sofa. Mrs. Alving wrings her hands and walks, in silent struggle, backwards and forwards. Oswald, after a while, looks up and remains resting upon his elbow.*) If it had only been something inherited, something one wasn't responsible for! But this! To have thrown away so shamefully, thoughtlessly, recklessly, one's own happiness, one's own health, everything in the world – one's future, one's very life!

MRS. ALVING: No, no, my dear, darling boy! It's impossible. (*Bends over him.*) Things are not so desperate as you think.

OSWALD: Oh! you don't know – (*Springs up.*) And then, mother, to cause you all this sorrow! Many a time I've almost wished and hoped that at bottom you didn't care so very much about me.

MRS. ALVING: I, Oswald? My only boy! You are all I have in the world! The only thing I care about!

OSWALD (*seizes both her hands and kisses them*): Yes, mother dear, I see it well enough. When I'm at home, I see it, of course; and that's the hardest part for me. But now you know the whole story, and now we won't talk any more about it today. I daren't think of it for long together. (*Goes up the room.*) Get me something to drink, mother.

MRS. ALVING: Drink? What do you want to drink now?

OSWALD: Oh! anything you like. You have some cold punch in the house.

MRS. ALVING: Yes, but my dear Oswald –

OSWALD: Don't refuse me, mother. Do be nice, now! I must have something to wash down all these gnawing thoughts. (*Goes into the conservatory.*) And then – it's so dark here! (*Mrs. Alving pulls a bell-rope on the right.*) And this ceaseless rain! It may go on week after week for months together. Never to get a glimpse of the sun! I can't recollect ever having seen the sun shine all the times I've been at home.

MRS. ALVING: Oswald, you're thinking of going away from me.

OSWALD: H'm – (*drawing a deep breath*) – I'm not thinking of anything. I can't think of anything. (*In a low voice.*) I let thinking alone.

REGINA (*from the dining room*): Did you ring, ma'am?

MRS. ALVING: Yes; let us have the lamp in.

REGINA: I will, directly. It's ready lighted. (*Goes out.*)

MRS. ALVING (*goes across to Oswald*): Oswald, be frank with me.

OSWALD: Well, so I am, mother. (*Goes to the table.*) I think I've told you enough.

(*Regina brings the lamp and sets it upon the table.*)

MRS. ALVING: Regina, you might fetch us a half-bottle of champagne.

REGINA: Very well, ma'am. (*Goes out.*)

OSWALD (*puts his arm round Mrs. Alving's neck*): That's just what I wanted. I knew mother wouldn't let her boy be thirsty.

MRS. ALVING: My own, poor, darling Oswald, how could I deny you anything now?

OSWALD (*eagerly*): Is that true, mother? Do you mean it?

MRS. ALVING: How? What?

OSWALD: That you couldn't deny me anything.

MRS. ALVING: My dear Oswald –

OSWALD: Hush!

REGINA (*brings a tray with a half-bottle of champagne and two glasses, which she sets on the table*): Shall I open it?

OSWALD: No, thanks. I'll do it myself.

(*Regina goes out again.*)

MRS. ALVING (*sits down by the table*): What was it you meant, I mustn't deny you?

OSWALD (*busy opening the bottle*): First let's have a glass – or two.

(*The cork pops; he pours wine into one glass, and is about to pour it into the other.*)

MRS. ALVING (*holding her hand over it*): Thanks; not for me.

OSWALD: Oh! won't you? Then I will!

(*He empties the glass, fills, and empties it again; then he sits down by the table.*)

MRS. ALVING (*in expectation*): Well?

OSWALD (*without looking at her*): Tell me – I thought you and Pastor Manders seemed so odd – so quiet – at dinner today.

MRS. ALVING: Did you notice it?

OSWALD: Yes. H'm – (*After a short silence.*) Tell me: what do you think of Regina?

MRS. ALVING: What I think?

OSWALD: Yes; isn't she splendid?

MRS. ALVING: My dear Oswald, you don't know her as I do –

OSWALD: Well?

MRS. ALVING: Regina, unfortunately, was allowed to stay at home too long. I ought to have taken her earlier into my house.

OSWALD: Yes, but isn't she splendid to look at, mother? (*He fills his glass.*)

MRS. ALVING: Regina has many serious faults.

OSWALD: Oh, what does it matter? (*He drinks again.*)

MRS. ALVING: But I'm fond of her, nevertheless, and I'm responsible for her. I wouldn't for all the world have any harm happen to her.

OSWALD (*springs up*): Mother! Regina is my only salvation.

MRS. ALVING (*rising*): What do you mean by that?

OSWALD: I can't go on bearing all this anguish of mind alone.

MRS. ALVING: Haven't you got your mother to share it with you?

OSWALD: Yes; that's what I thought; and so I came home to you. But that won't do. I see it won't do. I can't endure my life here.

MRS. ALVING: Oswald!

OSWALD: I must live differently, mother. That's why I must leave you. I won't have you looking on at it.

MRS. ALVING: My unhappy boy! But, Oswald, while you're so ill as this –

OSWALD: If it were only the illness, I should stay with you, mother, you may be sure; for you are the best friend I have in the world.

MRS. ALVING: Yes, indeed I am, Oswald; am I not?

OSWALD (*wanders restlessly about*): But it's all the torment, the remorse; and besides that, the great, killing dread. Oh! that awful dread!

MRS. ALVING (*walking after him*): Dread? What dread? What do you mean?

OSWALD: Oh, you musn't ask me any more! I don't know. I can't describe it. (*Mrs. Alving goes over to the right and pulls the bell.*) What is it you want?

MRS. ALVING: I want my boy to be happy – that's what I want. He shan't go on racking his brains. (*To Regina, who comes in at the door.*) More champagne – a whole bottle.

(*Regina goes.*)

OSWALD: Mother!

MRS. ALVING: Do you think we don't know how to live here at home?

OSWALD: Isn't she splendid to look at? How beautifully she's built! And so thoroughly healthy!

MRS. ALVING (*sits by the table*): Sit down, Oswald; let us talk quietly together.

OSWALD (*sits*): I daresay you don't know, mother, that I owe Regina some reparation.

MRS. ALVING: You?

OSWALD: For a bit of thoughtlessness, or whatever you like to call it – very innocent, anyhow. When I was home last time –

MRS. ALVING: Well?

OSWALD: She used often to ask me about Paris, and I used to tell her one thing and another. Then I recollect I happened to say to her one day, 'Wouldn't you like to go there yourself?'

MRS. ALVING: Well?

OSWALD: I saw her face flush, and then she said, 'Yes, I should like it of all things.' 'Ah, well,' I replied, 'it might perhaps be managed' – or something like that.

MRS. ALVING: And then?

OSWALD: Of course I'd forgotten the whole thing; but the day before yesterday I happened to ask her whether she was glad I was to stay at home so long –

MRS. ALVING: Yes?

OSWALD: And then she looked so strangely at me and asked, 'But what's to become of my trip to Paris?'

MRS. ALVING: Her trip!

OSWALD: And so I got out of her that she had taken the thing seriously; that she had been thinking of me the whole time, and had set to work to learn French –

MRS. ALVING: So that was why she did it!

OSWALD: Mother! when I saw that fresh, lovely, splendid girl standing there before me – till then I had hardly noticed her – but when she stood there as though with open arms ready to receive me –

MRS. ALVING: Oswald!

OSWALD: – then it flashed upon me that my salvation lay in her; for I saw that she was full of the joy of life.

MRS. ALVING (*starts*): The joy of life? Can there be salvation in that?

REGINA (*from the dining room, with a bottle of champagne*): I'm sorry to have been so long, but I had to go to the cellar. (*Puts the bottle on the table.*)

OSWALD: And now fetch another glass.

REGINA (*looks at him in surprise*): There is Mrs. Alving's glass, Mr. Alving.

OSWALD: Yes, but fetch one for yourself, Regina. (*Regina starts and gives a lightning-like side glance at Mrs. Alving.*) Why do you wait?

REGINA (*softly and hesitatingly*): Is it Mrs. Alving's wish?

MRS. ALVING: Fetch the glass, Regina.

(*Regina goes out into the dining room.*)

OSWALD (*follows her with his eyes*): Have you noticed how she walks? – so firmly and lightly!

MRS. ALVING: It can never be, Oswald!

OSWALD: It's a settled thing. Can't you see that? It's no use saying anything against it. (*Regina enters with an empty glass, which she keeps in her hand.*) Sit down, Regina. (*Regina looks inquiringly at Mrs. Alving.*)

MRS. ALVING: Sit down. (*Regina sits on a chair by the dining room door, still holding the empty glass in her hand.*) Oswald, what were you saying about the joy of life?

OSWALD: Ah! the joy of life, mother – that's a thing you don't know much about in these parts. I've never felt it here.

MRS. ALVING: Not when you're with me?

OSWALD: Not when I'm at home. But you don't understand that.

MRS. ALVING: Yes, yes; I think I almost understand it – now.

OSWALD: And then, too, the joy of work! At bottom, it's the same thing. But that, too, you know nothing about.

MRS. ALVING: Perhaps you're right, Oswald; tell me more about it.

OSWALD: Well, I only mean that here people are brought up to believe that work is a curse and a punishment for sin, and that life is something miserable, something we want to be done with, the sooner the better.

MRS. ALVING: 'A vale of tears,' yes; and we take care to make it one.

OSWALD: But in the great world people won't hear of such things. There, nobody really believes such doctrines any longer. There, you feel it bliss and ecstasy merely to draw the breath of life. Mother, have you noticed that everything I've painted has turned upon the joy of life? – always, always upon the joy of life? – light and sunshine and glorious air and faces radiant with happiness. That's why I'm afraid of remaining at home with you.

MRS. ALVING: Afraid? What are you afraid of here, with me?

OSWALD: I'm afraid lest all my instincts should be warped into ugliness.

MRS. ALVING (*looks steadily at him*): Do you think that would be the way of it?

OSWALD: I know it. You may live the same life here as there, and yet it won't be the same life.

MRS. ALVING (*who has been listening eagerly, rises, her eyes big with thought, and says:*) Now I see the connection.

OSWALD: What is it you see?

MRS. ALVING: I see it now for the first time. And now I can speak.

OSWALD (*rising*): Mother, I don't understand you.

REGINA (*who has also risen*): Perhaps I ought to go?

MRS. ALVING: No. Stay here. Now I can speak. Now, my boy, you shall know the whole truth. And then you can choose. Oswald! Regina!

OSWALD: Hush! Here's Manders –

MANDERS (*comes in by the hall door*): There! We've had a most edifying time down there.

OSWALD: So have we.

MANDERS: We must stand by Engstrand and his Sailors' Home. Regina must go to him and help him –

REGINA: No, thank you, sir.

MANDERS (*noticing her for the first time*): What? You here? and with a glass in your hand!

REGINA (*hastily putting the glass down*): *Pardon!*

OSWALD: Regina is going with me, Mr. Manders.

MANDERS: Going with you!

OSWALD: Yes; as my wife – if she wishes it.

MANDERS: But, good God – !

REGINA: I can't help it, sir.

OSWALD: Or she'll stay here, if I stay.

REGINA (*involuntarily*): Here!

MANDERS: I am thunderstuck at your conduct, Mrs. Alving.

MRS. ALVING: They will do neither one thing nor the other; for now I can speak out plainly.

MANDERS: You surely won't do that. No, no, no!

MRS. ALVING: Yes, I can speak and I will. And no ideal shall suffer after all.

OSWALD: Mother! What on earth are you hiding from me?

REGINA (*listening*): Oh, ma'am! listen! Don't you hear shouts outside? (*She goes into the conservatory and looks out.*)

OSWALD (*at the window on the left*): What's going on? Where does that light come from?

REGINA (*cries out*): The Orphanage is on fire!

MRS. ALVING (*rushing to the window*): On fire?

MANDERS: On fire! Impossible! I've just come from there.

OSWALD: Where's my hat? Oh, never mind it – Father's Orphanage! (*He rushes out through the garden door.*)

MRS. ALVING: My shawl, Regina! It's blazing!

MANDERS: Terrible! Mrs. Alving, it's a judgment upon this abode of sin.

MRS. ALVING: Yes, of course. Come, Regina. (*She and Regina hasten out through the hall.*)

MANDERS (*clasps his hands together*): And uninsured too! (*He goes out the same way.*)

Act Three

The room as before. All the doors stand open. The lamp is still burning on the table. It is dark out of doors; there is only a faint glow from the conflagration in the background to the left.

Mrs. Alving, with a shawl over her head, stands in the conservatory and looks out. Regina, also with a shawl on, stands a little behind her.

MRS. ALVING: All burnt! – burnt to the ground!

REGINA: The basement is still burning.

MRS. ALVING: How is it Oswald doesn't come home? There's nothing to be saved.

REGINA: Would you like me to take down his hat for him?

MRS. ALVING: Hasn't he even got his hat on?

REGINA (*pointing to the hall*): No; there it hangs.

MRS. ALVING: Let it be. He must come up now. I'll go and look for him myself. (*She goes out through the garden door.*)

MANDERS (*comes in from the hall*): Isn't Mrs. Alving here?

REGINA: She's just gone down the garden.

MANDERS: This is the most terrible night I ever went through.

REGINA: Yes; isn't it a dreadful misfortune, sir?

MANDERS: Oh, don't talk about it! I can hardly bear to think of it.

REGINA: How can it have happened?

MANDERS: Don't ask me, Regina. How should *I* know? Do you, too – ? Isn't it enough that your father – ?

REGINA: What about him?

MANDERS: Oh! he has driven me clean out of my mind. –

ENGSTRAND (*comes through the hall*): Your Reverence!

MANDERS (*turns round in terror*): Are you after me here, too?

ENGSTRAND: Yes, strike me dead, but I must – Oh, Lord! what am I saying? It's an awfully ugly business, your Reverence.

MANDERS (*walks to and fro*): Alas! alas!

REGINA: What's the matter?

ENGSTRAND: Why, it all came of that prayer-meeting, you see. (*Softly.*) The bird's limed, my girl. (*Aloud.*) And to think that it's my fault that it's his Reverence's fault!

MANDERS: But I assure you, Engstrand –

ENGSTRAND: There wasn't another soul except your Reverence that ever touched the candles down there.

MANDERS (*stops*): Ah! so you declare. But I certainly can't recollect that I ever had a candle in my hand.

ENGSTRAND: And I saw as clear as daylight how your Reverence took the candle and snuffed it with your fingers, and threw away the snuff among the shavings.

MANDERS: And you stood and looked on?

ENGSTRAND: Yes; I saw it as plain as a pike-staff.

MANDERS: It's quite beyond my comprehension. Besides, it's never been my habit to snuff candles with my fingers.

ENGSTRAND: And very risky it looked, that it did! But is there so much harm done after all, your Reverence?

MANDERS (*walks restlessly to and fro*): Oh, don't ask me!

ENGSTRAND (*walks with him*): And your Reverence hadn't insured it, neither?

MANDERS (*continuing to walk up and down*): No, no, no; you've heard that already.

ENGSTRAND (*following him*): Not insured! And then to go right down and set light to the whole thing. Lord! Lord! what a misfortune!

MANDERS (*wipes the sweat from his forehead*): Ay, you may well say that, Engstrand.

ENGSTRAND: And to think that such a thing should happen to a benevolent Institution, that was to have been a blessing both to town and country, as the saying is! The newspapers won't handle your Reverence very gently, I expect.

MANDERS: No; that's just what I'm thinking of. That's almost the worst of it. All the malignant attacks and accusations – ! Oh, it's terrible only to imagine it.

MRS. ALVING (*comes in from the garden*): He can't be got away from the fire.

MANDERS: Ah! there you are, Mrs. Alving!

MRS. ALVING: So you've escaped your Inaugural Address, Pastor Manders.

MANDERS: Oh! I should so gladly –

MRS. ALVING (*in an undertone*): It's all for the best. That Orphanage would have done no good to anybody.

MANDERS: Do you think not?

MRS. ALVING: Do you think it would?

MANDERS: It's a terrible misfortune, all the same.

MRS. ALVING: Let us speak plainly of it, as a piece of business. Are you waiting for Mr. Manders, Engstrand?

ENGSTRAND (*at the hall door*): Ay, ma'am; indeed I am.

MRS. ALVING: Then sit down meanwhile.

ENGSTRAND: Thank you, ma'am; I'd rather stand.

MRS. ALVING (*to Manders*): I suppose you're going by the steamer?

MANDERS: Yes; it starts in an hour.

MRS. ALVING: Be so good as to take all the papers with you. I won't hear another word about this affair. I have other things to think about.

MANDERS: Mrs. Alving –

MRS. ALVING: Later on I shall send you a Power of Attorney to settle everything as you please.

MANDERS: That I shall very readily undertake. The original destination of the endowment must now be completely changed, alas!

MRS. ALVING: Of course it must.

MANDERS: I think, first of all, I shall arrange that the Solvik property shall pass to the parish. The land is by no means without value. It can always be turned to account for some purpose or other. And the interest of the money in the Bank I could, perhaps, best apply for the benefit of some undertaking that has proved itself a blessing to the town.

MRS. ALVING: Do just as you please. The whole matter is now completely indifferent to me.

ENGSTRAND: Give a thought to my Sailor's Home, your Reverence.

MANDERS: Yes, that's not a bad suggestion. That must be considered.

ENGSTRAND: Oh, devil take considering – I beg your pardon!

MANDERS (*with a sigh*): And I'm sorry to say I don't know how long I shall be able to retain control of these things – whether public opinion may not compel me to retire. It entirely depends upon the result of the official inquiry into the fire –

MRS. ALVING: What are you talking about?

MANDERS: And the result can by no means be foretold.

ENGSTRAND (*comes close to him*): Ay, but it can, though. For here stands Jacob Engstrand.

MANDERS: Well, well, but – ?

ENGSTRAND (*more softly*): And Jacob Engstrand isn't the man to desert a noble benefactor in the hour of need, as the saying is.

MANDERS: Yes, but my good fellow – how – ?

ENGSTRAND: Jacob Engstrand may be likened to a guardian angel, he may, your Reverence.

MANDERS: No, no; I can't accept that.

ENGSTRAND: Oh! you will though, all the same. I know a man that's taken others' sins upon himself before now, I do.

MANDERS: Jacob! (*Wrings his hand.*) You are a rare character. Well, you shall be helped with your Sailors' Home. That you may rely upon. (*Engstrand tries to thank him, but cannot for emotion. Mr. Manders hangs his travelling bag over his shoulder.*) And now let's be off. We two go together.

ENGSTRAND (*at the dining room door, softly to Regina*): You come along too, girl. You shall live as snug as the yolk in an egg.

REGINA (*tosses her head*): *Merci!* (*She goes out into the hall and fetches Mander's overcoat.*)

MANDERS: Goodbye, Mrs. Alving! and may the spirit of Law and Order descend upon this house, and that quickly.

MRS. ALVING: Goodbye, Manders. (*She goes up towards the conservatory as she sees Oswald coming in through the garden door.*)

ENGSTRAND (*while he and Regina help Manders to get his coat on*): Goodbye, my child. And if any trouble should come to you, you know where Jacob Engstrand is to be found. (*Softly.*) Little Harbour Street, h'm – ! (*To Mrs. Alving and Oswald.*) And the refuge for wandering mariners shall be called 'Captain Alving's Home', that it shall! And if I'm spared to carry on that house in my own way, I venture to promise that it shall be worthy of his memory.

MANDERS (*in the doorway*): H'm – h'm! – Now come, my dear Engstrand. Goodbye! Goodbye! (*He and Engstrand go out through the hall.*)

OSWALD (*goes towards the table*): What house was he talking about?

MRS. ALVING: Oh, a kind of Home that he and Manders want to set up.

OSWALD: It will burn down like the other.

MRS. ALVING: What makes you think so?

OSWALD: Everything will burn. All that recalls father's memory is doomed. Here am I, too, burning down.

(*Regina starts and looks at him.*)

MRS. ALVING: Oswald! you oughtn't to have remained so long down there, my poor boy!

OSWALD (*sits down by the table*): I almost think you're right.

MRS. ALVING: Let me dry your face, Oswald; you're quite wet. (*She dries his face with her pocket-handkerchief.*)

OSWALD (*stares indifferently in front of him*): Thanks, mother.

MRS. ALVING: Aren't you tired, Oswald? Would you like to sleep?

OSWALD (*nervously*): No, no – I can't sleep. I never sleep. I only pretend to. (*Sadly.*) That will come soon enough.

MRS. ALVING (*looking sorrowfully at him*): Yes, you really are ill, my blessed boy.

REGINA (*eagerly*): Is Mr. Alving ill?

OSWALD (*impatiently*): Oh, do shut all the doors! This killing dread –

MRS. ALVING: Shut the doors, Regina.

(*Regina shuts them and remains standing by the hall door. Mrs. Alving takes her shawl off. Regina does the same. Mrs. Alving draws a chair across to Oswald's, and sits by him.*)

MRS. ALVING: There now! I'm going to sit beside you –

OSWALD: Ah! do. And Regina shall stay here, too. Regina shall be with me always. You'll come to the rescue, Regina, won't you?

REGINA: I don't understand –

MRS. ALVING: To the rescue?

OSWALD: Yes – in the hour of need.

MRS. ALVING: Oswald, have you not your mother to come to the rescue?

OSWALD: You? (*Smiles.*) No, mother; that rescue you will never bring me. (*Laughs sadly.*) You! ha! ha! (*Looks earnestly at her.*) Though, after all, it lies nearest to you. (*Impetuously.*) Why don't you say 'thou' to me, Regina? Why don't you call me 'Oswald'?

REGINA (*softly*): I don't think Mrs. Alving would like it.

MRS. ALVING: You shall soon have leave to do it. And sit over here beside us, won't you?

(*Regina sits down quietly and hesitatingly at the other side of the table.*)

MRS. ALVING: And now, my poor suffering boy, I'm going to take the burden off your mind –

OSWALD: You, mother?

MRS. ALVING: – All the gnawing remorse and self-reproach you speak of.

OSWALD: And you think you can do that?

MRS. ALVING: Yes, now I can, Oswald. You spoke of the joy of life; and at the word a new light burst for me over my life and all it has contained.

OSWALD (*shakes his head*): I don't understand you.

MRS. ALVING: You ought to have known your father when he was a young lieutenant. He was brimming over with the joy of life!

OSWALD: Yes, I know he was.

MRS. ALVING: It was like a breezy day only to look at him. And what exuberant strength and vitality there was in him!

OSWALD: Well – ?

MRS. ALVING: Well then, child of joy as he was – for he *was* like a child at that time – he had to live here at home in a half-grown town, which had no joys to offer him – only dissipations. He had no object in life – only an official position. He had no work into which he could throw himself heart and soul; he had only business. He had not a single comrade that knew what the joy of life meant – only loungers and boon-companions –

OSWALD: Mother!

MRS. ALVING: So the inevitable happened.

OSWALD: The inevitable?

MRS. ALVING: You said yourself, this evening, what would happen to you if you stayed at home.

OSWALD: Do you mean to say that father – ?

MRS. ALVING: Your poor father found no outlet for the overpowering joy of life that was in him. And I brought no brightness into his home.

OSWALD: Not even you?

MRS. ALVING: They had taught me a lot about duties and so on, which I had taken to be true. Everything was marked out into duties – into my duties, and his duties, and – I'm afraid I made home intolerable for your poor father, Oswald.

OSWALD: Why did you never write me anything about all this?

MRS. ALVING: I have never before seen it in such a light that I could speak of it to you, his son.

OSWALD: In what light did you see it then?

MRS. ALVING (*slowly*): I saw only this one thing, that your father was a broken-down man before you were born.

OSWALD (*softly*): Ah! (*He rises and walks away to the window.*)

MRS. ALVING: And then, day after day, I dwelt on the one thought that by rights Regina should be at home in this house – just like my own boy.

OSWALD (*turning round quickly*): Regina!

REGINA (*springs up and asks, with bated breath*): I?

MRS. ALVING: Yes, now you know it, both of you.

OSWALD: Regina!

REGINA (*to herself*): So mother was that kind of woman, after all.

MRS. ALVING: Your mother had many good qualities, Regina.

REGINA: Yes, but she was one of that sort, all the same. Oh! I've often suspected it; but – And now, if you please, ma'am, may I be allowed to go away at once?

MRS. ALVING: Do you really wish it, Regina?

REGINA: Yes, indeed I do.

MRS. ALVING: Of course you can do as you like; but –

OSWALD (*goes towards Regina*): Go away now? Isn't this your home?

REGINA: *Merci*, Mr. Alving! – or now, I suppose, I may say Oswald. But I can tell you this wasn't what I expected.

MRS. ALVING: Regina, I have not been frank with you –

REGINA: No, that you haven't, indeed. If I'd known that Oswald was ill, why – And now, too, that it can never come to anything serious between us – I really can't stop out here in the country and wear myself out nursing sick people.

OSWALD: Not even one who is so near to you?

REGINA: No, that I can't. A poor girl must make the best of her young days, or she'll be left out in the cold before she knows where she is. And I, too, have the joy of life in me, Mrs. Alving.

MRS. ALVING: Yes, I can see you have. But don't throw yourself away, Regina.

REGINA: Oh! what must be, must be. If Oswald takes after his father, I take after my mother, I daresay. May I ask, ma'am, if Mr. Manders knows all this about me?

MRS. ALVING: Mr. Manders knows all about it.

REGINA (*puts on her shawl hastily*): Well then, I'd better make haste and get away by this steamer. Pastor Manders is so nice to deal with; and I certainly think I've as much right to a little of that money as he has – that brute of a carpenter.

MRS. ALVING: You're heartily welcome to it, Regina.

REGINA (*looks hard at her*): I think you might have brought me up as a gentleman's daughter, ma'am; it would have suited me better. (*Tosses her head.*) But it's done now – it doesn't matter! (*With a bitter side glance at the corked bottle.*) All the same, I may come to drink champagne with gentlefolks yet.

MRS. ALVING: And if you ever need a home, Regina, come to me.

REGINA: No, thank you, ma'am. Mr. Manders will look after me, I know. And if the worst comes to the worst, I know of one house where I've every right to a place.

MRS. ALVING: Where is that?

REGINA: 'Captain Alving's Home.'

MRS. ALVING: Regina – now I see it – you're going to your ruin.

REGINA: Oh, stuff! Goodbye (*She nods and goes out through the hall.*)

OSWALD (*stands at the window and looks out*): Is she gone?

MRS. ALVING: Yes.

OSWALD (*murmuring aside to himself*): I think it's a great mistake, all this.

MRS. ALVING (*goes behind him and lays her hands on his shoulders*): Oswald, my dear boy; has it shaken you very much?

OSWALD (*turns his face towards her*): All that about father, do you mean?

MRS. ALVING: Yes, about your unhappy father. I'm so afraid it may have been too much for you.

OSWALD: Why should you fancy that? Of course it came upon me as a great surprise; but, after all, it can't matter much to me.

MRS. ALVING (*draws her hands away*): Can't matter! That your father was so infinitely miserable!

OSWALD: Of course I can pity him as I would anybody else; but –

MRS. ALVING: Nothing more? Your own father!

OSWALD (*impatiently*): Oh, there! 'father', 'father'! I never knew anything of father. I don't remember anything about him except that he once made me sick.

MRS. ALVING: That's a terrible way to speak! Should a son not love his father, all the same?

OSWALD: When a son has nothing to thank his father for? has never known him? Do you really cling to that old superstition? – you who are so enlightened in other ways?

MRS. ALVING: Is it only a superstition – ?

OSWALD: Yes; can't you see it, mother? It's one of those notions that are current in the world, and so –

MRS. ALVING (*deeply moved*): Ghosts!

OSWALD (*crossing the room*): Yes; you may well call them Ghosts.

MRS. ALVING (*wildly*): Oswald! – then you don't love me, either!

OSWALD: You I know, at any rate.

MRS. ALVING: Yes, you know me; but is that all?

OSWALD: And of course I know how fond you are of me, and I can't but be grateful to you. And you can be so very useful to me, now that I'm ill.

MRS. ALVING: Yes, can't I, Oswald? Oh! I could almost bless the illness that has driven you home to me. For I can see very plainly you are not mine; I have to win you.

OSWALD (*impatiently*): Yes, yes, yes; all these are just so many phrases. You must recollect I'm a sick man, mother. I can't be much taken up with other people! I have enough to do thinking about myself.

MRS. ALVING (*in a low voice*): I shall be patient and easily satisfied.

OSWALD: And cheerful too, mother.

MRS. ALVING: Yes, my dear boy, you're quite right. (*Goes towards him.*) Have I relieved you of all remorse and self-reproach now?

OSWALD: Yes, you have. But who's to relieve me of the dread?

MRS. ALVING: The dread?

OSWALD (*walks across the room*): Regina could have been got to do it.

MRS. ALVING: I don't understand you. What is all this about dread – and Regina?

OSWALD: Is it very late, mother?

MRS. ALVING: It's early morning. (*She looks out through the conservatory.*) The day is dawning over the hills; and the weather is fine, Oswald. In a little while you shall see the sun.

OSWALD: I'm glad of that. Oh! I may still have much to rejoice in and live for –

MRS. ALVING: Yes, much – much, indeed!

OSWALD: Even if I can't work –

MRS. ALVING: Oh! you'll soon be able to work again, my dear boy, now that you haven't got all those gnawing and depressing thoughts to brood over any longer.

OSWALD: Yes, I'm glad you were able to rid me of all those fancies; and when I've got one thing more arranged – (*Sits on the sofa.*) Now we'll have a little talk, mother.

MRS. ALVING: Yes, let us (*She pushes an armchair towards the sofa, and sits down close to him.*)

OSWALD: And meantime the sun will be rising. And then you'll know all. And then I shan't have that dread any longer.

MRS. ALVING: What am I to know?

OSWALD (*not listening to her*): Mother, didn't you say, a little while ago, that there was nothing in the world you wouldn't do for me, if I asked you.

MRS. ALVING: Yes, to be sure I said it.

OSWALD: And you'll stick to it, mother?

MRS. ALVING: You may rely on that, my dear and only boy! I have nothing in the world to live for but you alone.

OSWALD: All right, then; now you shall hear. Mother, you have a strong, steadfast mind, I know. Now you're to sit quite still when you hear it.

MRS. ALVING: What dreadful thing can it be – ?

OSWALD: You're not to scream out. Do you hear? Do you promise me that? We'll sit and talk about it quite quietly. Promise me, mother?

MRS. ALVING: Yes, yes; I promise. Only speak.

OSWALD: Well, you must know that all this fatigue, and my inability to think of work – all that is not the illness itself –

MRS. ALVING: Then what is the illness itself?

OSWALD: The disease I have as my birthright (*he point to his forehead and adds very softly*) – is seated here.

MRS. ALVING (*almost voiceless*): Oswald! No, no!

OSWALD: Don't scream. I can't bear it. Yes, it's seated here – waiting. And it may break out any day – at any moment.

MRS. ALVING: Oh! what horror!

OSWALD: Now, do be quiet. That's how it stands with me –

MRS. ALVING (*jumps up*): It's not true, Oswald. It's impossible. It can't be so.

OSWALD: I have had one attack down there already. It was soon over. But when I got to know what had been the matter with me, then the dread came upon me raging and tearing; and so I set off home to you as fast as I could.

MRS. ALVING: Then this is the dread – !

OSWALD: Yes, for it's so indescribably loathsome, you know. Oh! if it had only been an ordinary mortal disease – ! For I'm not so afraid of death – though I should like to live as long as I can.

MRS. ALVING: Yes, yes, Oswald, you must!

OSWALD: But this is so unutterably loathsome! To become a little baby again! To have to be fed! To have to – Oh, it's not to be spoken of!

MRS. ALVING: The child has his mother to nurse him.

OSWALD (*jumps up*): No, never; that's just what I won't have. I can't endure to think that perhaps I should lie in that state for many years – get old and grey. And in the meantime you might die and leave me. (*Sits in Mrs. Alving's chair.*) For the doctor said it wouldn't necessarily prove fatal at once. He called it a sort of softening of the brain – or something of the kind. (*Smiles sadly.*) I think that expression sounds so nice. It always sets me thinking of cherry-coloured velvet – something soft and delicate to stroke.

MRS. ALVING (*screams*): Oswald!

OSWALD (*springs up and paces the room*): And now you have taken Regina from me. If I'd only had her! She would have come to the rescue, I know.

MRS. ALVING (*goes to him*): What do you mean by that, my darling boy? Is there any help in the world that I wouldn't give you?

OSWALD: When I got over my attack in Paris, the doctor told me that when it came again – and it will come again – there would be no more hope.

MRS. ALVING: He was heartless enough to –

OSWALD: I demanded it of him. I told him I had preparations to make. (*He smiles cunningly.*) And so I had. (*He takes a little box from his inner breast pocket and opens it.*) Mother, do you see this?

MRS. ALVING: What is that?

OSWALD: Morphia.

MRS. ALVING (*looks horrified at him*): Oswald – my boy!

OSWALD: I've scraped together twelve pilules –

MRS. ALVING (*snatches at it*): Give me the box, Oswald.

OSWALD: Not yet, mother. (*He hides the box again in his pocket.*)

MRS. ALVING: I shall never survive this!

OSWALD: It must be survived. Now if I'd had Regina here, I should have told her how things stood with me, and begged her to come to the rescue at the last. She would have done it. I'm certain she would.

MRS. ALVING: Never!

OSWALD: When the horror had come upon me, and she saw me lying there helpless, like a little new-born baby, impotent, lost, hopeless, past all saving –

MRS. ALVING: Never in all the world would Regina have done this.

OSWALD: Regina would have done it. Regina was so splendidly light-hearted. And she would soon have wearied of nursing an invalid like me –

MRS. ALVING: Then heaven be praised that Regina is not here.

OSWALD: Well then, it's you that must come to the rescue, mother.

MRS. ALVING (*screams aloud*): I!

OSWALD: Who is nearer to it than you?

MRS. ALVING: I! your mother!

OSWALD: For that very reason.

MRS. ALVING: I, who gave you life!

OSWALD: I never asked you for life. And what sort of a life have you given me? I won't have it. You shall take it back again.

MRS. ALVING: Help! Help! (*She runs out into the hall.*)

OSWALD (*going after her*): Don't leave me. Where are you going?

MRS. ALVING (*in the hall*): To fetch the doctor, Oswald. Let me go.

OSWALD (*also outside*): You shall not go. And no one shall come in.

(*The locking of a door is heard.*)

MRS. ALVING (*comes in again*): Oswald – Oswald! – my child!

OSWALD (*follows her*): Have you a mother's heart for me, and yet can see me suffer from this unutterable dread?

MRS. ALVING (*after a moment's silence, commands herself, and says:*) Here's my hand upon it.

OSWALD: Will you – ?

MRS. ALVING: If it's ever necessary. But it will never be necessary. No, no; it's impossible.

OSWALD: Well, let us hope so, and let us live together as long as we can. Thank you, mother.

(*He seats himself in the armchair which Mrs. Alving has moved to the sofa. Day is breaking. The lamp is still burning on the table.*)

MRS. ALVING (*drawing near cautiously*): Do you feel calm now?

OSWALD: Yes.

MRS. ALVING (*bending over him*): It has been a dreadful fancy of yours, Oswald – nothing but a fancy. All this excitement has been too much for you. But now you shall have a long rest; at home with your mother, my own blessed boy. Everything you point to you shall have, just as when you were a little child. There now. That crisis is over now. You see how easily it passed. Oh! I was sure it would – And do you see, Oswald, what a lovely day we're going to have? Brilliant sunshine! Now you'll be really be able to see your home.

(*She goes to the table and puts the lamp out. Sunrise. The glacier and the snow-peaks in the background glow in the morning light.*)

OSWALD (*sits in the armchair with his back towards the landscape, without moving. Suddenly he says:*) Mother, give me the sun.

MRS. ALVING (*by the table, starts and looks at him*): What do you say?

OSWALD (*repeats, in a dull, toneless voice*): The sun. The sun.

MRS. ALVING (*goes to him*): Oswald, what's the matter with you? (*Oswald seems to shrink together in the chair; all his muscles relax; his face is expressionless, his eyes have a glassy stare. Mrs. Alving is quivering with terror.*) What is this? (*Shrieks.*) Oswald, what's the matter with you? (*Falls on her knees beside him and shakes him.*) Oswald, Oswald! look at me! Don't you know me?

OSWALD (*tonelessly as before*): The sun. The sun.

MRS. ALVING (*springs up in despair, entwines her hands in her hair and shrieks*): I can't bear it! (*Whispers, as though petrified.*) I can't bear it! Never! (*Suddenly.*) Where has he got them? (*Fumbles hastily in his breast.*) Here! (*Shrinks back a few steps and screams.*) No; no; no! Yes! – No; No! (*She stands a few steps from him with her hands twisted in her hair, and stares at him in speechless terror.*)

OSWALD (*sits motionless as before and says*): The sun. The sun.

Curtain

A Doll's House

Nora (Sharon Maughan) and Torvald (Peter McEnery):
Chichester Festival Theatre, 1994

Characters

TORVALD HELMER

NORA, *his wife*

DOCTOR RANK

MRS. LINDEN

NILS KROGSTAD

THE HELMERS' THREE CHILDREN

ANNA, *their nurse*

A MAID SERVANT (ELLEN)

A PORTER

The action passes in Helmer's house (a flat) in Christiania.

Act One

A room, comfortably and tastefully, but not expensively, furnished. In the back, on the right, a door leads to the hall; on the left another door leads to Helmer's study. Between the two doors a pianoforte. In the middle of the left wall a door, and nearer the front a window. Near the window a round table with armchairs and a small sofa. In the right wall, somewhat to the back, a door, and against the same wall, farther forward, a porcelain stove; in front of it a couple of armchairs and a rocking chair. Between the stove and the side door a small table. Engravings on the walls. A what-not with china and bric-à-brac. A small bookcase filled with handsomely bound books. Carpet. A fire in the stove. It is a winter day.

A bell rings in the hall outside. Presently the outer door of the flat is heard to open. Then Nora enters, humming gaily. She is in outdoor dress, and carries several parcels, which she lays on the right-hand table. She leaves the door into the hall open, and a Porter is seen outside, carrying a Christmas tree and a basket, which he gives to the maid servant who has opened the door.

NORA: Hide the Christmas tree carefully, Ellen; the children must on no account see it before this evening, when it's lighted up. (*To the Porter, taking out her purse.*) How much?

PORTER: Fifty öre.

NORA: There is a crown. No, keep the change.

(*The Porter thanks her and goes. Nora shuts the door. She continues smiling in quiet glee as she takes off her outdoor things. Taking from her pocket a bag of macaroons, she eats one or two. Then she goes on tiptoe to her husband's door and listens.*)

NORA: Yes, he is at home. (*She begins humming again, crossing to the table on the right.*)

HELMER (*in his room*): Is that my lark twittering there?

NORA (*busy opening some of her parcels*): Yes, it is.

HELMER: Is it the squirrel frisking around?

NORA: Yes!

HELMER: When did the squirrel get home?

NORA: Just this minute. (*Hides the bag of macaroons in her pocket and wipes her mouth.*) Come here, Torvald, and see what I've been buying.

HELMER: Don't interrupt me. (*A little later he opens the door and looks in, pen in hand.*) Buying, did you say? What! All that? Has my little spendthrift been making the money fly again?

NORA: Why, Torvald, surely we can afford to launch out a little now. It's the first Christmas we haven't had to pinch.

HELMER: Come, come; we can't afford to squander money.

NORA: Oh yes, Torvald, do let us squander a little, now – just the least little bit! You know you'll soon be earning heaps of money.

HELMER: Yes, from New Year's Day. But there's a whole quarter before my first salary is due.

NORA: Never mind; we can borrow in the meantime.

HELMER: Nora! (*He goes up to her and takes her playfully by the ear.*) Still my little featherbrain! Supposing I borrowed a thousand crowns today, and you made ducks and drakes of them during Christmas week, and then on New Year's Eve a tile blew off the roof and knocked my brains out –

NORA (*laying her hand on his mouth*): Hush! How can you talk so horribly?

HELMER: But supposing it were to happen – what then?

NORA: If anything so dreadful happened, it would be all the same to me whether I was in debt or not.

HELMER: But what about the creditors?

NORA: They! Who cares for them? They're only strangers.

HELMER: Nora, Nora! What a woman you are! But seriously, Nora, you know my principles on these points. No debts! No borrowing! Home life ceases to be free and beautiful as soon as it is founded on borrowing and debt. We two have held out bravely till now, and we are not going to give in at the last.

NORA (*going to the fireplace*): Very well – as you please, Torvald.

HELMER (*following her*): Come, come; my little lark mustn't drop her wings like that. What? Is my squirrel in the sulks? (*Takes out his purse.*) Nora, what do you think I have here?

NORA (*turning round quickly*): Money!

HELMER: There! (*Gives her some notes.*) Of course I know all sorts of things are wanted at Christmas.

NORA (*counting*): Ten, twenty, thirty, forty. Oh, thank you, thank you, Torvald! This will go a long way.

HELMER: I should hope so.

NORA: Yes, indeed; a long way! But come here, and let me show you all I've been buying. And so cheap! Look, here's a new suit for Ivar, and a little sword. Here are a horse and a trumpet for Bob. And here are a doll and a cradle for Emmy. They're only common, but they're good enough for her to pull to pieces. And dress-stuffs and kerchiefs for the servants. I ought to have got something better for old Anna.

HELMER: And what's in that other parcel?

NORA (*crying out*): No, Torvald, you're not to see that until this evening!

HELMER: Oh! Ah! But now tell me, you little spendthrift, have you thought of anything for yourself?

NORA: For myself! Oh, I don't want anything.

HELMER: Nonsense! Just tell me something sensible you would like to have.

NORA: No, really I don't know of anything – well, listen, Torvald –

HELMER: Well?

NORA (*playing with his coat buttons, without looking him in the face*): If you really want to give me something you might, you know – you might –

HELMER: Well? Out with it!

NORA (*quickly*): You might give me money, Torvald. Only just what you think you can spare; then I can buy something with it later on.

HELMER: But, Nora –

NORA: Oh, please do, dear Torvald, please do! I should hang the money in lovely gilt paper on the Christmas tree. Wouldn't that be fun?

HELMER: What do they call the birds that are always making the money fly?

NORA: Yes, I know – spendthrifts, of course. But please do as I ask you, Torvald. Then I shall have time to think what I want most. Isn't that very sensible, now?

HELMER (*smiling*): Certainly; that is to say, if you really kept the money I gave you, and really spent it on something for yourself. But it all goes in housekeeping, and for all manner of useless things, and then I have to pay up again.

NORA: But, Torvald –

HELMER: Can you deny it, Nora dear? (*He puts his arm round her.*) It's a sweet little lark, but it gets through a lot of money. No one would believe how much it costs a man to keep such a little bird as you.

NORA: For shame! How can you say so? Why, I save as much as ever I can.

HELMER (*laughing*): Very true – as much as you can – but that's precisely nothing.

NORA (*hums and smiles with covert glee*): H'm! If you only knew, Torvald, what expenses we larks and squirrels have.

HELMER: You're a strange little being! Just like your father – always on the lookout for all the money you can lay your hands on; but the moment you have it, it seems to slip through your fingers; you never know what becomes of it. Well, one must take you as you are. It's in the blood. Yes, Nora, that sort of thing is hereditary.

NORA: I wish I had inherited many of papa's qualities.

HELMER: And I don't wish you anything but just what you are – my own, sweet little songbird. But I say – it strikes me you look so – so – what shall I call it? – so suspicious today –

NORA: Do I?

HELMER: You do, indeed. Look me full in the face.

NORA (*looking at him*): Well?

HELMER (*threatening with his finger*): Hasn't the little sweet-tooth been playing pranks today?

NORA: No; how can you think such a thing!

HELMER: Didn't she just look in at the confectioner's?

NORA: No, Torvald; really –

HELMER: Not to sip a little jelly?

NORA: No, certainly not.

HELMER: Hasn't she even nibbled a macaroon or two?

NORA: No, Torvald, indeed, indeed!

HELMER: Well, well, well; of course I'm only joking.

NORA (*goes to the table on the right*): I shouldn't think of doing what you disapprove of.

HELMER: No, I'm sure of that; and, besides, you've given me your word – (*Going towards her.*) Well, keep your little Christmas secrets to yourself, Nora darling. The Christmas tree will bring them all to light, I daresay.

NORA: Have you remembered to invite Doctor Rank?

HELMER: No. But it's not necessary; he'll come as a matter of course. Besides, I shall ask him when he looks in today. I've ordered some capital wine. Nora, you can't think how I look forward to this evening.

NORA: And I too. How the children will enjoy themselves, Torvald!

HELMER: Ah, it's glorious to feel that one has an assured position and ample means. Isn't it delightful to think of?

NORA: Oh, it's wonderful!

HELMER: Do you remember last Christmas? For three whole weeks beforehand you shut yourself up every evening till long past midnight to make flowers for the Christmas tree, and all sorts of other marvels that were to have astonished us. I was never so bored in my life.

NORA: I didn't bore myself at all.

HELMER (*smiling*): But it came to little enough in the end, Nora.

NORA: Oh, are you going to tease me about that again? How could I help the cat getting in and pulling it all to pieces?

HELMER: To be sure you couldn't, my poor little Nora. You did your best to give us all pleasure, and that's the main point. But, all the same, it'a good thing the hard times are over.

NORA: Oh, isn't it wonderful?

HELMER: Now I needn't sit here boring myself all alone; and you needn't tire your blessed eyes and your delicate little fingers –

NORA (*clapping her hands*): No, I needn't, need I, Torvald? Oh, how wonderful it is to think of! (*Takes his arm.*) And now I'll tell you how I think we ought to manage, Torvald. As soon as Christmas is over – (*The hall-door bell rings.*) Oh, there's a ring! (*Arranging the room.*) That's somebody come to call. How tiresome!

HELMER: I'm 'not at home' to callers; remember that.

ELLEN (*in the doorway*): A lady to see you, ma'am.

NORA: Show her in.

ELLEN (*to Helmer*): And the doctor has just come, sir.

HELMER: Has he gone into my study?

ELLEN: Yes, sir.

(*Helmer goes into his study. Ellen ushers in Mrs. Linden, in travelling costume, and goes out, closing the door.*)

MRS. LINDEN (*embarrassed and hesitating*): How do you do, Nora?

NORA (*doubtfully*): How do you do?

MRS. LINDEN: I see you don't recognise me.

NORA: No, I don't think – oh yes! – I believe – (*Suddenly brightening.*) What, Christina! Is it really you!

MRS. LINDEN: Yes; really I!

NORA: Christina! And to think I didn't know you! But how could I – (*More softly.*) How changed you are, Christina!

MRS. LINDEN: Yes, no doubt. In nine or ten years –

NORA: Is it really so long since we met? Yes, so it is. Oh, the last eight years have been a happy time, I can tell you. And now you have come to town? All that long journey in midwinter! How brave of you!

MRS. LINDEN: I arrived by this morning's steamer.

NORA: To have a merry Christmas, of course. Oh, how delightful! Yes, we will have a merry Christmas? Do take your things off. Aren't you frozen? (*Helping her.*) There; now we'll sit cosily by the fire. No, you take the armchair; I shall sit in this rocking chair. (*Seizes her hands.*) Yes, now I can see the dear old face again. It was only at the first glance – But you're a little paler, Christina – and perhaps a little thinner.

MRS. LINDEN: And much, much older, Nora.

NORA: Yes, perhaps a little older – not much – ever so little. (*She suddenly checks herself; seriously.*) Oh, what a thoughtless wretch I am! Here I sit chattering on and – Dear, dear Christina, can you forgive me!

MRS. LINDEN: What do you mean, Nora?

NORA (*softly*): Poor Christina! I forgot: you are a widow.

MRS. LINDEN: Yes; my husband died three years ago.

NORA: I know, I know; I saw it in the papers. Oh, believe me, Christina, I did mean to write to you; but I kept putting it off, and something always came in the way.

MRS. LINDEN: I can quite understand that, Nora dear.

NORA: No, Christina; it was horrid of me. Oh, you poor darling! how much you must have gone through! – And he left you nothing?

MRS. LINDEN: Nothing.

NORA: And no children?

MRS. LINDEN: None.

NORA: Nothing, nothing at all?

MRS. LINDEN: Not even a sorrow or a longing to dwell upon.

NORA (*looking at her incredulously*): My dear Christina, how is that possible?

MRS. LINDEN (*smiling sadly and stroking her hair*): Oh, it happens so sometimes, Nora.

NORA: So utterly alone! How dreadful that must be! I have three of the loveliest children. I can't show them to you just now; they're out with their nurse. But now you must tell me everything.

MRS. LINDEN: No, no; I want you to tell me –

NORA: No, you must begin; I won't be egotistical today. Today I'll think only of you. Oh! but I must tell you one thing – perhaps you've heard of our great stroke of fortune?

MRS. LINDEN: No. What is it?

NORA: Only think! my husband has been made manager of the Joint Stock Bank.

MRS. LINDEN: Your husband! Oh, how fortunate!

NORA: Yes; isn't it? A lawyer's position is so uncertain, you see, especially when he won't touch any business that's the least bit – shady, as of course Torvald never would; and there I quite agree with him. Oh! you can imagine how glad we are. He is to enter on his new position at the New Year, and then he'll have a large salary, and percentages. In future we shall be able to live quite differently – just as we please, in fact. Oh, Christina, I feel so lighthearted and happy! It's delightful to have lots of money, and no need to worry about things, isn't it?

MRS. LINDEN: Yes; at any rate it must be delightful to have what you need.

NORA: No, not only what you need, but heaps of money – heaps!

MRS. LINDEN (*smiling*): Nora, Nora, haven't you learnt reason yet? In our schooldays you were a shocking little spendthrift.

NORA (*quietly smiling*): Yes; that's what Torvald says I am still. (*Holding up her forefinger.*) But 'Nora, Nora' is not so silly as you all think. Oh! I haven't had the chance to be much of a spendthrift. We have both had to work.

MRS. LINDEN: You too?

NORA: Yes, light fancy work: crochet, and embroidery, and things of that sort; (*Carelessly*) and other work too. You know, of course, that Torvald left the Government service when we were married. He had little chance of promotion, and of course he required to make more money. But in the first year after our marriage he overworked himself terribly. He had to undertake all sorts of extra work, you know, and to slave early and late. He couldn't stand it, and fell dangerously ill. Then the doctors declared he must go to the South.

MRS. LINDEN: You spent a whole year in Italy, didn't you?

NORA: Yes, we did. It wasn't easy to manage, I can tell you. It was just after Ivar's birth. But of course we had to go. Oh, it was a wonderful, delicious journey! And it saved Torvald's life. But it cost a frightful lot of money, Christina.

MRS. LINDEN: So I should think.

NORA: Twelve hundred dollars! Four thousand eight hundred crowns! Isn't that a lot of money?

MRS. LINDEN: How lucky you had the money to spend!

NORA: We got it from father, you must know.

MRS. LINDEN: Ah, I see. He died just about that time, didn't he?

NORA: Yes, Christina, just then. And only think! I couldn't go and nurse him! I was expecting little Ivar's birth daily; and then I had my poor sick Torvald to attend to. Dear, kind old father! I never saw him again, Christina. Oh! that's the hardest thing I have had to bear since my marriage.

MRS. LINDEN: I know how fond you were of him. But then you went to Italy?

NORA: Yes; you see, we had the money, and the doctors said we must lose no time. We started a month later.

MRS. LINDEN: And your husband came back completely cured?

NORA: Sound as a bell.

MRS. LINDEN: But – the doctor?

NORA: What do you mean?

MRS. LINDEN: I thought as I came in your servant announced the doctor –

NORA: Oh yes; Doctor Rank. But he doesn't come professionally. He is our best friend, and never lets a day pass without looking in. No, Torvald hasn't had an hour's illness since the time. And the children are so healthy and well, and so am I. (*Jumps up and claps her hands.*) Oh, Christina, Christina, what a wonderful thing it is to live and to be happy! – Oh, but it's really too horrid of me! Here am I talking about nothing but my own concerns. (*Seats herself upon a footstool close to Christina, and lays her arms on her friend's lap.*) Oh, don't be angry with me! Now tell me, is it really true that you didn't love your husband? What made you marry him, then?

MRS. LINDEN: My mother was still alive, you see, bedridden and helpless; and then I had my two younger brothers to think of. I didn't think it would be right for me to refuse him.

NORA: Perhaps it wouldn't have been. I suppose he was rich then?

MRS. LINDEN: Very well off, I believe. But his business was uncertain. It fell to pieces at his death, and there was nothing left.

NORA: And then – ?

MRS. LINDEN: Then I had to fight my way by keeping a shop, a little school, anything I could turn my hand to. The last three years have been one long struggle for me. But now it is over, Nora. My poor mother no longer needs me; she is at rest. And the boys are in business, and can look after themselves.

NORA: How free your life must feel!

MRS. LINDEN: No, Nora; only inexpressibly empty. No one to live for! (*Stands up restlessly.*) That's why I could not bear to stay any longer in that out-of-the way corner. Here it must be easier to find something to take one up – to occupy one's thoughts. If I could get some settled employment – some office work.

NORA: But, Christina, that's such drudgery, and you look worn-out already. It would be ever so much better for you to go to some watering place and rest.

MRS. LINDEN (*going to the window*): I have no father to give me the money, Nora.

NORA (*rising*): Oh, don't be vexed with me.

MRS. LINDEN (*going to her*): My dear Nora, don't you be vexed with me. The worst of a position like mine is that it makes one so bitter. You have no one to work for, yet you have to be always on the strain. You must live, and so you become selfish. When I heard of the happy change in your fortunes – can you believe it? – I was glad for my own sake more than for yours.

NORA: How do you mean? Ah, I see! You think Torvald can perhaps do something for you?

MRS. LINDEN: Yes, I thought so.

NORA: And so he shall, Christina. Just you leave it all to me. I shall lead up to it beautifully! – I shall think of some delightful plan to put him in a good humour! Oh, I should so love to help you.

MRS. LINDEN: How good of you, Nora, to stand by me so warmly! Doubly good in you, who know so little of the troubles and burdens of life.

NORA: I? I know so little of – ?

MRS. LINDEN (*smiling*): Oh, well – a little fancywork, and so forth. – You're a child, Nora.

NORA (*tosses her head and paces the room*): Oh, come, you mustn't be so patronising!

MRS. LINDEN: No?

NORA: You're like the rest. You all think I'm fit for nothing really serious –

MRS. LINDEN: Well, well –

NORA: You think I've had no troubles in this weary world.

MRS. LINDEN: My dear Nora, you've just told me all your troubles.

NORA: Pooh – those trifles! (*Softly.*) I haven't told you the great thing.

MRS. LINDEN: The great thing? What do you mean?

NORA: I know you look down upon me, Christina; but you have no right to. You are proud of having worked so hard and so long for your mother.

MRS. LINDEN: I am sure I don't look down upon anyone; but it's true I am both proud and glad when I remember that I was able to keep my mother's last days free from care.

NORA: And you're proud to think of what you have done for your brothers, too.

MRS. LINDEN: Have I not the right to be?

NORA: Yes, indeed. But now let me tell you, Christina – I, too, have something to be proud and glad of.

MRS. LINDEN: I don't doubt it. But what do you mean?

NORA: Hush! Not so loud. Only think, if Torvald were to hear! He mustn't – not for worlds! No one must know about it, Christina – no one but you.

MRS. LINDEN: Why, what can it be?

NORA: Come over here. (*Draws her down beside her on the sofa.*) Yes, Christina – I, too, have something to be proud and glad of. I saved Torvald's life.

MRS. LINDEN: Saved his life? How?

NORA: I told you about our going to Italy. Torvald would have died but for that.

MRS. LINDEN: Well – and your father gave you the money.

NORA (*smiling*): Yes, so Torvald and every one believes; but –

MRS. LINDEN: But – ?

NORA: Papa didn't give us one penny. It was *I* that found the money.

MRS. LINDEN: You? All that money?

NORA: Twelve hundred dollars. Four thousand eight hundred crowns. What do you say to that?

MRS. LINDEN: My dear Nora, how did you manage it? Did you win it in the lottery?

NORA (*contemptuously*): In the lottery? Pooh! Anyone could have done that!

MRS. LINDEN: Then wherever did you get it from?

NORA (*hums and smiles mysteriously*): H'm; tra-la-la-la!

MRS. LINDEN: Of course you couldn't borrow it.

NORA: No? Why not?

MRS. LINDEN: Why, a wife can't borrow without her husband's consent.

NORA (*tossing her head*): Oh! when the wife has some idea of business, and knows how to set about things –

MRS. LINDEN: But, Nora, I don't undestand –

NORA: Well, you needn't. I never said I borrowed the money. There are many ways I may have got it. (*Throws herself back on the sofa.*) I may have got it from some admirer. When one is so – attractive as I am –

MRS. LINDEN: You're too silly, Nora.

NORA: Now I'm sure you're dying of curiosity, Christina –

MRS. LINDEN: Listen to me, Nora dear: haven't you been a little rash?

NORA (sitting upright again): Is it rash to save one's husband's life?

MRS. LINDEN: I think it was rash of you, without his knowledge –

NORA: But it would have been fatal for him to know! Can't you understand that? He wasn't even to suspect how ill he was. The doctors came to me privately and told me his life was in danger – that nothing could save him but a winter in the South. Do you think I didn't try diplomacy first? I told him how I longed to have a trip abroad, like other young wives; I wept and prayed; I said he ought to think of my condition, and not to thwart me: and then I hinted that he could borrow the money. But then, Christina, he got almost angry. He said I was frivolous, and that it was his duty as a husband not to yield to my whims and fancies – so he called them. Very well, thought I, but saved you must be; and then I found the way to do it.

MRS. LINDEN: And did your husband never learn from your father that the money was not from him?

NORA: No; never. Papa died at that very time. I meant to have told him all about it, and begged him to say nothing. But he was so ill – unhappily, it wasn't necessary.

MRS. LINDEN: And you have never confessed to your husband?

NORA: Good heavens! What can you be thinking of? Tell him, when he has such a loathing of debt! And besides – how painful and humiliating it would be for Torvald, with his manly self-respect, to know that he owed anything to me! It would utterly upset the relation between us; our beautiful, happy home would never again be what it is.

MRS. LINDEN: Will you never tell him?

NORA (*thoughtfully, half-smiling*): Yes, some time perhaps – many, many years hence, when I'm – not so pretty. You mustn't laugh at me! Of course I mean when Torvald is not so much in love with me as he is now; when it doesn't amuse him any longer to see me dancing about, and dressing up and acting. Then it might be well to have something in reserve. (*Breaking off.*) Nonsense! nonsense! That time will never come. Now, what do you say to my grand secret, Christina? Am I fit for nothing now? You may believe it has cost me a lot of anxiety. It has been no joke to meet my engagements punctually. You must know, Christina, that in business there are things called instalments, and quarterly interest, that are terribly hard to provide for. So I've had to pinch a little here and there, wherever I could. I couldn't save much out of the housekeeping, for of course Torvald had to live well. And I couldn't let the children go about badly dressed; all I got for them, I spent on them, the blessed darlings!

MRS. LINDEN: Poor Nora! So it had to come out of your own pocket-money?

NORA: Yes, of course. After all, the whole thing was my doing. When Torvald gave me money for clothes, and so on, I never spent more than half of it; I always bought the simplest and cheapest things. It's a mercy that everything suits me so well – Torvald never had any suspicions. But it was often very hard, Christina dear. For it's nice to be beautifully dressed – now, isn't it?

MRS. LINDEN: Indeed it is.

NORA: Well, and besides that, I made money in other ways. Last winter I was so lucky – I got a heap of copying to do. I shut myself up every evening, and wrote far into the night. Oh, sometimes I was so tired, so tired. And yet it was splendid to work in that way and earn money. I almost felt as if I was a man.

MRS. LINDEN: Then how much have you been able to pay off?

NORA: Well, I can't precisely say. It's difficult to keep that sort of business clear. I only know that I've paid everything I could scrape together. Sometimes I really didn't know where to turn. (*Smiles.*) Then I used to sit here and pretend that a rich old gentleman was in love with me –

MRS. LINDEN: What! What gentleman?

NORA: Oh, nobody? – that he was dead now, and that when his will was opened, there stood in large letters: 'Pay over at once everything of which I die possessed to that charming person, Mrs. Nora Helmer.'

MRS. LINDEN: But, my dear Nora – what gentleman do you mean?

NORA: Oh dear, can't you understand? There wasn't any old gentleman: it was only what I used to dream and dream when I was at my wits' end for money. But it doesn't matter now – the tiresome old creature may stay where he is for me. I care nothing for him or his will; for now my troubles are over. (*Springing up.*) Oh, Christina, how glorious it is to think of! Free from all anxiety! Free, quite free. To be able to play and romp about with the children; to have things tasteful and pretty in the house, exactly as Torvald likes it! And then the spring will soon be here, with the great blue sky. Perhaps then we shall have a little holiday. Perhaps I shall see the sea again. Oh, what a wonderful thing it is to live and to be happy!

(*The hall doorbell rings.*)

MRS. LINDEN (*rising*): There's a ring. Perhaps I had better go.

NORA: No; do stay. No one will come here. It's sure to be some one for Torvald.

ELLEN (*in the doorway*): If you please, ma'am there's a gentleman to speak to Mr. Helmer.

NORA: Who is the gentleman?

KROGSTAD (*in the doorway*): It is I, Mrs. Helmer.

(*Mrs. Linden starts, and turns away to the window.*)

NORA (*goes a step towards him, anxiously, speaking low.*) You? What is it? What do you want with my husband?

KROGSTAD: Bank Business – in a way. I hold a small post in the Joint Stock Bank, and your husband is to be our new chief, I hear.

NORA: Then it is – ?

KROGSTAD: Only tiresome business, Mrs. Helmer; nothing more.

NORA: Then will you please go to his study?

(*Krogstad goes. She bows indifferently while she closes the door into the hall. Then she goes to the stove and looks to the fire.*)

MRS. LINDEN: Nora – who was that man?

NORA: A Mr. Krogstad – a lawyer.

MRS. LINDEN: Then it was really he?

NORA: Do you know him?

MRS. LINDEN: I used to know him – many years ago. He was in a lawyer's office in our town.

NORA: Yes, so he was.

MRS. LINDEN: How he has changed!

NORA: I believe his marriage was unhappy.

MRS. LINDEN: And he is a widower now?

NORA: With a lot of children. There! Now it will burn up. (*She closes the stove, and pushes the rocking-chair a little aside.*)

MRS. LINDEN: His business is not of the most creditable, they say?

NORA: Isn't it? I daresay not. I don't know. But don't let us think of business – it's so tiresome.

(*Dr. Rank comes out of Helmer's room.*)

RANK (*still in the doorway*): No, no; I'm in your way. I shall go and have a chat with your wife. (*Shuts the door and sees Mrs. Linden.*) Oh, I beg your pardon. I'm in the way here too.

NORA: No, not in the least. (*Introduces them.*) Doctor Rank – Mrs. Linden.

RANK: Oh, indeed; I've often heard Mrs. Linden's name. I think I passed you on the stairs as I came up.

MRS. LINDEN: Yes; I go so very slowly. Stairs try me so much.

RANK: Ah – you are not very strong?

MRS. LINDEN: Only overworked.

RANK: Nothing more? Then no doubt you've come to town to find rest in a round of dissipation?

MRS. LINDEN: I have come to look for employment.

RANK: Is that an approved remedy for overwork?

MRS. LINDEN: One must live, Doctor Rank.

RANK: Yes, that seems to be the general opinion.

NORA: Come, Doctor Rank – you want to live yourself.

RANK: To be sure I do. However wretched I may be, I want to drag on as long as possible. All my patients, too, have the same mania. And it's the same with people whose complaint is moral. At this very moment Helmer is talking to just such a moral incurable –

MRS. LINDEN (*softly*): Ah!

NORA: Whom do you mean?

RANK: Oh, a fellow named Krogstad, a man you know nothing about – corrupt to the very core of his character. But even he began by announcing, as a matter of vast importance, that he must live.

NORA: Indeed? And what did he want with Torvald?

RANK: I haven't an idea; I only gathered that it was some bank business.

NORA: I didn't know that Krog – that this Mr. Krogstad had anything to do with the Bank?

RANK: Yes. He has got some sort of place there. (*To Mrs. Linden.*) I don't know whether, in your part of the country, you have people who go grubbing and sniffing around in search of moral rottenness – and then, when they have found a 'case', don't rest till they have got their man into some good position, where they can keep a watch upon him. Men with a clean bill of health they leave out in the cold.

MRS. LINDEN: Well, I suppose the – delicate characters require most care.

RANK (*shrugs his shoulders*): There we have it! It's that notion that makes society a hospital.

(*Nora, deep in her own thoughts, breaks into half-stifled laughter, and claps her hands.*)

RANK: Why do you laugh at that? Have you any idea what 'society' is?

NORA: What do I care for your tiresome society? I was laughing at something else – something excessively amusing. Tell me, Doctor Rank, are all the employees at the Bank dependent on Torvald now?

RANK: Is that what strikes you as excessively amusing?

NORA (*smiles and hums*): Never mind, never mind! (*Walks about the room.*) Yes, it is funny to think that we – that Torvald has such power over so many people. (*Takes the bag from her pocket.*) Doctor Rank, will you have a macaroon?

RANK: What! – macaroons! I thought they were contra-band here?

NORA: Yes; but Christina brought me these.

MRS. LINDEN: What! I –

NORA: Oh, well! Don't be frightened. You couldn't possibly know that Torvald had forbidden them. The fact is, he's afraid of me spoiling my teeth. But, oh bother, just for once! – That's for you, Doctor Rank! (*Puts a macaroon into his mouth.*) And you too, Christina. And I'll have one while we're about it – only a tiny one, or at most two. (*Walks about again.*) Oh dear, I am happy! There's only one thing in the world I really want.

RANK: Well, what's that?

NORA: There's something I should so like to say – in Torvald's hearing.

RANK: Then why don't you say it?

NORA: Because I daren't, it's so ugly.

MRS. LINDEN: Ugly?

RANK: In that case you'd better not. But to us you might – What is it you would so like to say in Helmer's hearing?

NORA: I should so love to say, 'Damn it all!'

RANK: Are you out of your mind?

MRS. LINDEN: Good gracious, Nora – !

RANK: Say it – there he is!

NORA (*hides the macaroons*): Hush – sh – sh.

(*Helmer comes out of his room, hat in hand, with his overcoat on his arm.*)

NORA (*going to him*): Well, Torvald dear, have you got rid of him?

HELMER: Yes; he has just gone.

NORA: Let me introduce you – this is Christina, who has come to town –

HELMER: Christina? Pardon me, I don't know –

NORA: Mrs. Linden, Torvald dear – Christina Linden.

HELMER (*to Mrs. Linden*): Indeed! A school friend of my wife's, no doubt?

MRS. LINDEN: Yes, we knew each other as girls.

NORA: And only think! She has taken this long journey on purpose to speak to you.

HELMER: To speak to me!

MRS. LINDEN: Well, not quite –

NORA: You see, Christina is tremendously clever at office work, and she's so anxious to work under a first-rate man of business in order to learn still more –

HELMER (*to Mrs. Linden*): Very sensible indeed.

NORA: And when she heard you were appointed manager – it was telegraphed, you know – she started off at once, and – Torvald dear, for my sake, you must do something for Christina. Now, can't you?

HELMER: It's not impossible. I presume Mrs. Linden is a widow?

MRS. LINDEN: Yes.

HELMER: And you have already had some experience of business?

MRS. LINDEN: A good deal.

HELMER: Well, then, it's very likely I may be able to find a place for you.

NORA (*clapping her hands*): There now! There now!

HELMER: You have come at a fortunate moment, Mrs. Linden.

MRS. LINDEN: Oh, how can I thank you – ?

HELMER (*smiling*): There is no occasion. (*Puts on his overcoat.*) But for the present you must excuse me –

RANK: Wait; I am going with you.

(*Fetches his fur coat from the hall and warms it at the fire.*)

NORA: Don't be long, Torvald dear.

HELMER: Only an hour; not more.

NORA: Are you going too, Christina?

MRS. LINDEN (*putting on her walking things*): Yes; I must set about looking for lodgings.

HELMER: Then perhaps we can go together?

NORA (*helping her*): What a pity we haven't a spare room for you; but it's impossible –

MRS. LINDEN: I shouldn't think of troubling you. Goodbye, dear Nora, and thank you for all your kindness.

NORA: Goodbye for the present. Of course you'll come back this evening. And you, too, Doctor Rank. What! If you're well enough? Of course you'll be well enough. Only wrap up warmly. (*They go out, talking, into the hall. Outside on the stairs are heard children's voices.*) There they are! There they are! (*She runs to the outer door and opens it. The Nurse, Anna, enters the hall with the children.*) Come in! Come in! (*Stoops down and kisses the children.*) Oh, my sweet darlings! Do you see them, Christina? Aren't they lovely?

RANK: Don't let us stand here chattering in the draught.

HELMER: Come, Mrs. Linden; only mothers can stand such a temperature.

(*Dr. Rank, Helmer, and Mrs. Linden go down the stairs; Anna enters the room with the children; Nora also, shutting the door.*)

NORA: How fresh and bright you look! And what red cheeks you've got! Like apples and roses. (*The children chatter to her during what follows.*) Have you had great fun? That's splendid! Oh, really! You've been giving Emmy and Bob a ride on your sledge! – both at once, only think! Why, you're quite a man, Ivar. Oh, give her to me a little, Anna. My sweet little dolly! (*Takes the smallest from the Nurse and dances with her.*) Yes, yes; mother will dance with Bob too. What! Did you have a game of snowballs? Oh, I wish I'd been there. No; leave them, Anna; I'll take their things off. Oh yes, let me do it; it's such fun. Go to the nursery; you look frozen. You'll find some hot coffee on the stove.

(*The Nurse goes into the room on the left. Nora takes off the children's things and throws them down anywhere, while the children talk all together.*)

Really! A big dog ran after you? But he didn't bite you? No; dogs don't bite dear little dolly children. Don't peep into those parcels, Ivar. What is it? Wouldn't you like to know? Take care – it'll bite! What? Shall we have a game? What shall we play at? Hide-and-seek? Yes, let's play hide-and-seek. Bob shall hide first. Am I to? Yes, let me hide first.

(*She and the children play, with laughter and shouting, in the room and the adjacent one to the right. At last Nora hides under the table; the children come rushing in, look for her, but cannot find her, hear her half-choked laughter, rush to the table, lift up the cover and see her. Loud shouts. She creeps out, as though to frighten them. Fresh shouts. Meanwhile there has been a knock at the door leading into the hall. No one has heard it. Now the door is half opened, and Krogstad appears. He waits a little; the game is renewed.*)

KROGSTAD: I beg your pardon, Mrs. Helmer –

NORA (*with a suppressed cry, turns round and half jumps up*): Ah! What do you want?

KROGSTAD: Excuse me; the outer door was ajar – somebody must have forgotten to shut it –

NORA (*standing up*): My husband is not at home, Mr. Krogstad.

KROGSTAD: I know it.

NORA: Then what do you want here?

KROGSTAD: To say a few words to you.

NORA: To me? (*To the children, softly.*) Go in to Anna. What? No, the strange man won't hurt mamma. When he's gone we'll go on playing. (*She leads the children into the left-hand room, and shuts the door behind them. Uneasy, in suspense.*) It is to me you wish to speak?

KROGSTAD: Yes, to you.

NORA: Today? But it's not the first yet –

KROGSTAD: No, today is Christmas Eve. It will depend upon yourself whether you have a merry Christmas.

NORA: What do you want? I'm not ready today –

KROGSTAD: Never mind that just now. I have come about another matter. You have a minute to spare?

NORA: Oh yes, I suppose so; although –

KROGSTAD: Good. I was sitting in the restaurant opposite, and I saw your husband go down the street –

NORA: Well?

KROGSTAD: – with a lady.

NORA: What then?

KROGSTAD: May I ask if the lady was a Mrs. Linden?

NORA: Yes.

KROGSTAD: Who has just come to town?

NORA: Yes. today.

KROGSTAD: I believe she is an intimate friend of yours?

NORA: Certainly. But I don't understand –

KROGSTAD: I used to know her too.

NORA: I know you did.

KROGSTAD: Ah! You know all about it. I thought as much. Now, frankly, is Mrs. Linden to have a place in the Bank?

NORA: How dare you catechise me in this way, Mr. Krogstad – you, a subordinate of my husband's? But since you ask, you shall know. Yes, Mrs. Linden is to be employed. And it is I who recommended her, Mr. Krogstad. Now you know.

KROGSTAD: Then my guess was right.

NORA (*walking up and down*): You see one has a wee bit of influence, after all. It doesn't follow because one's only a woman – When people are in subordinate position, Mr. Krogstad, they ought really to be careful how they offend anybody who – h'm –

KROGSTAD: – who has influence?

NORA: Exactly.

KROGSTAD (*taking another tone*): Mrs. Helmer, will you have the kindness to employ your influence on my behalf?

NORA: What? How do you mean?

KROGSTAD: Will you be so good as to see that I retain my subordinate position in the Bank?

NORA: What do you mean? Who wants to take it from you?

KROGSTAD: Oh, you needn't pretend ignorance. I can very well understand that it cannot be pleasant for your friend to meet me; and I can also understand now for whose sake I am to be hounded out.

NORA: But I assure you –

KROGSTAD: Come, come now, once for all: there is time yet, and I advise you to use your influence to prevent it.

NORA: But, Mr. Krogstad, I have no influence – absolutely none.

KROGSTAD: None? I thought you said a moment ago –

NORA: Of course not in that sense. I! How can you imagine that I should have any influence over my husband?

KROGSTAD: Oh, I know your husband from our college days. I don't think he is any more inflexible than other husbands.

NORA: If you talk disrespectfully of my husband, I must request you to leave the house.

KROGSTAD: You are bold, madam.

NORA: I am afraid of you no longer. When New Year's Day is over, I shall soon be out of the whole business.

KROGSTAD (*controlling himself*): Listen to me, Mrs. Helmer. If need be, I shall fight as though for my life to keep my little place in the Bank.

NORA: Yes, so it seems.

KROGSTAD: It's not only for the salary; that is what I care least about. It's something else – Well, I had better make a clean breast of it. Of course you know, like every one else, that some years ago I – got into trouble.

NORA: I think I've heard something of the sort.

KROGSTAD: The matter never came into court; but from that moment all paths were barred to me. Then I took up the business you know about. I had to turn my hand to something; and I don't think I've been one of the worst. But now I must get clear of it all. My sons are growing up; for their sake I must try to recover my character as well as I can. This place in the Bank was the first step; and now your husband wants to kick me off the ladder, back into the mire.

NORA: But I assure you, Mr. Krogstad, I haven't the least power to help you.

KROGSTAD: That is because you have not the will; but I can compel you.

NORA: You won't tell my husband that I owe you money?

KROGSTAD: H'm; suppose I were to?

NORA: It would be shameful of you. (*With tears in her voice.*) The secret that is my joy and my pride – that he should learn it in such an ugly, coarse way – and from you. It would involve me in all sorts of unpleasantness –

KROGSTAD: Only unpleasantness?

NORA (*hotly*): But just do it. It's you that will come off worst, for then my husband will see what a bad man you are, and then you certainly won't keep your place.

KROGSTAD: I asked whether it was only domestic unpleasantness you feared?

NORA: If my husband gets to know about it, he will of course pay you off at once, and then we shall have nothing more to do with you.

KROGSTAD (*coming a pace nearer*): Listen, Mrs. Helmer; either your memory is defective, or you don't know much about business. I must make the position a little clearer to you.

NORA: How so?

KROGSTAD: When your husband was ill, you came to me to borrow twelve hundred dollars.

NORA: I knew of nobody else.

KROGSTAD: I promised to find you the money –

NORA: And you did find it.

KROGSTAD: I promised to find you the money, on certain conditions. You were so much taken up at the time about your husband's illness, and so eager to have the wherewithal for your journey, that you probably did not give much thought to the details. Allow me to remind you of them. I promised to find you the amount in exchange for a note of hand, which I drew up.

NORA: Yes, and I signed it.

KROGSTAD: Quite right. But then I added a few lines, making your father security for the debt. Your father was to sign this.

NORA: Was to – ? He did sign it!

KROGSTAD: I had left the date blank. That is to say, your father was himself to date his signature. Do you recollect that?

NORA: Yes, I believe –

KROGSTAD: Then I gave you the paper to send to your father, by post. Is not that so?

NORA: Yes.

KROGSTAD: And of course you did so at once; for within five or six days you brought me back the document with your father's signature; and I handed you the money.

NORA: Well? Have I not made my payments punctually?

KROGSTAD: Fairly – yes. But to return to the point: you were in great trouble at the time, Mrs. Helmer.

NORA: I was indeed!

KROGSTAD: Your father was very ill, I believe?

NORA: He was on his deathbed.

KROGSTAD: And died soon after?

NORA: Yes.

KROGSTAD: Tell me, Mrs. Helmer: do you happen to recollect the day of his death? The day of the month, I mean?

NORA: Father died on the 29th of September.

KROGSTAD: Quite correct. I have made inquiries. And here comes in the remarkable point – (*produces a paper*) – which I cannot explain.

NORA: What remarkable point? I don't know –

KROGSTAD: The remarkable point, madam, that your father signed this paper three days after this death!

NORA: What! I don't understand –

KROGSTAD: Your father died on the 29th of September. But look here: he has dated his signature October 2nd! Is not that remarkable, Mrs. Helmer? (*Nora is silent.*) Can you explain it? (*Nora continues silent.*) It is noteworthy, too, that the words 'October 2nd' and the year are not in your father's handwriting, but in one which I believe I know. Well, this may be explained; your father may have forgotten to date his signature, and somebody may have added the date at random, before the fact of your father's death was known. There is nothing wrong in that. Everything depends on the signature. Of course it is genuine, Mrs. Helmer? It was really your father himself who wrote his name here?

NORA (*after a short silence, throws her head back and looks defiantly at him*): No, it was not. *I* wrote father's name.

KROGSTAD: Ah! – Are you aware, madam, that that is a dangerous admission?

NORA: How so? You will soon get your money.

KROGSTAD: May I ask you one more question? Why did you not send the paper to your father?

NORA: It was impossible. Father was ill. If I had asked him for his signature, I should have had to tell him why I wanted the money; but he was so ill I really could not tell him that my husband's life was in danger. It was impossible.

KROGSTAD: Then it would have been better to have given up your tour.

NORA: No, I couldn't do that; my husband's life depended on that journey. I couldn't give it up.

KROGSTAD: And did it never occur to you that you were playing me false?

NORA: That was nothing to me. I didn't care in the least about you. I couldn't endure you for all the cruel difficulties you made, although you knew how ill my husband was.

KROGSTAD: Mrs. Helmer, you evidently do not realise what you have been guilty of. But I can assure you it was nothing more and nothing worse that made me an outcast from society.

NORA: You! You want me to believe that you did a brave thing to save your wife's life?

KROGSTAD: The law takes no account of motives.

NORA: Then it must be a very bad law.

KROGSTAD: Bad or not, if I produce this document in court, you will be condemned according to law.

NORA: I don't believe that. Do you mean to tell me that a daughter has no right to spare her dying father trouble and anxiety? – that a wife has no right to save her husband's life? I don't know much about the law, but I'm sure you'll find, somewhere or another, that that is allowed. And you don't know that – you, a lawyer! You must be a bad one, Mr. Krogstad.

KROGSTAD: Possibly. But business – such business as ours – I do understand. You believe that? Very well; now do as you please. But this I may tell you, that if I am flung into the gutter a second time, you shall keep me company. (*Bows and goes out through hall.*)

NORA (*stands a while thinking, then tosses her head*): Oh, nonsense! He wants to frighten me. I'm not so foolish as that. (*Begins folding the children's clothes. Pauses.*) But – ? No, it's impossible! Why, I did it for love!

CHILDREN (*at the door, left*): Mamma, the strange man has gone now.

NORA: Yes, yes, I know. But don't tell anyone about the strange man. Do you hear? Not even papa!

CHILDREN: No, mamma; and now will you play with us again?

NORA: No, no; not now.

CHILDREN: Oh, do, mamma; you know you promised.

NORA: Yes, but I can't just now. Run to the nursery; I have so much to do. Run along, run along, and be good, my darlings! (*She pushes them gently into the inner room, and closes the door behind them. Sits on the sofa, embroiders a few stitches, but soon pauses.*) No! (*Throws down the work, rises, goes to the hall door and calls out.*) Ellen, bring in the Christmas tree! (*Goes to table, left, and opens the drawer; again pauses.*) No, it's quite impossible!

ELLEN (*with Christmas tree*): Where shall I stand it, ma'am?

NORA: There, in the middle of the room.

ELLEN: Shall I bring in anything else?

NORA: No, thank you, I have all I want.

(*Ellen, having put down the tree, goes out.*)

NORA (*busy dressing the tree*): There must be a candle here – and flowers there. – That horrible man! Nonsense, nonsense! there's nothing to be afraid of. The Christmas tree shall be beautiful. I'll do everything to please you, Torvald; I'll sing and dance, and –

(*Enter Helmer by the hall door, with a bundle of documents.*)

NORA: Oh! You're back already?

HELMER: Yes. Has anybody been here?

NORA: Here? No.

HELMER: That's odd. I saw Krogstad come out of the house.

NORA: Did you? Oh yes, by the by, he was here for a minute.

HELMER: Nora, I can see by your manner that he has been begging you to put in a good word for him.

NORA: Yes.

HELMER: And you were to do it as if of your own accord? You were to say nothing to me of his having been here. Didn't he suggest that too?

NORA: Yes, Torvald; but –

HELMER: Nora, Nora! And you could condescend to that! To speak to such a man, to make him a promise! And then to tell me an untruth about it!

NORA: An untruth!

HELMER: Didn't you say that nobody had been here? (*Threatens with his finger.*) My little bird must never do that again! A songbird must sing clear and true; no false notes. (*Puts his arm round her.*) That's so, isn't it? Yes, I was sure of it. (*Lets her go.*) And now we'll say no more about it. (*Sits down before the fire.*) Oh, how cosy and quiet it is here! (*Glances into his documents.*)

NORA (*busy with the tree, after a short silence*): Torvald!

HELMER: Yes.

NORA: I'm looking forward so much to the Stenborgs' fancy ball the day after tomorrow.

HELMER: And I'm on tenterhooks to see what surprise you have in store for me.

NORA: Oh, it's too tiresome!

HELMER: What is?

NORA: I can't think of anything good. Everything seems so foolish and meaningless.

HELMER: Has little Nora made that discovery?

NORA (*behind his chair, with her arms on the back*): Are you very busy, Torvald?

HELMER: Well –

NORA: What papers are those?

HELMER: Bank business.

NORA: Already!

HELMER: I have got the retiring manager to let me make some necessary changes in the staff and the organisation. I can do this during Christmas week. I want to have everything straight by the New Year.

NORA: Then that's why that poor Krogstad –

HELMER: H'm.

NORA (*still leaning over the chair-back and slowly stroking his hair*): If you hadn't been so very busy, I should have asked you a great, great favour, Torvald.

HELMER: What can it be? Out with it.

NORA: Nobody has such perfect taste as you; and I should so love to look well at the fancy ball. Torvald dear, couldn't you take me in hand, and settle what I'm to be, and arrange my costume for me?

HELMER: Aha! So my wilful little woman is at a loss, and making signals of distress.

NORA: Yes, please, Torvald. I can't get on without your help.

HELMER: Well, well, I'll think it over, and we'll soon hit upon something.

NORA: Oh, how good that is of you! (*Goes to the tree again; pause.*) How well the red flowers show. – Tell me, was it anything so very dreadful this Krogstad got into trouble about?

HELMER: Forgery, that's all. Don't you know what that means?

NORA: Mayn't he have been driven to it by need?

HELMER: Yes, or, like so many others, he may have done it in pure heedlessness. I am not so hardhearted as to condemn a man absolutely for a single fault.

NORA: No, surely not, Torvald!

HELMER: Many a man can retrieve his character, if he owns his crime and takes the punishment.

NORA: Punishment – ?

HELMER: But Krogstad didn't do that. He evaded the law by means of tricks and subterfuges; and that is what has morally ruined him.

NORA: Do you think that – ?

HELMER: Just think how a man with a thing of that sort on his conscience must be always lying and canting and shamming. Think of the mask he must wear even towards those who stand nearest him – towards his own wife and children. The effect on the children – that's the most terrible part of it, Nora.

NORA: Why?

HELMER: Because in such an atmosphere of lies home life is poisoned and contaminated in every fibre. Every breath the children draw contains some germ of evil.

NORA (*closer behind him*): Are you sure of that?

HELMER: As a lawyer, my dear, I have seen it often enough. Nearly all cases of early corruption may be traced to lying mothers.

NORA: Why – mothers?

HELMER: It generally comes from the mother's side; but of course the father's influence may act in the same way. Every lawyer knows it too well. And here has this Krogstad been poisoning his own children for years past by a life of lies and hypocrisy – that is why I call him morally ruined. (*Holds out both hands to her.*) So my sweet little Nora must promise not to plead his cause. Shake hands upon it. Come, come, what's this? Give me your hand. That's right. Then it's a bargain. I assure you it would have been impossible for me to work with him. It gives me a positive sense of physical discomfort to come in contact with such people.

(*Nora draws her hand away, and moves to the other side of the Christmas tree.*)

NORA: How warm it is here. And I have so much to do.

HELMER (*rises and gathers up his papers*): Yes, and I must try to get some of these papers looked through before dinner. And I shall think over your costume too. Perhaps I may even find something to hang in gilt paper on the Christmas tree. (*Lays his hand on her head.*) My precious little songbird! (*He goes into his room and shuts the door.*)

NORA (*softly, after a pause*): It can't be. Impossible. It must be impossible!

ANNA (*at the door, left*): The little ones are begging so prettily to come to mamma.

NORA: No, no, no; don't let them come to me! Keep them with you, Anna.

ANNA: Very well, ma'am. (*Shuts the door.*)

NORA (*pale with terror*): Corrupt my children! – Poison my home! (*Short pause. She throws back her head.*) It's not true! It can never, never be true!

Act Two

The same room. In the corner, beside the piano, stands the Christmas tree, stripped, and with the candles burnt out.

Nora's outdoor things lie on the sofa.

Nora, alone, is walking about restlessly. At last she stops by the sofa, and takes up her cloak.

NORA (*dropping the cloak*): There's somebody coming! (*Goes to the hall door and listens.*) Nobody; of course nobody will come today, Christmas Day; nor tomorrow either. But perhaps – (*Opens the door and looks out.*) – No, nothing in the letter box; quite empty. (*Comes forward.*) Stuff and nonsense! Of course he won't really do anything. Such a thing couldn't happen. It's impossible! Why, I have three little children.

(*Anna enters from the left, with a large cardboard box.*)

ANNA: I've found the box with the fancy dress at last.

NORA: Thanks; put it down on the table.

ANNA (*does so*): But I'm afraid it's very much out of order.

NORA: Oh, I wish I could tear it into a hundred thousand pieces!

ANNA: Oh no. It can easily be put to rights – just a little patience.

NORA: I shall go and get Mrs. Linden to help me.

ANNA: Going out again? In such weather as this! You'll catch cold, ma'am, and be ill.

NORA: Worse things might happen. – What are the children doing?

ANNA: They're playing with their Christmas presents, poor little dears; but –

NORA: Do they often ask for me?

ANNA: You see, they've been so used to having their mamma with them.

NORA: Yes; but, Anna, I can't have them so much with me in future.

ANNA: Well, little children get used to anything.

NORA: Do you think they do? Do you believe they would forget their mother if she went quite away?

ANNA: Gracious me! Quite away?

NORA: Tell me, Anna – I've so often wondered about it – how could you bring yourself to give your child up to strangers?

ANNA: I had to when I came to nurse my little Miss Nora.

NORA: But how could you make up your mind to it?

ANNA: When I had the chance of such a good place? A poor girl who's been in trouble must take what comes. That wicked man did nothing for me.

NORA: But your daughter must have forgotten you.

ANNA: Oh no, ma'am, that she hasn't. She wrote to me both when she was confirmed and when she was married.

NORA (*embracing her*): Dear old Anna – you were a good mother to me when I was little.

ANNA: My poor little Nora had no mother but me.

NORA: And if my little ones had nobody else, I'm sure you would – Nonsense, nonsense! (*Opens the box.*) Go in to the children. Now I must – You'll see how lovely I shall be tomorrow.

ANNA: I'm sure there will be no one at the ball so lovely as my Miss Nora. (*She goes into the room on the left.*)

NORA (*takes the costume out of the box, but soon throws it down again*): Oh, if I dared go out. If only nobody would come. If only nothing would happen here in the meantime. Rubbish; nobody is coming. Only not to think. What a delicious muff!

Beautiful gloves, beautiful gloves! To forget – to forget! One, two, three, four, five, six – (*With a scream.*) Ah, there they come.

(*Goes towards the door, then stands irresolute. Mrs. Linden enters from the hall, where she has taken off her things.*)

NORA: Oh, it's you, Christina. There's nobody else there? I'm so glad you have come.

MRS. LINDEN: I hear you called at my lodgings.

NORA: Yes, I was just passing. There's something you must help me with. Let us sit here on the sofa – so. Tomorrow evening there's to be a fancy ball at Consul Stenborg's overhead, and Torvald wants me to appear as a Neapolitan fishergirl, and dance the tarantella; I learned it at Capri.

MRS. LINDEN: I see – quite a performance.

NORA: Yes, Torvald wishes it. Look, this is the costume; Torvald had it made for me in Italy. But now it's all so torn, I don't know –

MRS. LINDEN: Oh, we shall soon set that to rights. It's only the trimming that has come loose here and there. Have you a needle and thread? Ah, here's the very thing.

NORA: Oh, how kind of you.

MRS. LINDEN (*sewing*): So you're to be in costume tomorrow, Nora? I'll tell you what – I shall come in for a moment to see you in all your glory. But I've quite forgotten to thank you for the pleasant evening yesterday.

NORA (*rises and walks across the room*): Oh, yesterday; it didn't seem so pleasant as usual. – You should have come to town a little sooner, Christina. – Torvald has certainly the art of making home bright and beautiful.

MRS. LINDEN: You too, I should think, or you wouldn't be your father's daughter. But tell me – is Doctor Rank always so depressed as he was last evening?

NORA: No, yesterday it was particularly noticeable. You see, he suffers from a dreadful illness. He has spinal consumption, poor fellow. They say his father was a horrible man, so the son has been sickly from his childhood, you understand.

MRS. LINDEN (*lets her sewing fall into her lap*): Why, my darling Nora, how do you come to know such things?

NORA (*moving about the room*): Oh, when one has three children, one sometimes has visits from women who are half – half doctors – and they talk of one thing and another.

MRS. LINDEN (*goes on sewing; a short pause*): Does Doctor Rank come here every day?

NORA: Every day of his life. He has been Torvald's most intimate friend from boyhood, and he's a good friend of mine too. Doctor Rank is quite one of the family.

MRS. LINDEN: But tell me – is he quite sincere? I mean, isn't he rather given to flattering people?

NORA: No, quite the contrary. Why should you think so?

MRS. LINDEN: When you introduced us yesterday he said he had often heard my name; but I noticed afterwards that your husband had no notion who I was. How could Doctor Rank – ?

NORA: He was quite right, Christina. You see, Torvald loves me so indescribably, he wants to have me all to himself, as he says. When we were first married he was almost jealous if I even mentioned any of my old friends at home; so naturally I gave up doing it. But I often talk of the old times to Doctor Rank, for he like to hear about them.

MRS. LINDEN: Listen to me, Nora! You are still a child in many ways. I'll tell you something. You ought to get clear of all this with Doctor Rank.

NORA: Get clear of what?

MRS. LINDEN: The whole affair, I should say. You were talking yesterday of a rich admirer who was to find you money –

NORA: Yes, one who never existed, worse luck! What then?

MRS. LINDEN: Has Doctor Rank money?

NORA: Yes, he has.

MRS. LINDEN: And nobody to provide for?

NORA: Nobody. But – ?

MRS. LINDEN: And he comes here every day?

NORA: Yes, I told you so.

MRS. LINDEN: I should have thought he would have had better taste.

NORA: I don't understand you a bit.

MRS. LINDEN: Don't pretend, Nora. Do you suppose I can't guess who lent you the twelve hundred dollars?

NORA: Are you out of your senses? How can you think such a thing? A friend who comes here every day! Why, the position would be unbearable!

MRS. LINDEN: Then it really is not he?

NORA: No, I assure you. It never for a moment occurred to me – Besides, at that time he had nothing to lend; he came into his property afterwards.

MRS. LINDEN: Well, I believe that was lucky for you, Nora dear.

NORA: No, really, it would never have struck me to ask Doctor Rank – And yet, I'm certain that if I did –

MRS. LINDEN: But of course you never would.

NORA: Of course not. It's inconceivable that it should ever be necessary. But I'm quite sure that if I spoke to Doctor Rank –

MRS. LINDEN: Behind your husband's back?

NORA: I must get clear of the other thing; that's behind his back too. I must get clear of that.

MRS. LINDEN: Yes, yes, I told you so yesterday; but –

NORA (*walking up and down*): A man can manage these things much better than a woman.

MRS. LINDEN: One's own husband, yes.

NORA: Nonsense, (*Stands still.*) When everything is paid, one gets back the paper.

MRS. LINDEN: Of course.

NORA: And can tear it into a hundred thousand pieces, and burn it up, the nasty, filthy thing!

MRS. LINDEN (*looks at her fixedly, lays down her work, and rises slowly*): Nora, you are hiding something from me.

NORA: Can you see it in my face?

MRS. LINDEN: Something has happened since yesterday morning. Nora, what is it?

NORA (*going towards her*): Christina – ! (*Listens.*) Hush! There's Torvald coming home. Do you mind going into the nursery for the present? Torvald can't bear to see dressmaking going on. Get Anna to help you.

MRS. LINDEN (*gathers some of the things together*): Very well; but I shan't go away until you have told me all about it. (*She goes out to the left, as Helmer enters from the hall.*)

NORA (*runs to meet him*): Oh, how I've been longing for you to come, Torvald dear!

HELMER: Was that the dressmaker – ?

NORA: No, Christina. She's helping me with my costume. You'll see how nice I shall look.

HELMER: Yes, wasn't that a happy thought of mine?

NORA: Splendid! But isn't it good of me too, to have given in to you about the tarantella?

HELMER (*takes her under the chin*): Good of you! To give in to your own husband? Well, well, you little madcap. I know you don't mean it. But I won't disturb you. I daresay you want to be 'trying on'.

NORA: And you are going to work, I suppose?

HELMER: Yes. (*Shows her a bundle of papers.*) Look here. I've just come from the Bank – (*Goes towards his room.*)

NORA: Torvald.

HELMER (*stopping*): Yes?

NORA: If your little squirrel were to beg you for something so prettily –

HELMER: Well?

NORA: Would you do it?

HELMER: I must know first what it is.

NORA: The squirrel would skip about and play all sorts of tricks if you would only be nice and kind.

HELMER: Come, then, out with it.

NORA: Your lark would twitter from morning till night –

HELMER: Oh, that she does in any case.

NORA: I'll be an elf and dance in the moonlight for you, Torvald.

HELMER: Nora – you can't mean what you were hinting at this morning?

NORA (*coming nearer*): Yes, Torvald, I beg and implore you!

HELMER: Have you really the courage to begin that again?

NORA: Yes, yes; for my sake, you must let Krogstad keep his place in the Bank.

HELMER: My dear Nora, it's his place I intend for Mrs. Linden.

NORA: Yes, that's so good of you. But instead of Krogstad, you could dismiss some other clerk.

HELMER: Why, this is incredible obstinacy! Because you have thoughtlessly promised to put in a word for him, I am to – !

NORA: It's not that, Torvald. It's for your own sake. This man writes for the most scurrilous newspapers; you said so yourself. He can do you no end of harm. I'm so terribly afraid of him –

HELMER: Ah, I understand; it's old recollections that are frightening you.

NORA: What do you mean?

HELMER: Of course you're thinking of your father.

NORA: Yes – yes, of course. Only think of the shameful slanders wicked people used to write about father. I believe they would have got him dismissed if you hadn't been sent to look into the thing, and been kind to him, and helped him.

HELMER: My little Nora, between your father and me there is all the difference in the world. You father was not altogether unimpeachable. I am; and I hope to remain so.

NORA: Oh, no one knows what wicked men may hit upon. We could live so quietly and happily now, in our cosy, peaceful home, you and I and the children, Torvald! That's why I beg and implore you –

HELMER: And it is just by pleading his cause that you make it impossible for me to keep him. It's already known at the Bank that I intend to dismiss Krogstad. If it were now reported that the new manager let himself be turned round his wife's little finger –

NORA: What then?

HELMER: Oh, nothing, so long as a wilful woman can have her way –! I am to make myself a laughing-stock to the whole staff, and set people saying that I am open to all sorts of outside influence? Take my word for it, I should soon feel the consequences. And besides – there is one thing that makes Krogstad impossible for me to work with –

NORA: What thing?

HELMER: I could perhaps have overlooked his moral failings at a pinch –

NORA: Yes, couldn't you, Torvald?

HELMER: And I hear he is good at his work. But the fact is, he was a college chum of mine – there was one of those rash friendships between us that one so often repents of later. I may as well confess it at once – he calls me by my Christian name; and he is tactless enough to do it even when others are present. He delights in putting on airs of familiarity – Torvald here, Torvald there! I assure you it's most painful to me. He would make my position at the Bank perfectly unendurable.

NORA: Torvald, surely you're not serious?

NORA: No, on the contrary, Torvald, dear; and that's just why –

HELMER: Never mind; you call my motives petty; then I must be petty too. Petty! Very well! – Now we'll put an end to this, once for all. (*Goes to the door into the hall and calls.*) Ellen!

NORA: What do you want?

HELMER (*searching among his papers*): To settle the thing. (*Ellen enters.*) Here, take this letter; give it to a messenger. See that he takes it at once. The address is on it. Here's the money.

ELLEN: Very well, sir. (*Goes with the letter.*)

HELMER (*putting his papers together*): There, Madam Obstinacy.

NORA (*breathless*): Torvald – what was in the letter?

HELMER: Krogstad's dismissal.

NORA: Call it back again, Torvald! There's still time. Oh, Torvald, call it back again! For my sake, for your own, for the children' sake! Do you hear, Torvald? Do it! You don't know what that letter may bring upon us all.

HELMER: Too late.

NORA: Yes, too late.

HELMER: My dear Nora, I forgive your anxiety, though it's anything but flattering to me. Why should you suppose that *I* would be afraid of a wretched scribbler's spite? But I forgive you all the same, for it's a proof of your great love for me. (*Takes her in his arms.*) That's as it should be, my own dear Nora. Let what will happen – when it comes to the pinch, I shall have strength and courage enough. You shall see: my shoulders are broad enough to bear the whole burden.

NORA (*terror-struck*): What do you mean by that?

HELMER: The whole burden, I say –

NORA (*with decision*): That you shall never, never do!

HELMER: Very well; then we'll share it, Nora, as man and wife. That is how it should be. (*Petting her.*) Are you satisfied now? Come, come, come, don't look like a scared dove. It's all nothing – foolish fancies. – Now you ought to play the tarantella through and practise with the tambourine. I shall sit in my inner room and shut both doors, so that I shall hear nothing. You can make as much noise as you please. (*Turns round in doorway.*) And when Rank comes, just tell him where I'm to be found.

(*He nods to her, and goes with his papers into his room, closing the door.*)

NORA (*bewildered with terror, stands as though rooted to the ground, and whispers*): He would do it. Yes, he would do it. He would do it, in spite of all the world. – No, never that, never, never! Anything rather than that! Oh, for some way of escape! What shall I do – ! (*Hall bell rings.*) Doctor Rank – ! Anything, anything, rather than – !

(*Nora draws her hands over her face, pulls herself together, goes to the door and opens it. Rank stands outside hanging up his fur coat. During what follows it begins to grow dark.*)

NORA: Good afternoon, Doctor Rank. I knew you by your ring. But you mustn't go to Torvald now. I believe he's busy.

RANK: And you? (*Enters and closes the door.*)

NORA: Oh, you know very well, I have always time for you.

RANK: Thank you. I shall avail myself of your kindness as long as I can.

NORA: What do you mean? As long as you can?

RANK: Yes. Does that frighten you?

NORA: I think it's an odd expression. Do you expect anything to happen?

RANK: Something I have long been prepared for; but I didn't think it would come so soon.

NORA (*catching at his arm*): What have you discovered? Doctor Rank, you must tell me!

RANK (*sitting down by the stove*): I am running down hill. There's no help for it.

NORA (*draws a long breath of relief*): It's you – ?

RANK: Who else should it be? – Why lie to one's self? I am the most wretched of all my patients, Mrs. Helmer. In these last days I have been auditing my life account – bankrupt! Perhaps before a month is over I shall lie rotting in the churchyard.

NORA: Oh! What an ugly way to talk.

RANK: The thing itself is so confoundedly ugly, you see. But the worst of it is, so many other ugly things have to be gone through first. There is only one last investigation to be made, and when that is over I shall know pretty certainly when the breakup will begin. There's one thing I want to say to you: Helmer's delicate nature shrinks so from all that is horrible: I will not have him in my sick-room –

NORA: But, Doctor Rank –

RANK: I won't have him, I say – not on any account! I shall lock my door against him. As soon as I am quite certain of the worst, I shall send you my visiting card with a black cross on it; and then you will know that the final horror has begun.

NORA: Why, you're perfectly unreasonable today; and I did so want you to be in a really good humour.

RANK: With death staring me in the face? – And to suffer thus for another's sin! Where's the justice of it? And in one way or another you can trace in every family some such inexorable retribution –

NORA (*stopping her ears*): Nonsense, nonsense! Now cheer up!

RANK: Well, after all, the whole thing's only worth laughing at. My poor innocent spine must do penance for my father's wild oats.

NORA (*at table, left*): I suppose he was too fond of asparagus and Strasbourg pâté, wasn't he?

RANK: Yes; and truffles.

NORA: Yes, truffles, to be sure. And oysters, I believe?

RANK: Yes, oysters; oysters, of course.

NORA: And then all the port and champagne! It's sad that all these good things should attack the spine.

RANK: Especially when the luckless spine attacked never had any good of them.

NORA: Ah yes, that's the worst of it.

RANK (*looks at her searchingly*): H'm –

NORA (*a moment later*): Why did you smile?

RANK: No; it was you that laughed.

NORA: No; it was you that smiled, Doctor Rank.

RANK (*standing up*): I see you're deeper than I thought.

NORA: I'm in such a crazy mood today.

RANK: So it seems.

NORA (*with her hands on his shoulders*): Dear, dear Doctor Rank, death shall not take you away from Torvald and me.

RANK: Oh, you'll easily get over the loss. The absent are soon forgotten.

NORA (*looks at him anxiously*): Do you think so?

RANK: People make fresh ties, and then –

NORA: Who make fresh ties?

RANK: You and Helmer will, when I am gone. You yourself are taking time by the forelock, it seems to me. What was that Mrs. Linden doing here yesterday?

NORA: Oh! – you're surely not jealous of poor Christina?

RANK: Yes, I am. She will be my successor in this house. When I am out of the way, this woman will perhaps –

NORA: Hush! Not so loud! She's in there.

RANK: Today as well? You see!

NORA: Only to put my costume in order – dear me, how unreasonable you are! (*Sits on sofa.*) Now do be good, Doctor Rank! Tomorrow you shall see how beautifully I shall dance; and then you may fancy that I'm doing it all to please you – and of course Torvald as well. (*Takes various things out of box.*) Doctor Rank, sit down here, and I'll show you something.

RANK (*sitting*): What is it?

NORA: Look here. Look!

RANK: Silk stockings.

NORA: Flesh-coloured. Aren't they lovely? It's so dark here now; but tomorrow – No, no, no; you must only look at the feet. Oh, well, I suppose you may look at the rest too.

RANK: H'm –

NORA: What are you looking so critical about? Do you think they won't fit me?

RANK: I can't possibly give any competent opinion on that point.

NORA (*looking at him a moment*): For shame! (*Hits him lightly on the ear with the stockings.*) Take that. (*Rolls them up again.*)

RANK: And what other wonders am I to see?

NORA: You shan't see any more; for you don't behave nicely. (*She hums a little, and searches among the things.*)

RANK (*after a short silence*): When I sit here gossiping with you, I can't imagine – I simply cannot conceive – what would have become of me if I had never entered this house.

NORA (*smiling*): Yes, I think you do feel at home with us.

RANK (*more softly – looking straight before him*): And now to have to leave it all –

NORA: Nonsense. You shan't leave us.

RANK (*in the same tone*): And not to be able to leave behind the slightest token of gratitude; scarcely even a passing regret – nothing but an empty place, that can be filled by the first comer.

NORA: And if I were to ask you for – ? No –

RANK: For what?

NORA: For a great proof of your friendship.

RANK: Yes – yes?

NORA: I mean – for a very, very great service –

RANK: Would you really, for once, make me so happy?

NORA: Oh, you don't know what it is.

RANK: Then tell me.

NORA: No, I really can't, Doctor Rank. It's far, far too much – not only a service, but help and advice besides –

RANK: So much the better. I can't think what you can mean. But go on. Don't you trust me?

NORA: As I trust no one else. I know you are my best and truest friend. So I will tell you. Well then, Doctor Rank, there is something you must help me to prevent. You know how deeply, how wonderfully Torvald loves me; he wouldn't hesitate a moment to give his very life for my sake.

RANK (*bending towards her*): Nora – do you think he is the only one who – ?

NORA (*with a slight start*): Who – ?

RANK: Who would gladly give his life for you?

NORA (*sadly*): Oh!

RANK: I have sworn that you shall know it before I – go. I shall never find a better opportunity. – Yes, Nora, now I have told you; and now you know that you can trust me as you can no one else.

NORA (*standing up; simply and calmly*): Let me pass, please.

RANK (*makes way for her, but remains sitting*): Nora –

NORA (*in the doorway*): Ellen, bring the lamp. (*Crosses to the stove.*) Oh dear, Doctor Rank, that was too bad of you.

RANK (*rising*): That I have loved you as deeply as – any one else? Was that too bad to me?

NORA: No, but that you should have told me so. It was so unnecessary –

RANK: What do you mean? Did you know – ?

(*Ellen enters with the lamp; sets it on the table and goes out again.*)

RANK: Nora – Mrs. Helmer – I ask you, did you know?

NORA: Oh, how can I tell what I knew or didn't know? I really can't say – How could you be so clumsy, Doctor Rank? It was all so nice!

RANK: Well, at any rate, you know now that I am at your service, body and soul. And now, go on.

NORA (*looking at him*): Go on – now?

RANK: I beg you to tell me what you want.

NORA: I can tell you nothing now.

RANK: Yes, yes! You musn't punish me in that way. Let me do for you whatever a man can.

NORA: You can do nothing for me now. – Besides, I really want no help. You shall see it was only my fancy. Yes, it must be so. Of course! (*Sits in the rocking chair, looks at him and smiles.*) You are a nice person, Doctor Rank! Aren't you ashamed of yourself, now that the lamp is on the table?

RANK: No; not exactly. But perhaps I ought to go – forever.

NORA: No, indeed you mustn't. Of course you must come and go as you've always done. You know very well that Torvald can't do without you.

RANK: Yes, but you?

NORA: Oh, you know I always like to have you here.

RANK: That is just what led me astray. You are a riddle to me. It has often seemed to me as if you liked being with me almost as much as being with Helmer.

NORA: Yes; don't you see? There are people one loves, and others one likes to talk to.

RANK: Yes – there's something in that.

NORA: When I was a girl, of course I loved papa best. But it always delighted me to steal into the servants' room. In the first place, they never lectured me, and, in the second, it was such fun to hear them talk.

RANK: Ah, I see; then it's their place I have taken?

NORA (*jumps up and hurries towards him*): Oh, my dear Doctor Rank, I don't mean that. But you understand, with Torvald it's the same as with papa –

(*Ellen enters from the hall.*)

ELLEN: Please ma'am – (*Whispers to Nora, and gives her a card.*)

NORA (*glancing at card*): Ah! (*Puts it in her pocket.*)

RANK: Anything wrong?

NORA: No, no, not in the least. It's only – it's my new costume –

RANK: Your costume? Why, it's there.

NORA: Oh, that one, yes. But this is another that – I have ordered it – Torvald mustn't know –

RANK: Aha! So that's the great secret.

NORA: Yes, of course. Please go to him; he's in the inner room. Do keep him while I –

RANK: Don't be alarmed; he shan't escape. (*Goes into Helmer's room.*)

NORA (*to Ellen*): Is he waiting in the kitchen?

ELLEN: Yes, he came up the back stair –

NORA: Didn't you tell him I was engaged?

ELLEN: Yes, but it was no use.

NORA: He won't go away?

ELLEN: No, ma'am, not until he has spoken to you.

NORA: Then let him come in; but quietly. And, Ellen – say nothing about it; it's a surprise for my husband.

ELLEN: Oh, yes, ma'am, I understand. (*She goes out.*)

NORA: It is coming! The dreadful thing is coming, after all. No, no, no, it can never be; it shall not!

(*She goes to Helmer's door and slips the bolt. Ellen opens the hall door for Krogstad, and shuts it after him. He wears a travelling coat, high boots, and a fur cap.*)

NORA (*goes towards him*): Speak softly; my husband is at home.

KROGSTAD: All right. That's nothing to me.

NORA: What do you want?

KROGSTAD: A little information.

NORA: Be quick, then. What is it?

KROGSTAD: You know I have got my dismissal?

NORA: I couldn't prevent it, Mr. Krogstad. I fought for you to the last, but it was of no use.

KROGSTAD: Does your husband care for you so little? He knows what I can bring upon you, and yet he dares –

NORA: How could you think I should tell him?

KROGSTAD: Well, as a matter of fact, I didn't think it. It wasn't like my friend Torvald Helmer to show so much courage –

NORA: Mr. Krogstad, be good enough to speak respectfully of my husband.

KROGSTAD: Certainly, with all due respect. But since you are so anxious to keep the matter secret, I suppose you are a little clearer than yesterday as to what you have done.

NORA: Clearer than you could ever make me.

KROGSTAD: Yes, such a bad lawyer as I –

NORA: What is it you want?

KROGSTAD: Only to see how you are getting on, Mrs. Helmer. I've been thinking about you all day. Even a mere money-lender, a gutter journalist, a – in short, a creature like me – has a little bit of what people call feeling.

NORA: Then show it; think of my little children.

KROGSTAD: Did you and your husband think of mine? But enough of that. I only wanted to tell you that you needn't take this matter too seriously. I shall not lodge any information, for the present.

NORA: No, surely not. I knew you wouldn't.

KROGSTAD: The whole thing can be settled quite amicably. Nobody need know. It can remain among us three.

NORA: My husband must never know.

KROGSTAD: How can you prevent it? Can you pay off the balance?

NORA: No, not at once.

KROGSTAD: Or have you any means of raising the money in the next few days?

NORA: None – that I will make use of.

KROGSTAD: And if you had, it would not help you now. If you offered me ever so much money down, you should not get back your I O U.

NORA: Tell me what you want to do with it.

KROGSTAD: I only want to keep it – to have it in my possession. No outsider shall hear anything of it. So, if you have any desperate scheme in your head –

NORA: What if I have?

KROGSTAD: If you should think of leaving your husband and children –

NORA: What if I do?

KROGSTAD: Or if you should think of – something worse –

NORA: How do you know that?

KROGSTAD: Put all that out of your head.

NORA: How did you know what I had in my mind?

KROGSTAD: Most of us think of that at first. I thought of it, too; but I hadn't the courage –

NORA (*tonelessly*): Nor I.

KROGSTAD (*relieved*): No, one hasn't. You haven't the courage either, have you?

NORA: I haven't, I haven't.

KROGSTAD: Besides, it would be very foolish. – Just one domestic storm, and it's all over. I have a letter in my pocket for your husband –

NORA: Telling him everything?

KROGSTAD: Sparing you as much as possible.

NORA (*quickly*): He must never read that letter. Tear it up. I will manage to get the money somehow –

KROGSTAD: Pardon me, Mrs. Helmer, but I believe I told you –

NORA: Oh, I am not talking about the money I owe you. Tell me how much you demand from my husband – I will get it.

KROGSTAD: I demand no money from your husband.

NORA: What do you demand, then?

KROGSTAD: I will tell you. I want to regain my footing in the world. I want to rise; and your husband shall help me to do it. For the last eighteen months my record has been spotless; I have been in bitter need all the time; but I was content to fight my way up, step by step. Now, I've been thrust down again, and I will not be satified with merely being reinstated as a matter of grace. I want to rise, I tell you. I must get into the Bank again, in a higher position than before. Your husband shall create a place on purpose for me –

NORA: He will never do that!

KROGSTAD: He will do it; I know him – he won't dare to show fight! And when he and I are together there, you shall soon see! Before a year is out I shall be the manager's right hand. It won't be Torvald Helmer, but Nils Krogstad, that manages the Joint Stock Bank.

NORA: That shall never be.

KROGSTAD: Perhaps you will – ?

NORA: Now I have the courage for it.

KROGSTAD: Oh, you don't frighten me! A sensitive, petted creature like you –

NORA: You shall see, you shall see!

KROGSTAD: Under the ice, perhaps? Down into the cold, black water? And next spring to come up again, ugly, hairless, unrecognisable –

NORA: You can't terrify me.

KROGSTAD: Nor you me. People don't do that sort of thing, Mrs. Helmer. And after all, what would be the use of it? I have your husband in my pocket all the same.

NORA: Afterwards? When I am no longer – ?

KROGSTAD: You forget, your reputation remains in my hands! (*Nora stands speechless and looks at him.*) Well, now you are prepared. Do nothing foolish. As soon as Helmer has received my letter, I shall expect to hear from him. And remember that it is your husband himself who has forced me back again into such paths. That I will never forgive him. Goodbye, Mrs. Helmer.

(*Goes out through the hall. Nora hurries to the door, opens it a little, and listens.*)

NORA: He's going. He's not putting the letter into the box. No, no, it would be impossible! (*Opens the door farther and farther.*) What's that? He's standing still; not going downstairs. Has he changed his mind? Is he – ? (*A letter falls into the box. Krogstad's footsteps are heard gradually receding down the stair. Nora utters a suppressed shriek, and rushes forward towards the sofa-table; pause.*) In the letter box! (*Slips shrinkingly up to the hall door.*) There it lies. – Torvald, Torvald – now we are lost!

(*Mrs. Linden enters from the left with the costume.*)

MRS. LINDEN: There, I think it's all right now. Shall we just try it on?

NORA (*hoarsely and softly*): Christina, come here.

MRS. LINDEN (*throws down the dress on the sofa*): What's the matter? You look quite distracted.

NORA: Come here. Do you see that letter? There, see – through the glass of the letter box.

MRS. LINDEN: Yes, yes, I see it.

NORA: That letter is from Krogstad –

MRS. LINDEN: Nora – it was Krogstad who lent you the money?

NORA: Yes; and now Torvald will know everything.

MRS. LINDEN: Believe me, Nora, it's the best thing for both of you.

NORA: You don't know all yet. I have forged a name –

MRS. LINDEN: Good heavens!

NORA: Now, listen to me, Christina; you shall bear me witness –

MRS. LINDEN: How "witness"? What am I to – ?

NORA: If I should go out of my mind – it might easily happen –

MRS. LINDEN: Nora!

NORA: Or if anything else should happen to me – so that I couldn't be here – !

MRS. LINDEN: Nora, Nora, you're quite beside yourself!

NORA: In case any one wanted to take it all upon himself – the whole blame – you understand –

MRS. LINDEN: Yes, yes; but how can you think – ?

NORA: You shall bear witness that it's not true, Christina. I'm not out of my mind at all; I know quite well what I'm saying; and I tell you nobody else knew anything about it; I did the whole thing, I myself. Remember that.

MRS. LINDEN: I shall remember. But I don't understand what you mean –

NORA: Oh, how should you? It's the miracle coming to pass.

MRS. LINDEN: The miracle?

NORA: Yes, the miracle. But it's so terrible, Christina; it mustn't happen for all the world.

MRS. LINDEN: I shall go straight to Krogstad and talk to him.

NORA: Don't; he'll do you some harm.

MRS. LINDEN: Once he would have done anything for me.

NORA: He?

MRS. LINDEN: Where does he live?

NORA: Oh, how can I tell – ? Yes – (*Feels in her pocket.*) Here's his card. But the letter, the letter – !

HELMER (*knocking outside*): Nora!

NORA (*shrieks in terror*): Oh, what is it? What do you want?

HELMER: Well, well, don't be frightened. We're not coming in; you've bolted the door. Are you trying on your dress?

NORA: Yes, yes, I'm trying it on. It suits me so well, Torvald.

MRS. LINDEN (*who has read the card*): Why, he lives close by here.

NORA: Yes, but it's no use now. We are lost. The letter is there in the box.

MRS. LINDEN: And your husband has the key?

NORA: Always.

MRS. LINDEN: Krogstad must demand his letter back, unread. He must find some pretext –

NORA: But this is the very time when Torvald generally –

MRS. LINDEN: Prevent him. Keep him occupied. I shall come back as quickly as I can. (*She goes out hastily by the hall door.*)

NORA (*opens Helmer's door and peeps in*): Torvald!

HELMER: Well, may one come into one's own room again at last? Come, Rank, we'll have a look – (*In the doorway.*) But how's this?

NORA: What, Torvald dear?

HELMER: Rank led me to expect a grand transformation.

RANK (*in the doorway*): So I understood. I suppose I was mistaken.

NORA: No, no one shall see me in my glory till tomorrow evening.

HELMER: Why, Nora dear, you look so tired. Have you been practising too hard?

NORA: No, I haven't practised at all yet.

HELMER: But you'll have to –

NORA: Oh yes, I must, I must! But, Torvald, I can't get on at all without your help. I've forgotten everything.

HELMER: Oh, we shall soon freshen it up again.

NORA: Yes, do help me, Torvald. You must promise me – Oh, I'm so nervous about it. Before so many people – This evening you must give yourself up entirely to me. You mustn't do a stroke of work; you mustn't even touch a pen. Do promise, Torvald dear!

HELMER: I promise. All this evening I shall be your slave. Little helpless thing – ! But, by the by, I must just – (*Going to hall door.*)

NORA: What do you want there?

HELMER: Only to see if there are any letters.

NORA: No, no, don't do that, Torvald.

HELMER: Why not?

NORA: Torvald, I beg you not to. There are none there.

HELMER: Let me just see. (*Is going. Nora, at the piano, plays the first bars of the tarantella.*)

HELMER (*at the door, stops*): Aha!

NORA: I can't dance tomorrow if I don't rehearse with you first.

HELMER (*going to her*): Are you really so nervous, dear Nora?

NORA: Yes, dreadfully! Let me rehearse at once. We have time before dinner. Oh, do sit down and play for me, Torvald dear; direct me and put me right, as you used to do.

HELMER: With all the pleasure in life, since you wish it. (*Sits at the piano. Nora snatches the tambourine out of the box, and hurriedly drapes herself in a long parti-coloured shawl; then, with a bound, stands in the middle of the floor.*)

NORA: Now play for me! Now I'll dance!

(*Helmer plays and Nora dances. Rank stands at the piano behind Helmer and looks on.*)

HELMER (*playing*): Slower! Slower!

NORA: Can't do it slower!

HELMER: Not so violently, Nora.

NORA: I must! I must!

HELMER (*stops*): No, no, Nora – that will never do.

NORA (*laughs and swings her tambourine*): Didn't I tell you so!

RANK: Let me play for her.

HELMER (*rising*): Yes, do – then I can direct her better.

(*Rank sits down to the piano and plays; Nora dances more and more wildly. Helmer stands by the stove and addresses frequent directions to her; she seems not to hear. Her hair breaks loose, and falls over her shoulders. She does not notice it, but goes on dancing. Mrs. Linden enters, and stands spellbound in the doorway.*)

MRS. LINDEN: Ah – !

NORA (*dancing*): We're having such fun here, Christina!

HELMER: Why, Nora dear, you're dancing as if it were a matter of life and death.

NORA: So it is.

HELMER: Rank, stop! This is the merest madness. Stop, I say!

(*Rank stops playing, and Nora comes to a sudden standstill.*)

HELMER (*going towards her*): I couldn't have believed it. You've positively forgotten all I taught you.

NORA (*throws the tambourine away*): You see for yourself.

HELMER: You really do want teaching.

NORA: Yes, you see how much I need it. You must practise with me up to the last moment. Will you promise me, Torvald?

HELMER: Certainly, certainly.

NORA: Neither today nor tomorrow must you think of anything but me. You mustn't open a single letter – mustn't look at the letter box.

HELMER: Ah, you're still afraid of that man –

NORA: Oh yes, yes, I am.

HELMER: Nora, I can see it in your face – there's a letter from him in the box.

NORA: I don't know, I believe so. But you're not to read anything now; nothing ugly must come between us until all is over.

RANK (*softly, to Helmer*): You mustn't contradict her.

HELMER (*putting his arm around her*): The child shall have her own way. But tomorrow night, when the dance is over –

NORA: Then you shall be free.

(*Ellen appears in the doorway, right.*)

ELLEN: Dinner is on the table, ma'am.

NORA: We'll have some champagne, Ellen.

ELLEN: Yes, ma'am. (*Goes out.*)

HELMER: Dear me! Quite a banquet.

NORA: Yes, and we'll keep it up till morning. (*Calling out.*) And macaroons, Ellen – plenty – just this once.

HELMER (*seizing her hand*): Come, come, don't let us have this wild excitement! Be my own little lark again.

NORA: Oh yes, I will. But now go into the dining room; and you too, Doctor Rank. Christina, you must help me to do up my hair.

RANK (*softly, as they go*): There's nothing in the wind? Nothing – I mean – ?

HELMER: Oh no, nothing of the kind. It's merely this babyish anxiety I was telling you about.

(*They go out to the right.*)

NORA: Well?

MRS. LINDEN: He's gone out of town.

NORA: I saw it in your face.

MRS. LINDEN: He comes back tomorrow evening. I left a note for him.

NORA: You shouldn't have done that. Things must take their course. After all, there's something glorious in waiting for the miracle.

MRS. LINDEN: What is it you're waiting for?

NORA: Oh, you can't understand. Go to them in the dining room; I shall come in a moment.

(*Mrs. Linden goes into the dining room. Nora stands for a moment as though collecting her thoughts; then looks at her watch.*)

NORA: Five. Seven hours till midnight. Then twenty-four hours till the next midnight. Then the tarantella will be over. Twenty-four and seven? Thirty-one hours to live.

(*Helmer appears at the door, right.*)

HELMER: What has become of my little lark?

NORA (*runs to him with open arms*): Here she is!

Act Three

The same room. The table, with the chairs around it, in the middle. A lighted lamp on the table. The door to the hall stands open. Dance music is heard from the floor above.

Mrs. Linden sits by the table and absently turns the pages of a book. She tries to read, but seems unable to fix her attention; she frequently listens, and looks anxiously towards the hall door.

MRS. LINDEN (*looks at her watch*): Not here yet; and the time is nearly up. If only he hasn't – (*Listens again.*) Ah, there he is. (*She goes into the hall and cautiously opens the outer door; soft footsteps are heard on the stairs; she whispers.*) Come in; there is no one here.

KROGSTAD (*in the doorway*): I found a note from you at my house. What does it mean?

MRS. LINDEN: I must speak to you.

KROGSTAD: Indeed? And in this house?

MRS. LINDEN: I could not see you at my rooms. They have no separate entrance. Come in; we are quite alone. The servants are asleep, and the Helmers are at the ball upstairs.

KROGSTAD (*coming into the room*): Ah! So the Helmers are dancing this evening? Really?

MRS. LINDEN: Yes. Why not?

KROGSTAD: Quite right. Why not?

MRS. LINDEN: And now let us talk a little.

KROGSTAD: Have we two anything to say to each other?

MRS. LINDEN: A great deal.

KROGSTAD: I should not have thought so.

MRS. LINDEN: Because you have never really understood me.

KROGSTAD: What was there to understand? The most natural thing in the world – a heartless woman throws a man over when a better match offers.

MRS. LINDEN: Do you really think me so heartless? Do you think I broke with you lightly?

KROGSTAD: Did you not?

MRS. LINDEN: Do you really think so?

KROGSTAD: If not, why did you write me that letter?

MRS. LINDEN: Was it not best? Since I had to break with you, was it not right that I should try to put an end to all that you felt for me?

KROGSTAD (*clenching his hands together*): So that was it? And all this – for the sake of money!

MRS. LINDEN: You ought not to forget that I had a helpless mother and two little brothers. We could not wait for you, Nils, as your prospects then stood.

KROGSTAD: Perhaps not; but you had no right to cast me off for the sake of others, whoever the others might be.

MRS. LINDEN: I don't know. I have often asked myself whether I had the right.

KROGSTAD (*more softly*): When I had lost you, I seemed to have no firm ground left under my feet. Look at me now. I am a shipwrecked man, clinging to a spar.

MRS. LINDEN: Rescue may be at hand.

KROGSTAD: It was at hand; but then you came and stood in the way.

MRS. LINDEN: Without my knowledge, Nils. I did not know till today that it was you I was to replace in the Bank.

KROGSTAD: Well, I take your word for it. But now that you do know, do you mean to give way?

MRS. LINDEN: No, for that would not help you in the least.

KROGSTAD: Oh, help, help – ! I should do it whether or no.

MRS. LINDEN: I have learnt prudence. Life and bitter necessity have schooled me.

KROGSTAD: And life has taught me not to trust fine speeches.

MRS. LINDEN: Then life has taught you a very sensible thing. But deeds you will trust?

KROGSTAD: What do you mean?

MRS. LINDEN: You said you were a shipwrecked man, clinging to a spar.

KROGSTAD: I have good reason to say so.

MRS. LINDEN: I too am shipwrecked, and clinging to a spar. I have no one to mourn for, no one to care for.

KROGSTAD: You made your own choice.

MRS. LINDEN: No choice was left me.

KROGSTAD: Well, what then?

MRS. LINDEN: Nils, how if we two shipwrecked people could join hands?

KROGSTAD: What!

MRS. LINDEN: Two on a raft have a better chance than if each clings to a separate spar.

KROGSTAD: Christina!

MRS. LINDEN: What do you think brought me to town?

KROGSTAD: Had you any thought of me?

MRS. LINDEN: I must have work or I can't bear to live. All my life, as long as I can remember, I have worked; work has been my one great joy. Now I stand quite alone in the world, aimless and forlorn. There is no happiness in working for one's self. Nils, give me somebody and something to work for.

KROGSTAD: I cannot believe in all this. It is simply a woman's romantic craving for self-sacrifice.

MRS. LINDEN: Have you ever found me romantic?

KROGSTAD: Would you really – ? Tell me: do you know all my past?

MRS. LINDEN: Yes.

KROGSTAD: And do you know what people say of me?

MRS. LINDEN: Did you not say just now that with me you could have been another man?

KROGSTAD: I am sure of it.

MRS. LINDEN: Is it too late?

KROGSTAD: Christina, do you know what you are doing? Yes, you do; I see it in your face. Have you the courage, then – ?

MRS. LINDEN: I need some one to be a mother to, and your children need a mother. You need me, and I – I need you. Nils, I believe in your better self. With you I fear nothing.

KROGSTAD (*seizing her hands*): Thank you – thank you, Christina. Now I shall make others see me as you do. – Ah, I forgot –

MRS. LINDEN (*listening*): Hush! The tarantella! Go! go!

KROGSTAD: Why? What is it?

MRS. LINDEN: Don't you hear the dancing overhead? As soon as that is over they will be here.

KROGSTAD: Oh yes, I shall go. Nothing will come of this, after all. Of course, you don't know the step I have taken against the Helmers.

MRS. LINDEN: Yes, Nils, I do know.

KROGSTAD: And yet you have the courage to – ?

MRS. LINDEN: I know to what lengths despair can drive a man.

KROGSTAD: Oh, if I could only undo it!

MRS. LINDEN: You could. Your letter is still in the box.

KROGSTAD: Are you sure?

MRS. LINDEN: Yes; but –

KROGSTAD (*looking at her searchingly*): Is that what it all means?

You want to save your friend at any price. Say it out – is that your idea?

MRS. LINDEN: Nils, a woman who has once sold herself for the sake of others, does not do so again.

KROGSTAD: I shall demand my letter back again.

MRS. LINDEN: No, no.

KROGSTAD: Yes, of course. I shall wait till Helmer comes; I shall tell him to give it back to me – that it's only about my dismissal – that I don't want it read –

MRS. LINDEN: No, Nils, you must not recall the letter.

KROGSTAD: But tell me, wasn't that just why you got me to come here?

MRS. LINDEN: Yes, in my first alarm. But a day has passed since then, and in that day I have seen incredible things in this house. Helmer must know everything; there must be an end to this unhappy secret. These two must come to a full understanding. They must have done with all these shifts and subterfuges.

KROGSTAD: Very well, if you like to risk it. But one thing I can do, and at once –

MRS. LINDEN (*listening*): Make haste! Go, go! The dance is over; we're not safe another moment.

KROGSTAD: I shall wait for you in the street.

MRS. LINDEN: Yes, do; you must see me home.

KROGSTAD: I never was so happy in all my life!

(*Krogstad goes out by the outer door. The door between the room and the hall remains open.*)

MRS. LINDEN (*arranging the room and getting her outdoor things together*): What a change! What a change! To have someone to work for, to live for; a home to make happy! Well, it shall not be my fault if I fail. – I wish they would come. – (*Listens.*) Ah, here they are! I must get my things on.

(*Takes bonnet and cloak. Helmer's and Nora's voices are heard outside, a key is turned in the lock, and Helmer drags Nora almost by force into the hall. She wears the Italian costume with a large black shawl over it. He is in evening dress, and wears a black domino, open.*)

NORA (*struggling with him in the doorway*): No, no, no! I won't go in! I want to go upstairs again; I don't want to leave so early!

HELMER: But, my dearest girl – !

NORA: Oh, please, please, Torvald, I beseech you – only one hour more!

HELMER: Not one minute more, Nora dear; you know what we agreed. Come, come in; you're catching cold here. (*He leads her gently into the room in spite of her resistance.*)

MRS. LINDEN: Good evening.

NORA: Christina!

HELMER: What, Mrs. Linden! You here so late?

MRS. LINDEN: Good evening.

MRS. LINDEN: Yes, I ought to apologise. I did so want to see Nora in her costume.

NORA: Have you been sitting here waiting for me?

MRS. LINDEN: Yes; unfortunately I came too late. You had gone upstairs already, and I felt I couldn't go away without seeing you.

HELMER (*taking Nora's shawl off*): Well then, just look at her! I assure you she's worth it. Isn't she lovely, Mrs. Linden?

MRS. LINDEN: Yes, I must say –

HELMER: Isn't she exquisite? Every one said so. But she's dreadfully obstinate, dear little creature. What's to be done with her? Just think, I had almost to force her away.

NORA: Oh, Torvald, you'll be sorry some day that you didn't let me stay, if only for one half-hour more.

HELMER: There! You hear her, Mrs. Linden? She dances her

tarantella with wild applause, and well she deserved it, I must say – though there was, perhaps, a little too much nature in her rendering of the idea – more than was, strictly speaking, artistic. But never mind – the point is, she made a great success, a tremendous success. Was I to let her remain after that – to weaken the impression? Not if I know it. I took my sweet little Capri girl – my capricious little Capri girl, I might say – under my arm; a rapid turn round the room, a curtsey to all sides, and – as they say in novels – the lovely apparition vanished! An exit should always be effective, Mrs. Linden; but I can't get Nora to see it. By Jove! it's warm here. (*Throws his domino on a chair and opens the door to his room.*) What! No light there? Oh, of course. Excuse me – (*Goes in and lights candles.*)

NORA (*whispering breathlessly*): Well?

MRS. LINDEN (*softly*): I've spoken to him.

NORA: And – ?

MRS. LINDEN: Nora – you must tell your husband everything –

NORA (*tonelessly*): I knew it!

MRS. LINDEN: You have nothing to fear from Krogstad; but you must speak out.

NORA: I shall not speak.

MRS. LINDEN: Then the letter will.

NORA: Thank you, Christina. Now I know what I have to do. Hush – !

HELMER (*coming back*): Well, Mrs. Linden, have you admired her?

MRS. LINDEN: Yes; and now I must say goodnight.

HELMER: What, already? Does this knitting belong to you?

MRS. LINDEN (*takes it*): Yes, thanks; I was nearly forgetting it.

HELMER: Then you do knit?

MRS. LINDEN: Yes.

HELMER: Then you do knit?

MRS. LINDEN: Yes.

HELMER: Do you know, you ought to embroider instead?

MRS. LINDEN: Indeed! Why?

HELMER: Because it's so much prettier. Look now! You hold the embroidery in the left hand so, and then work the needle with the right hand, in a long, graceful curve – don't you?

MRS. LINDEN: Yes, I suppose so.

HELMER: But knitting is always ugly. Just look – your arms close to your sides, and the needles going up and down – there's something Chinese about it – They really gave us splendid champagne tonight.

MRS. LINDEN: Well, goodnight, Nora, and don't be obstinate any more.

HELMER: Well said, Mrs. Linden!

MRS. LINDEN: Goodnight, Mr. Helmer.

HELMER (*accompanying her to the door*): Goodnight, goodnight; I hope you'll get safely home. I should be glad to – but you have such a short way to go. Goodnight, goodnight. (*She goes; Helmer shuts the door after her, and comes forward again.*) At last we've got rid of her: she's a terrible bore.

NORA: Aren't you very tired, Torvald?

HELMER: No, not in the least.

NORA: Nor sleepy?

HELMER: Not a bit. I feel particularly lively. But you? You do look tired and sleepy.

NORA: Yes, very tired. I shall soon sleep now.

HELMER: There, you see. I was right after all not to let you stay longer.

NORA: Oh, everything you do is right.

HELMER (*kissing her forehead*): Now my lark is speaking like a reasonable being. Did you notice how jolly Rank was this evening?

NORA: Indeed? Was he? I had no chance of speaking to him.

HELMER: Nor I, much; but I haven't seen him in such good spirits for a long time. (*Looks at Nora a little, then comes nearer her.*) It's splendid to be back in our own home, to be quite alone together! – Oh, you enchanting creature!

NORA: Don't look at me in that way, Torvald.

HELMER: I am not to look at my dearest treasure? – at all the loveliness that is mine, mine only, wholly and entirely mine?

NORA (*goes to the other side of the table*): You mustn't say these things to me this evening.

HELMER (*following*): I see you have the tarantella still in your blood – and that makes you all the more enticing. Listen! the other people are going now. (*More softly.*) Nora – soon the whole house will be still.

NORA: Yes, I hope so.

HELMER: Yes, don't you, Nora darling! When we are among strangers, do you know why I speak so little to you, and keep so far away, and only steal a glance at you now and then – do you know why I do it? Because I am fancying that we love each other in secret, that I am secretly betrothed to you, and that no one dreams that there is anything between us.

NORA: Yes, yes, yes. I know all your thoughts are with me.

HELMER: And then, when the time comes to go, and I put the shawl about your smooth, soft shoulders, and this glorious neck of yours, I imagine you are my bride, that our marriage is just over, that I am bringing you for the first time to my home – that I am alone with you for the first time – quite alone with you, in your trembling loveliness! All this evening I have been longing for you, and you only. When I watched you swaying and whirling in the tarantella – my blood boiled

– I could endure it no longer; and that's why I made you come home with me so early –

NORA: Go now, Torvald! Go away from me. I won't have all this.

HELMER: What do you mean? Ah, I see you're teasing me, little Nora! Won't – won't! Am I not your husband – ?

(*A knock at the outer door.*)

NORA (*starts*): Did you hear – ?

HELMER (*going towards the hall*): Who's there?

RANK (*outside*): It is I; may I came in for a moment?

HELMER (*in a low tone, annoyed*): Oh! what can he want just now? (*Aloud.*) Wait a moment. (*Opens door.*) Come, it's nice of you to look in.

RANK: I thought I heard your voice, and that put it into my head. (*Looks round.*) Ah, this dear old place! How cosy you two are here!

HELMER: You seemed to find it pleasant enough upstairs, too.

RANK: Exceedingly. Why not? Why shouldn't one take one's share of everything in this world? All one can, at least, and as long as one can. The wine was splendid –

HELMER: Especially the champagne.

RANK: Did you notice it? It's incredible the quantity I contrived to get down.

NORA: Torvald drank plenty of champagne, too.

RANK: Did he?

NORA: Yes, and it always puts him in such spirits.

RANK: Well, why shouldn't one have a jolly evening after a well-spent day?

HELMER: Well spent! Well, I haven't much to boast of in that respect.

RANK (*slapping him on the shoulder*): But I have, don't you see?

NORA: I suppose you have been engaged in a scientific investigation, Doctor Rank?

RANK: Quite right.

HELMER: Bless me! Little Nora talking about scientific investigations?

NORA: Am I to congratulate you on the result?

RANK: By all means.

NORA: It was good, then?

RANK: The best possible, both for doctor and patient – certainty.

NORA (*quickly and searchingly*): Certainty?

RANK: Absolute certainty. Wasn't I right to enjoy myself after that?

NORA: Yes, quite right, Doctor Rank.

HELMER: And so say I, provided you don't have to pay for it tomorrow.

RANK: Well, in this life nothing is to be had for nothing.

NORA: Doctor Rank – I'm sure you are very fond of masquerades?

RANK: Yes, when there are plenty of amusing disguises –

NORA: Tell me, what shall we two be at our next masquerade?

HELMER: Little featherbrain! Thinking of your next already!

RANK: We two? I'll tell you. You must go as a good fairy.

HELMER: Ah, but what costume would indicate that?

RANK: She has simply to wear her everyday dress.

HELMER: Capital! But don't you know what you will be yourself?

RANK: Yes, my dear friend, I am perfectly clear upon that point.

HELMER: Well?

RANK: At the next masquerade I shall be invisible.

HELMER: What a comical idea!

RANK: There's a big black hat – haven't you heard of the invisible hat? It comes down all over you, and then no one can see you.

HELMER (*with a suppressed smile*): No, you're right there.

RANK: But I'm quite forgetting what I came for. Helmer, give me a cigar – one of the dark Havanas.

HELMER: With the greatest pleasure. (*Hands cigar-case.*)

RANK (*takes one and cuts the end off*): Thank you.

NORA (*striking a wax match*): Let me give you a light.

RANK: A thousand thanks.

(*She holds the match. He lights his cigar at it.*)

RANK: And now, goodbye!

HELMER: Goodbye, goodbye, my dear fellow.

NORA: Sleep well, Doctor Rank.

RANK: Thanks for the wish.

NORA: Wish me the same.

RANK: You? Very well, since you ask me – Sleep well. And thanks for the light. (*He nods to them both and goes out.*)

HELMER (*in an undertone*): He's been drinking a good deal.

NORA (*absently*): I daresay. (*Helmer takes his bunch of keys from his pocket and goes into the hall.*) Torvald, what are you doing there?

HELMER: I must empty the letter box; it's quite full; there will be no room for the newspapers tomorrow morning.

NORA: Are you going to work tonight?

HELMER: You know very well I am not. – Why, how is this? Someone has been at the lock.

NORA: The lock – ?

HELMER: I'm sure of it. What does it mean? I can't think that the servants – ? Here's a broken hairpin. Nora, it's one of yours.

NORA (*quickly*): It must have been the children –

HELMER: Then you must break them of such tricks. – There! At last I've got it open. (*Takes contents out and calls into the kitchen.*) Ellen! – Ellen, just put the hall door lamp out.

(*He returns with letters in his hand, and shuts the inner door.*)

HELMER: Just see how they've accumulated. (*Turning them over.*) Why, what's this?

NORA (*at the window*): The letter! Oh no, no, Torvald!

HELMER: Two visiting cards – from Rank.

NORA: From Doctor Rank?

HELMER (*looking at them*): Doctor Rank. They were on the top. He must just have put them in.

NORA: Is there anything on them?

HELMER: There's a black cross over the name. Look at it. What an unpleasant idea! It looks just as if he were announcing his own death.

NORA: So he is.

HELMER: What! Do you know anything? Has he told you anything?

NORA: Yes. These cards mean that he has taken his last leave of us. He is going to shut himself up and die.

HELMER: Poor fellow! Of course I knew we couldn't hope to keep him long. But so soon – ! And to go and creep into his lair like a wounded animal –

NORA: When we must go, it is best to go silently. Don't you think so, Torvald?

HELMER (*walking up and down*): He has so grown into our lives, I can't realise that he is gone. He and his sufferings and his loneliness formed a sort of cloudy background to the sunshine of our happiness. – Well, perhaps it's best as it is – at any rate for him. (*Stands still.*) And perhaps for us too, Nora. Now we two are thrown entirely upon each other. (*Takes her in his arms.*) My darling wife! I feel as if I could never hold you close enough. Do you know, Nora, I often wish some danger might threaten you, that I might risk body and soul, and everything, everything, for your dear sake.

NORA (*tears herself from him, and says firmly*): Now you shall read your letters, Torvald.

HELMER: No, no; not tonight. I want to be with you, my sweet wife.

NORA: With the thought of your dying friend – ?

HELMER: You are right. This has shaken us both. Unloveliness has come between us – thoughts of death and decay. We must seek to cast them off. Till then – we will remain apart.

NORA (*her arms round his neck*): Torvald! Goodnight! goodnight!

HELMER (*kissing her forehead*): Goodnight, my little songbird. Sleep well, Nora. Now I shall go and read my letters. (*He goes with the letters in his hand into his room and shuts the door.*)

NORA (*with wild eyes, gropes about her, seizes Helmer's domino, throws it round her, and whispers quickly, hoarsely, and brokenly*): Never to see him again. Never never, never. (*Throws her shawl over her head.*) Never to see the children again. Never, never. – Oh, that black, icy water! Oh, that bottomless – ! If it were only over! Now he has it; he's reading it. Oh, no, no, no, not yet. Torvald, goodbye – ! Goodbye my little ones – !

(*She is rushing out by the hall; at the same moment Helmer flings his door open, and stands there with an open letter in his hand.*)

HELMER: Nora!

NORA (*shrieks*): Ah – !

HELMER: What is this? Do you know what is in this letter?

NORA: Yes, I know. Let me go! Let me pass!

HELMER (*holds her back*): Where do you want to go?

NORA (*tries to break away from him*): You shall not save me, Torvald.

HELMER (*falling back*): True! Is what he writes true? No, no, it is impossible that this can be true.

NORA: It is true. I have loved you beyond all else in the world.

HELMER: Pshaw – no silly evasions!

NORA (*a step nearer him*): Torvald – !

HELMER: Wretched woman – what have you done!

NORA: Let me go – you shall not save me! You shall not take my guilt upon yourself!

HELMER: I don't want any melodramatic airs. (*Locks the outer door.*) Here you shall stay and give an account of yourself. Do you understand what you have done? Answer! Do you understand it?

NORA (*looks at him fixedly, and says with a stiffening expression*): Yes; now I begin fully to understand it.

HELMER (*walking up and down*): Oh! what an awful awakening! During all these eight years – she who was my pride and my joy – a hypocrite, a liar – worse, worse – a criminal. Oh, the unfathomable hideousness of it all! Ugh! Ugh!

(*Nora says nothing, and continues to look fixedly at him.*)

HELMER: I ought to have known how it would be. I ought to have forseen it. All your father's want of principle – be silent! – all your father's want of principle you have inherited – no religion, nor morality, no sense of duty. How I am punished for screening him! I did it for your sake; and you reward me like this.

NORA: Yes – like this!

HELMER: You have destroyed my whole happiness. You have ruined my future. Oh, it's frightful to think of! I am in the power of a scoundrel; he can do whatever he pleases with me, demand whatever he chooses; he can domineer over me as much as he likes, and I must submit. And all this disaster and ruin is brought upon me by an unprincipled woman!

NORA: When I am out of the world you will be free.

HELMER: Oh, no fine phrases. Your father, too, was always ready with them. What good would it do me, if you were "out of the world," as you say? No good whatever! He can publish the story all the same; I might even be suspected of collusion. People will think I was at the bottom of it all and egged you on. And for all this I have you to thank – you whom I have done nothing but pet and spoil during our whole married life. Do you understand now what you have done to me?

NORA (*with cold calmness*): Yes.

HELMER: The thing is so incredible, I can't grasp it. But we must come to an understanding. Take that shawl off. Take it off, I say! I must try to pacify him in one way or another – the matter must be hushed up, cost what it may. – As for you and me, we must make no outward change in our way of life – no outward change, you understand. Of course, you will continue to live here. But the children cannot be left in your care. I dare not trust them to you. – Oh, to have to say this to one I have loved so tenderly – whom I still – ! But that must be a thing of the past. Henceforward there can be no question of happiness, but merely of saving the ruins, the shreds, the show – (*A ring; Helmer starts.*) What's that? So late! Can it be the worst? Can he – ? Hide yourself, Nora; say you are ill.

(*Nora stands motionless. Helmer goes to the door and opens it.*)

ELLEN: (*half dressed, in the hall*) Here is a letter for you, ma'am.

HELMER: Give it to me. (*Seizes the letter and shuts the door.*) Yes, from him. You shall not have it. I shall read it.

NORA: Read it!

HELMER (*by the lamp*): I have hardly the courage to. We may both be lost, both you and I. Ah! I must know. (*Hastily tears the letter open; reads a few lines, looks at an enclosure; with a cry of joy.)* Nora!

(*Nora looks enquiringly at him.*)

HELMER: Nora! – Oh! I must read it again. – Yes, yes, it is so. I am saved! Nora, I am saved!

NORA: And I?

HELMER: You too, of course; we are both saved, both of us. Look here – he sends you back your promissory note. He writes that he regrets and apologises, that a happy turn in his life – Oh, what matter what he writes! We are saved, Nora! No one can harm you. Oh, Nora, Nora – ; but first to get rid of this hateful thing. I'll just see – (*Glances at the I O U.*) No, I will not look at it; the whole thing shall be nothing but a dream to me. (*Tears the I O U and both letters in pieces. Throws them into the fire and watches them burn.*) There! it's gone! – He said that ever since Christmas Eve – Oh, Nora, they must have been three terrible days for you!

NORA: I have fought a hard fight for he last three days.

HELMER: And in your agony you saw no other outlet but – No; we won't think of that horror. We will only rejoice and repeat – it's over, all over! Don't you hear, Nora? You don't seem able to grasp it. Yes, it's over. What is this set look on your face? Oh, my poor Nora, I understand; you cannot believe that I have forgiven you. But I have, Nora; I swear it. I have forgiven everything. I know that what you did was all for love of me.

NORA: That is true.

HELMER: You loved me as a wife should love her husband. It was only the means that, in your inexperience, you misjudged. But do you think I love you the less because you cannot do without guidance? No, no. Only lean on me; I will counsel you, and guide you. I should be no true man if this very womanly helplessness did not make you doubly dear in my eyes. You mustn't dwell upon the hard things I said in my first moment of terror, when the world seemed to be tumbling about my ears. I have forgiven you, Nora – I swear I have forgiven you.

NORA: I thank you for your forgiveness. (*Goes out, to the right.*)

HELMER: No, stay – ! (*Looking through the doorway.*) What are you going to do?

NORA (*inside*): To take off my masquerade dress.

HELMER (*in the doorway*): Yes, do, dear. Try to calm down, and recover your balance, my scared little songbird. You may rest secure. I have broad wings to shield you. (*Walking up and down near the door.*) Oh, how lovely – how cosy our home is, Nora! Here you are safe; here I can shelter you like a hunted dove whom I have saved from the claws of the hawk. I shall soon bring your poor beating heart to rest; believe me, Nora, very soon. Tomorrow all this will seem quite different – everything will be as before. I shall not need to tell you again that I forgive you; you will feel for yourself that it is true. How could you think I could find it in my heart to drive you away, or even so much as to reproach you? Oh, you don't know a true man's heart, Nora. There is something indescribably sweet and soothing to a man in having forgiven his wife – honestly forgiven her, from the bottom of his heart. She becomes his property in a double sense. She is as though born again; she has become, so to speak, at once his wife and his child. That is what you shall henceforth be to me, my bewildered, helpless darling. Don't be troubled about anything, Nora; only open your heart to me, and I will be both will and conscience to you. (*Nora enters in everyday dress.*) Why, what's this? Not gone to bed? You have changed your dress?

NORA: Yes, Torvald; now I have changed my dress.

HELMER: But why now, so late – ?

NORA: I shall not sleep tonight.

HELMER: But, Nora dear –

NORA (*looking at her watch*): It's not so late yet. Sit down, Torvald; you and I have much to say to each other.

(*She sits at one side of the table.*)

HELMER: Nora – what does this mean? Your cold, set face –

NORA: Sit down. It will take some time. I have much to talk over with you.

(*Helmer sits at the other side of the table.*)

HELMER: You alarm me, Nora. I don't understand you.

NORA: No, that is just it. You don't understand me; and I have never understood you – till tonight. No, don't interrupt. Only listen to what I say. – I must come to a final settlement, Torvald.

HELMER: How do you mean?

NORA (*after a short silence*): Does not one thing strike you as we sit here?

HELMER: What should strike me?

NORA: We have been married eight years. Does it not strike you that this is the first time we two, you and I, man and wife, have talked together seriously?

HELMER: Seriously! What do you call seriously?

NORA: During eight whole years, and more – ever since the day we first met – we have never exchanged one serious word about serious things.

HELMER: Was I always to trouble you with the cares you could not help me to bear?

NORA: I am not talking of cares. I say that we have never yet set ourselves seriously to get to the bottom of anything.

HELMER: Why, my dearest Nora, what have you to do with serious things?

NORA: There we have it! You have never understood me. – I have had great injustice done me, Torvald; first by father, and then by you.

HELMER: What! By your father and me? – By us, who have loved you more than all the world?

NORA (*shaking her head*): You have never loved me. You only thought it amusing to be in love with me.

HELMER: Why, Nora, what a thing to say!

NORA: Yes, it is so, Torvald. While I was at home with father, he used to tell me all his opinions, and I held the same opinions. If I had others I said nothing about them, because he wouldn't have liked it. He used to call me his doll-child, and played with me as I played with my dolls. Then I came to live in your house –

HELMER: What an expression to use about our marriage!

NORA (*undisturbed*): I mean I passed from father's hands into yours. You arranged everything according to your taste; and I got the same tastes as you; or I pretended to – I don't know which – both ways, perhaps; sometimes one and sometimes the other. When I look back on it now, I seem to have been living here like a beggar, from hand to mouth. I lived by performing tricks for you, Torvald. But you would have it so. You and father have done me a great wrong. It is your fault that my life has come to nothing.

HELMER: Why, Nora, how unreasonable and ungrateful you are! Have you not been happy here?

NORA: No, never. I thought I was; but I never was.

HELMER: Not – not happy!

NORA: No; only merry. And you have always been so kind to me. But our house has been nothing but a playroom. Here I have been your doll-wife, just as at home I used to be papa's doll-child. And the children, in their turn, have been my dolls. I thought it fun when you played with me, just as the children did when I played with them. That has been our marriage, Torvald.

HELMER: There is some truth in what you say, exaggerated and overstrained though it be. But henceforth it shall be different. Playtime is over; now comes the time for education.

NORA: Whose education? Mine, or the children's?

HELMER: Both, my dear Nora.

NORA: Oh, Torvald, you are not the man to teach me to be a fit wife for you.

HELMER: And you can say that?

NORA: And I – how have I prepared myself to educate the children?

HELMER: Nora!

NORA: Did you not say yourself, a few minutes ago, you dared not trust them to me?

HELMER: In the excitement of the moment! Why should you dwell upon that?

NORA: No – you were perfectly right. That problem is beyond me. There is another to be solved first – I must try to educate myself. You are not the man to help me in that. I must set about it alone. And that is why I am leaving you.

HELMER (*jumping up*): What – do you mean to say –?

NORA: I must stand quite alone if I am ever to know myself and my surroundings; so I cannot stay with you.

HELMER: Nora! Nora!

NORA: I am going at once. I daresay Christina will take me in for tonight –

HELMER: You are mad! I shall now allow it! I forbid it!

NORA: It is of no use your forbidding me anything now. I shall take with me what belongs to me. From you I will accept nothing, either now or afterwards.

HELMER: What madness is this!

NORA: Tomorrow I shall go home – I mean to what was my home. It will be easier for me to find some opening there.

HELMER: Oh, in your blind inexperience –

NORA: I must try to gain experience, Torvald.

HELMER: To forsake your home, your husband, and your children! And you don't consider what the world will say!

NORA: I can pay no heed to that. I only know that I must do it.

HELMER: This is monstrous! Can you forsake your holiest duties in this way?

NORA: What do you consider my holiest duties?

HELMER: Do I need to tell you that? Your duties to your husband and your children.

NORA: I have other duties equally sacred.

HELMER: Impossible! What duties do you mean?

NORA: My duties towards myself.

HELMER: Before all else you are a wife and a mother.

NORA: That I no longer believe. I believe that before all else I am a human being, just as much as you are – or at least that I should try to become one. I know that most people agree with you, Torvald, and that they say so in books. But henceforth I can't be satisfied with what most people say, and what is in books. I must think things out for myself, and try to get clear about them.

HELMER: Are you not clear about your place in your own home? Have you not an infallible guide in questions like these? Have you not religion?

NORA: Oh, Torvald, I don't really know what religion is.

HELMER: What do you mean?

NORA: I know nothing but what Pastor Hansen told me when I was confirmed. He explained that religion was this and that. When I get away from all this and stand alone, I will look into that matter too. I will see whether what he taught me is right, or, at any rate, whether it is right for me.

HELMER: Oh, this is unheard-of! And from so young a woman!

But if religion cannot keep you right, let me appeal to your conscience – for I suppose you have some moral feeling? Or, answer me: perhaps you have none?

NORA: Well, Torvald, it's not easy to say. I really don't know – I am all at sea about these things. I only know that I think quite differently from you about them. I hear, too, that the laws are different from what I thought; but I can't believe that they can be right. It appears that a woman has no right to spare her dying father, or to save her husband's life! I don't believe that.

HELMER: You talk like a child. You don't understand the society in which you live.

NORA: No, I do not. But now I shall try to learn. I must make up my mind which is right – society or I.

HELMER: Nora, you are ill; you are feverish; I almost think you are out of your senses.

NORA: I have never felt so much clearness and certainty as tonight.

HELMER: You are clear and certain enough to forsake husband and children?

NORA: Yes, I am.

HELMER: Then there is only one explanation possible.

NORA: What is that?

HELMER: You no longer love me.

NORA: No; that is just it.

HELMER: Nora! – Can you say so!

NORA: Oh, I'm so sorry, Torvald; for you've always been so kind to me. But I can't help it. I do not love you any longer.

HELMER (*mastering himself with difficulty*): Are you clear and certain on this point too?

NORA: Yes, quite. That is why I will not stay here any longer.

HELMER: And can you also make clear to me how I have forfeited your love?

NORA: Yes, I can. It was this evening, when the miracle did not happen; for then I saw you were not the man I had imagined.

HELMER: Explain yourself more clearly; I don't understand.

NORA: I have waited so patiently all these eight years; for of course I saw clearly enough that miracles don't happen every day. When this crushing blow threatened me, I said to myself so confidently, 'Now comes the miracle!' When Krogstad's letter lay in the box, it never for a moment occurred to me that you would think of submitting to that man's conditions. I was convinced that you would say to him, 'Make it known to all the world'; and that then –

HELMER: Well? When I had given my own wife's name up to disgrace and shame – ?

NORA: Then I firmly believed that you would come forward, take everything upon yourself, and say, 'I am the guilty one.'

HELMER: Nora – !

NORA: You mean I would never have accepted such a sacrifice? No, certainly not? But what would my assertions have been worth in opposition to your? – That was the miracle that I hoped for and dreaded. And it was to hinder that that I wanted to die.

HELMER: I would gladly work for you day and night, Nora – bear sorrow and want for your sake. But no man sacrifices his honour, even for one he loves.

NORA: Millions of women have done so.

HELMER: Oh, you think and talk like a silly child.

NORA: Very likely. But you neither think nor talk like the man I can share my life with. When your terror was over – not for what threatened me, but for yourself – when there was nothing more to fear – then it seemed to you as though nothing had happened. I was your lark again, your doll, just as before – whom you would take twice as much care of in future, because she was so weak and fragile. (*Stands up.*) Torvald – in that moment it burst upon me that I had been living here these eight years with a strange man, and had borne him three children. – Oh, I can't bear to think of it! I could tear myself to pieces!

HELMER (*sadly*): I see it, I see it; an abyss has opened between us. – But, Nora, can it never be filled up?

NORA: As I now am, I am no wife for you.

HELMER: I have strength to become another man.

NORA: Perhaps – when your doll is taken away from you.

HELMER: To part – to part from you! No, Nora, no; I can't grasp the thought.

NORA (*going into the room on the right*): The more reason for the thing to happen.

(*She comes back with outdoor things and a small travelling bag, which she places on a chair.*)

HELMER: Nora, Nora, not now! Wait till tomorrow.

NORA (*putting on cloak*): I can't spend the night in a strange man's house.

HELMER: But can we not live here, as brother and sister – ?

NORA (*fastening her hat*): You know very well that wouldn't last long. (*Puts on the shawl.*) Goodbye, Torvald. No, I won't go to the children. I know they are in better hands than mine. As I now am, I can be nothing to them.

HELMER: But sometime, Nora – sometime – ?

NORA: How can I tell? I have no idea what will become of me.

HELMER: But you are my wife, now and always!

NORA: Listen, Torvald – when a wife leaves her husband's house, as I am doing, I have heard that in the eyes of the law he is free from all duties towards her. At any rate I release you from all duties. You must not feel yourself bound, any more than I shall. There must be perfect freedom on both sides. There, I give you back your ring. Give me mine.

HELMER: That too?

NORA: That too.

HELMER: Here it is.

NORA: Very well. Now it is all over. I lay the keys here. The servants know about everything in the house – better than I do. Tomorrow, when I have started, Christina will come to pack up the things I brought with me from home. I will have them sent after me.

HELMER: All over! all over! Nora, will you never think of me again?

NORA: Oh, I shall often think of you, and the children, and this house.

HELMER: May I write to you, Nora?

NORA: No – never. You must not.

HELMER: But I must send you –

NORA: Nothing, nothing.

HELMER: I must help you if you need it.

NORA: No, I say. I take nothing from strangers.

HELMER: Nora – can I never be more than a stranger to you?

NORA (*taking her travelling bag*): Oh, Torvald, then the miracle of miracles would have to happen –

HELMER: What is the miracle of miracles?

NORA: Both of us would have to change so that – Oh, Torvald, I no longer believe in miracles.

HELMER: But *I* will believe. Tell me! We must so change that – ?

NORA: That communion between us shall be a marriage. Goodbye. (*She goes out by the hall door.*)

HELMER (*sinks into a chair by the door with his face in his hands*): Nora! Nora! (*He looks round and rises.*) Empty. She is gone. (*A hope springs up in him.*) Ah! The miracle of miracles – ?

(*From below is heard the reverberation of a heavy door closing.*)

Curtain

Glossary: reading the text

The Wild Duck

Act I

3 ***upholstered*** (stage direction – s.d.) covered with material and cushions.

lamps (s.d.) oil lamps (no electricity in use then).

branching condlesticks (s.d.) candelabra (a frame holding many branches on which to place candles).

baize (s.d.) covered with green material.

livery (s.d.) uniform for servants.

old man referring to Mr Werle.

customer an innuendo of an existing relationship between Werle and Mrs Sörby.

4 ***threadbare*** (s.d.) with the material completely worn through.

5 ***bitters*** a liquid made from bitter herbs, often mixed with alcohol.

bankrupt left with no money – associated with financial loss after business failure.

Penitentiary a type of prison, house of correction.

maraschino a cherry liqueur.

6 ***outside his set*** of a different class.

portly stocky, plump.

outer man outward appearance.

7 ***How is your... on now?*** neither Hialmar nor Gregers would have been aware of Old Ekdal's appearance at the start of the act.

8 ***And my father... money?*** the conversation between Hialmar and

Gregers continuously reveals the influence of Mr Werle on the Ekdal family.

9 ***compunction*** conscience, sympathetic feeling.

Her daily intercourse Hialmar's comment reveals his arrogance by assuming that his wife can learn from *him* in their daily conversations.

who kept house for us . . . a typical device of Ibsen's to reveal information about the past.

10 ***it was your father that recommended it to me*** again, Mr Werle's influence is evident in all arrangements.

chimed in worked out. It becomes apparent that a photographic business is particularly ironic in view of the allusions to sight, blindness and re-touching in the play.

providence divine spirit.

He has a good heart, you see this comment will be seen to be *ironic* as the plot is revealed. (See 'Introduction', pages xx–xxi.)

11 ***staring at the lights*** one of many references to sight and blindness in the play.

punch a drink; a mixture of alcohol and fruit juices.

Chamberlain an honourary title in Norway conferred by the king; used to be the official in charge of royal private chambers.

stringent severe.

12 ***Tokay*** Hungarian wine.

13 ***The old vintages*** double meaning: old wines and older men.

14 ***deuce*** devil

deny that you knew him! an element of Christian symbolism here, referring to Peter's denial of Christ.

15 ***the crushing hand of Fate*** destiny. In classical mythology there were three goddesses of fate who ruled the birth, life and death of humans.

melancholy sad, depressing.

16 ***cognac*** French brandy.

pianoforte piano.

to go so miserably to the wall deteriorate so badly.

17 ***quite in the dark*** one of many references to light and dark in the play.

acquitted let off.

There are people in the world... to the surface again one of many references to the symbol of the wild duck.

18 ***laugh of derision*** (s.d.) scornful laugh.

19 ***alluding to*** referring to, suggesting.

burrow into Mr Werle's description of Gregers here as a dog is a recurring image.

21 ***you have everything just as you wish*** Gregers remains cynical during their conversation.

22 ***concurrence*** agreement, support.

a tableau of filial devotion a picture of a son's love and duty.

filial piety a sense of holy (religious) duty from the child.

vestige trace.

annihilates destroys completely.

you, and all these – ! Gregers refers to his father's reputation with women.

23 ***he sits*** Gregers uses the third person in disgust.

what he calls his home is built upon a lie! a recurring theme of lies, truth and illusions.

battle-field use of a metaphor – describing the effects of Mr Werle's past actions in terms of a war which has wounded so many.

chasm large gap.

mission Gregers's purpose in life is another recurring subject.

1 What has happened in the past between Mr Werle and Old Ekdal?
2 Why does Hialmar feel so uncomfortable at the dinner party?
3 In what ways has Mr Werle influenced the life of Hialmar and his family?
4 How could the relationship between Werle and his son be described?
5 Explain what has been learned about past events so far.
6 How are the father/son relationships between Hialmar/Old Ekdal and Werle/Gregers presented?

Act 2

24 *camel's-hair pencils* (s.d.) the hair of camels was used for paint brushes.

shading her eyes (s.d.) one of many references to the state of Hedvig's eyes.

25 *We've nothing to do with that Mr Werle* Gina's emphatic statement is ironic.

26 *that's nothing* referring to the cognac he had been given (see note to page 16).

she's gone into the basket referring to the wild duck.

forenoon morning.

27 *for then we have a pleasanter time* Hedvig understands Hialmar's moods.

Gina and Hedvig look at each other (s.d.) they realise the water is for alcohol.

28 *We were about twelve or fourteen at table* he avoids saying thirteen (see Act 1, page 6).

29 ***Aha! Then he's –*** Hialmar also acknowledges the fact that his father drinks.

genteel refined, well-bred, fashionable.

30 ***I gave them a bit of my mind*** he did nothing of the sort. Hialmar is being arrogant and snobbish. The conversation in Act 1 (pages 12–13) shows he knew nothing about the seasonal effect on wines.

they got that in their pipes too that sorted them out!

31 ***A free-and-easy indoor costume . . . personality better*** another way of saying he cannot really afford anything better.

No one knows how much . . . sour faces at once throughout this conversation Hialmar acts the martyr. The audience will realise that Gina is the real worker in the family.

34 ***I'm a man beset by a host of cares*** Hialmar makes it sound as if he has all the responsibility, whereas Gina ensures the family survives.

35 ***Bohemian*** (s.d.) Czech.

plaintive (s.d.) sad.

No, I'm like my mother Gregers virtually disowns his father here.

36 ***countrified cut*** (s.d.) ordinary, plain, unsophisticated.

capital excellent.

37 ***inexorably*** not to be prevented.

Hereditary inherited from parent to child (an important theme in all these Ibsen plays).

Ekdal's mother had weak eyes Gina is quick to point out that Hedvig has probably inherited her weak eyes from her grandmother. Her comment will be important.

plenty of butter on it an example of how most of the money coming in to the household seems to be spent on Hialmar (see Act 2, page 25).

38 ***fifteen years*** the precise timing of Hedvig's birth becomes all important. Gina appears to avoid the details.

39 ***The woods avenge themselves*** a recurring saying – used here in relation to Ekdal's changed circumstances and status since the fraud (see Act 1, pages 17 and Act 5, page 118).

41 ***garret*** (s.d.) room just under the roof (attic).

poultry chickens, hens.

42 ***That man wasn't my father, was he?*** Gregers discovers yet more to attribute to his father in relation to the Ekdal family.

43 ***They shoot to the bottom ... never come up again*** this description of a wounded wild duck is used as a factual explanation and a symbolic representation of a type of person (see Werle's comment in Act 1, page 17).

45 ***they're not always quite –*** the suggestion is they are sometimes drunk.

5–6 ***Yes, an extraordinarily clever ... among the ooze*** this becomes Gregers mission (see Act 1, page 23 and Act 2, page 47). He believes he can save a 'wild duck' (here, meaning Hedvig and the Ekdal family.) The central image now becomes pivotal to the whole play.

46 ***it seemed to me he meant ... what he said*** Hedvig understands that Gregers had been talking metaphorically, but is puzzled all the same.

47 ***if it had only been to someone else*** possibly because she realises the trouble Gregers could cause, or perhaps because she wants nothing more to do with the Werle family.

pariah social outcast.

independent the word is ironic as Hialmar wrongly thinks himself to be independent.

1. Give examples of the self-centred and arrogant nature of Hialmar.
2. What differences are there between the facts of the dinner party in Act 1 and the way Hialmar describes them?
3. What events led to the Ekdal family having the wild duck?
4. How does Ibsen portray the marriage of Hialmar and Gina?
5. What examples can you find to illustrate Gina as the driving force of the family?
6. Explain what Gregers means by wanting to be 'an extraordinarily clever dog'.
7. What do think Old Ekdal means when he says 'The woods avenge themselves'?

Act 3

49 ***must needs*** had to.

damper a valve on the stove to regulate the draught of air. The stove was the central means of heat in the house.

ewer large water jug.

50 ***on the loose*** out drinking.

toiling away Hialmar makes it sound as though he is working much harder than is the case (note the stage directions of 'lazily and listlessly' just above).

51 ***dodge*** apparatus.

52 ***sailcloth*** (s.d.) strong, coarse fishing net.

I must bear the whole burden... strength holds out Hialmar acts the martyr whilst Gina gets on with the work.

you must take the responsibility upon yourself Hialmar again shirks his responsibility.

55 *Father has promised to read ... hasn't had time yet* an example of Hialmar's laziness.

56 *'Harrison's History of London'* the illustrated book by Harrison was one which Ibsen himself had found in the loft when the family moved to Venstøp.

57 *basket-making and straw-plaiting* the irony is that Hedvig does not understand the implications of these being activities associated with the blind.

Why do you say 'the depths of the sea'? Hedvig is the mouthpiece of the audience, wondering at the deeper meanings of Gregers's pronouncements.

59 *when Ekdal hasn't time himself* Gina is being modest (she uses Hialmar's surname as a matter of formality).

60 *One of the barrels is loaded* an ominous warning.

fiddle-faddles plays around with.

a charge of shot pellets from a shooting rifle.

61 *I generally leave the details ... think of more important things* Hialmar does not appear to *do* anything!

I haven't quite completed it yet the audience might doubt its completion.

62 *it's my life's mission ... to save shipwrecked man* Hialmar's mission, explained in terms of the shipwreck metaphor can be compared to Gregers's mission in Act 2, pages 45–6.

His courage failed him Old Ekdal had attempted suicide.

63 *Hialmar Ekdal pointed the pistol at his own breast* Hialmar also attempted suicide. His description is melodramatic. The idea of suicide is important in the play.

64 *goaded* persuaded.

I almost think you have something of the wild duck in you Gregers extends the symbol here.

insidious treacherous, deceptive.

65 *melancholy* depression, sadness.

marsh vapours as well as meaning the mists and smells which come from the marshes, Gregers also speaks metaphorically here and later: the vapours mean mists which prevent Hialmar from seeing the truth.

breadwinner the one who earns the money to keep the family.

exalts raises.

66 *screwed* drunk.

dæmonic possessed by the devil.

67 *meander* wander, not in a straight line.

claim of the ideal the phrase recurs throughout the play; it shows Gregers's strong belief in 'will' and living according to ideals.

knock a little discount off not be so demanding in your ideals.

68 *one can get through the world with a wig* go through life with some kind of false prop.

69 *taint* stench.

I have a strong suspicion ... in your coat-tail pocket Relling makes the abstract concept of Gregers's 'claim of the ideal' into something concrete.

70 *dunning us with it* demanding it from us.

Oh – oh dear! a violent reaction from Gina upon seeing Werle.

71 *I intend to open Hialmar Ekdal's eyes* metaphorically – to reveal the truth.

but Hialmar I can rescue ... doing him a kindness the central debate about whether it is better to tell a person the truth or let them live with their illusions is examined here.

72 *sick conscience* Gregers's motives become apparent.

right scent the hunting metaphor is sustained.

73 *You shouldn't go out with him, Ekdal* Gina's warning to Hialmar suggests she knows exactly what is likely to happen.

74 *chronic integrity in an acute form* Relling uses medical terminology to explain Gregers's 'illness' of a bad case of 'conscience'.

sporadically here and there; now and again.

1 Give examples of Hialmar acting like a martyr.
2 Why does Gregers appear so strange to Hedvig?
3 Why might an audience come to believe that Hialmar will never invent anything?
4 What are the different 'missions' of Hialmar and Gregers?
5 What is meant by the phrase 'claim of the ideal'?
6 Explain the reasons for the argument between Gregers and Werle.
7 What is the difference in outlook between Gregers and Relling?
8 What further information does Ibsen reveal in this act about the relationship between the Ekdal and Werle families?

Act 4

75 *everything seems so queer today* there is a sense of dramatic change for Hedvig.

76 *I mean to do everything myself* there is a sudden change in Hialmar.

77 *The air is heavy under this roof* Hialmar now uses Gregers's metaphor of the 'marsh vapours'. (See note to Act 3, page 65.)

78 *he gets it from Mr Werle* yet more for the Ekdal family from Werle.

79 *hocus-pocus and hurly-burly* such an almighty fuss.

until he'd had his way Gina admits her past relationship with Werle.

80 *penitence and remorse* guilty repentance.

callous cruel.

81 *swamp of deceit* the image of the marsh again.

presentiment idea, vision of the future.

sap my vitality draw all my strength.

82 ***ennobling*** Gregers assumes that Hialmar must feel noble, having discovered the truth.

communion . . . transfiguration . . . consecration spiritual conversation, transformation, holiness.

83 ***quack-salver*** boastful pretender of medicinal remedies.

84 ***circumspectly*** cautiously.

you may do her a great injury an ominous warning.

85 ***inopportunely*** at an inconvenient time.

emissary someone sent on a mission (often used as a spy).

86 ***franker*** more honest. The contrast is made between Mrs Sörby/Werle and Gina/Hialmar.

88 ***He's going blind*** Werle's impending blindness now makes Hialmar wonder but he simply feels it is Fate's punishment for Werle's past actions.

90 ***indubitable*** certain.

moral homilies sermons on the proper way to conduct oneself.

92 ***deed of gift*** at this point Hialmar suddenly realises Hedvig must be Werle's daughter.

93 ***The eyes! The eyes!*** Hialmar realises that Hedvig's eye condition is inherited from Werle.

vistas avenues, prospects.

benefactions deeds of gifts.

95 ***You three must be together*** Gregers tries to control events.

96 ***Mother might have found me*** an example of Hedvig's innocence.

97 ***leeches*** blood-sucking worms – used in medicine to drain poisons from wounds.

sacrifice the wild duck Gregers puts the idea of self-sacrifice into Hedvig's mind.

the claims of the what-do-you-call-it Gina is cynical towards Gregers's ideals.

1. What immediate changes are noticeable in Hialmar between the end of Act 3 and the beginning of Act 4?
2. Explain the relationship between Werle and Gina.
3. How does Ibsen make sure that the audience remains sympathetic towards Gina in her dialogue with Hialmar (pages 78–83)?
4. Why is Relling so concerned about Hedvig?
5. What makes Mrs Sörby feel she will have a successful marriage?
6. What factors contribute towards Hialmar's realisation that Hedvig is not his daughter?
7. How does Gregers try to control events in the Ekdal family? What does he want each member of the family to do and why?

Act 5

102 *spiritual tumult* chaos of conscience.

extirpated destroyed, rooted out.

humour mood.

rhetoric eloquent speech.

103 *integrity-fever* illness of the conscience.

phoenix the mythical bird which rises from its own ashes.

cotter's cabin cottage.

insolvent bankrupt.

104 *inoculated* continuing the medical image.

infallible bound to succeed.

hocus-pocus trickery.

105 ***typhus and putrid fever*** names for the same illness.

Rob the average man of his life-illusion . . . at the same time the central argument from Relling to oppose Gregers's 'mission' and 'claims of the ideal'.

106 ***if only your eyes had been opened*** a metaphorical use of the sight image.

109 ***memoranda*** notes.

interlopers intruders.

110 ***portmanteau*** (s.d.) large travelling case.

111 ***He must have taken it in with him*** an ironic statement as on the previous page the stage direction noted that Hedvig took it.

113 ***firm ground to build upon now*** nothing could be further from the truth for the Ekdal family now.

blackguard villain.

aptitude ability.

blot out the sunlight another example of the light/dark contrast used throughout Ibsen's plays.

116 ***It was a child's act of sacrifice*** a moment of great tension as the audience will know (see stage direction on page 107) that Old Ekdal has been in his room. Only Hedvig would have known that as well. Old Ekdal appears moments later.

119 ***Internal haemorrhage*** unstoppable internal bleeding.

120 ***declamation*** speech.

121 ***duns*** people who ask for their money.

thirteenth at table see Act 1, page 6 and Act 3, page 66.

1. Explain the differences of opinion between Relling and Gregers (pages 102–105). What do you think they mean by 'life-illusion' and 'claims of the ideal'?
2. Which stage directions are particularly important in this act, and why?
3. What is ironic about Gregers's comment on pages 113–4 ('It seems to me you have firm ground to build on... you have your invention to live for')?
4. How is Hialmar portrayed in this act?
5. What do you think the meaning is of Old Ekdal's comment: 'The woods avenge themselves' (pages 39 and 118)?
6. Explain what has happened to the Ekdal family by the end of the play.
7. What do you think Gregers means by his final comment of the play?

Ghosts

Characters

124 *Chamberlain* see note to Act 1, page 17, ***The Wild Duck***.

Pastor a clergyman.

Act I

125 *periodicals* (s.d.) weekly or monthly magazines.

conservatory (s.d.) an additional room at the back or side of a house – usually with glass walls for plants.

garden syringe (s.d.) for watering the plants.

young master meaning Oswald.

126 *manifold* many in quantity.

Asylum also referred to as the Orphanage.

swells important officials.

127 *I, who am treated almost as a daughter here!* the words take on significance.

Fi donc! (French) one of many expressions from Regina trying to show a refined upbringing. It is an empty expression to avoid words used previously by her father.

a bit on drunk.

to twit her with pull her to her senses.

128 *Pied de mouton* (French) with feet like a sheep – devil-like.

129 *there must be a petticoat in the house* there must be women. (There is a possibility that the sailors' tavern could be in part a brothel as well.)

130 *Savoir vivre* (French) knowledge of life.

131 *I can prove it from the church register* this would prove that he is named legally as her father.

turning round, surprised and pleased (s.d.) a contrived action by Regina as the stage direction above shows that she had already seen him.

Oh, mayn't I help you? There! Why, how wet it is! a very different manner from the way she greeted her father when he entered the house with wet clothes!

133 *a daughter's duty* one of many references concerned with family duty. The short pause that follows suggests strongly that Pastor Manders is looking closely at Regina.

134 *H'm – indeed!* disapproval at the type of books belonging to Mrs Alving.

135 *even now* the audience would be led to wonder why *even* now.

136 *most people either don't formulate... keep quiet about it* Mrs Alving immediately establishes herself as a free-thinking woman.

surely not in this country Pastor Manders is voicing the kind of parochial narrow-mindedness against which Ibsen himself struggled so much.

137 *legal fiat for the endowment* a legal order for the fund for the money coming from the interest gained from Alving's estate.

138 *pretentious* seems rather over the top.

the capital the original sum of money which has been invested. This money is in a bank and has been earning interest.

a good mortgage . . . and an undoubted security he suggests using the money for a mortgage as the interest would be much higher than interest from a bank. In other words, all the money from Alving's estate will go into the new Orphanage building.

Shall the Orphanage buildings be insured or not? an important discussion at this point in view of later events.

139 *consecrated* made holy.

impropriety unsuitable action.

contingencies plans in case anything goes wrong.

my colleagues' adherents followers of mine in the Church.

Higher Providence he argues that if the Orphanage is insured people will attack him for seeming not to trust in the Hand of God.

140 *the brunt of fanaticism* the suggestion that there are already enough people who are against the Church.

Then you do not wish the Orphanage insured? he makes it sound as if the idea had been Mrs Alving's!

make good the damage pay for any repairs following a disaster.

Special Providence rather than having the building insured Pastor Manders is prepared to put his faith in God.

141 *nearly had a fire* ominous words.

142 *meerschaum* (s.d.) clay pipe.

Prodigal Son referring to the New Testament story of the son who returns home after a dissolute life away.

Reclaimed Son Oswald is now back with his family.

144 *Oswald takes after me* Mrs Alving is anxious that Oswald should take after her.

145 *yet he managed to do ... so young, too* these words are ironic.

146 *in the eyes of all the world!* Pastor Manders is concerned about the views of 'society' and what people think.

147 *No, it wouldn't go far* her comment shows that she agrees with Oswald.

respectable the men to whom Oswald refers as the most immoral are seen by Pastor Manders as being 'respectable', simply because they appear so (good jobs, family, etc.).

148 *I've never dared to say anything* an example of Mrs Alving's 'free-thinking' being stifled by society.

149 *verge of an abyss* on the edge of a great gulf, emotional upheaval.

we have to do our duty the central argument between happiness and duty.

humility modesty, state of being humble.

150 *vouchsafed* guaranteed.

yoke chain, burden.

pestilent evil.

emancipation freedom.

sent your child forth among strangers the style of talking has become almost biblical.

151 *Bethink* think.

yonder over there.

verily truly.

Helen a sudden change to informality.

152 *dissolute* with loose morals (with a reputation for womanising and drinking).

153 *unseemly levity* shocking lightness. Pastor Manders is still convinced that shocking as Captain Alving's behaviour may have been, it must have just been a silly game.

that connection had consequences the 'consequences' become apparent.

154 *boon companion* favoured friend.

ribald rude.

the child must be poisoned... polluted home this idea recurs in *A Doll's House*.

querulous wretchedness argumentative self-pity.

155 *I did not wish that Oswald... from his father* the theme of inheritance is used in all three plays.

my purchase-money the money with which she was 'bought' for marriage.

156 *Ah!* the recollections of the past (Captain Alving's actions with the housemaid – see page 153)

Is she – ?... Yes Ibsen ends the act with the 'consequence of the connection' (see page 153): Regina is the illegitimate daughter of Captain Alving and, therefore, Oswald's half-sister.

1 What is the difference in the way Regina responds towards Engstrand and Pastor Manders?
2 How is Mrs Alving presented at the start of Act 1?
3 Why does Pastor Manders think it would be better for the Orphanage to be uninsured?
4 How do Oswald and Pastor Manders differ in their views of a moral way of living?
5 What past actions of Mrs Alving had caused Pastor Manders to be shocked and not set foot in the Alving home for so long?
6 What was it about Captain Alving that Mrs Alving had kept hidden from Pastor Manders, Oswald and from public knowledge?
7 What has Mrs Alving done to make sure that Oswald will inherit money only from her?
8 What are the 'ghosts' mentioned by Mrs Alving (page 156)? Who exactly is Regina?

Act 2

157 ***Velbekomme*** a colloquial expression – she hopes he enjoyed the meal.

garlands decorations.

no mischief has been done meaning that the relationship between Oswald and Regina has not become too intimate.

158 ***Johanna*** the name of the housemaid (referred to in Act 1, page 153).

misbehaviour Engstrand had obviously lied and told Pastor Manders that *he* had made Johanna pregnant before they got married.

159 *duplicity* deceit.

fallen woman meaning a woman who had indulged in a sexual relationship before marriage.

a world of difference between the two cases this idea of society's different rules for men and women occurs also in ***A Doll's House*** and is one which concerned Ibsen (see quotation from ***Notes for a Modern Tragedy*** in 'The writer on writing' on pages x–xi).

counsel advice.

160 *Oh! that perpetual law and order! . . . in the world* Mrs Alving and Pastor Manders again clash on the central principle of what is considered proper conduct by society.

161 *Do not despise ideals . . . avenge themselves cruelly* here Pastor Manders and Mrs Alving argue about duty, truth, ideal, illusions – common themes in each play.

162 *would you let them marry!* it would be incest – a sin.

So far as that goes . . . arranged the world so Mrs Alving presents a logical, but shocking argument to Pastor Manders by placing all relationships as the responsibility of God in the first place.

163 *scruples* moral behaviour.

I almost think we're all of us Ghosts . . . afraid of the light the central speech, placed almost exactly half way through the play, also using the recurring light/dark images.

revolutionary, free-thinking books! the discussion on Mrs Alving's books in Act 1, pages 135–7.

I wanted only to pick at a single knot . . . all machine-sewn the image is of a garment which has been machine sewn, so that if one thread is pulled all the stitching will unravel itself. Using this metaphor, Mrs Alving attacks the ideas of duty and obligation from the seemingly mindless doctrine.

164 *the victory over myself* Pastor Manders is proud of his self-restraint.

Was that a crime? the discussion points out the difference in their outlooks.

166 *prevarication* evasion of the truth.

167 *a man to raise up the fallen* a Christian ideal.

Johanna had got into trouble through that Englishman ironic – as even Engstrand is unaware that Captain Alving is the real father of Regina.

admonition warning.

puffed up about it proud.

169 *mammon . . . wages of sin* the heathen god devoted only to riches, the embodiment of evil.

Scripture Bible

170 *I who ought to beg your pardon* Pastor Manders feels humble after what Engstrand has told him – but will not reveal the truth about about Captain Alving.

171 *I think you are . . . a great baby, Manders* because Manders has become quite sentimental and changed his opinion about Engstrand. Of course not all the truth about Regina's parentage has been revealed and Manders has left Engstrand to his 'illusions'.

172 *Without a single ray of sunlight* an important reference to the light.

174 *fatigue* exhaustion.

dissipated life a life spent wastefully in personal amusements.

175 *worm eaten . . .* **vermoulu** Oswald explains that the illness has been inherited and is eating away at him from the inside. This reference to the sexually-transmitted disease syphilis caused a furore on the publication of the play. Syphilis can be inherited by a child from its parents and although it is initially a disease of the sexual organs, it manifests itself later in increasingly bad headaches and could (at the time Ibsen was writing – without proper medication) lead to a form of dementia, insanity, loss of all bodily functions and, finally, death.

'The sins of the fathers, are visited upon the children' a reference to the Old Testament Deuteronomy 5:9: 'For I the Lord thy God am a jealous God, visiting the iniquity of the fathers upon the children.'

176 ***your letters*** Mrs Alving had kept up the pretence of Captain Alving as a good, respectable man in her correspondence with Oswald. This is the 'happy illusion' referred to by Pastor Manders (see Act 2, page 161).

I got to know the truth Oswald does not see the irony of his statement. He feels his own lifestyle brought about his illness but this is not so. His illness had been inherited because of his father's sexual promiscuity.

If only it had been something inherited an added irony.

179 ***I'm fond of her... responsible for her*** Oswald does not understand the real significance of this statement. Mrs Alving has been trying to ensure that Regina will leave the house.

180 ***reparation*** repayment.

181 ***salvation*** that which can save Oswald.

182 ***here people are... a punishment for sin*** Oswald looks at society's 'rules of conduct'.

'A vale of tears' an old saying, suggesting that life is nothing but misery.

182–3 ***But in the great world... radiant with happiness*** Oswald's reference to the 'joy of life' is in contrast to the darkness pervading the play and is ironic in view of what has happened.

184 ***I can speak... no ideal shall suffer after all*** Mrs Alving must speak the truth now – to save Oswald from feeling he has brought his doom upon himself and because she has hidden the truth for so long.

1 What happened to Johanna (Regina's mother)? Look at pages 157–65.
2 Why does Pastor Manders think there is a difference between the cases of Engstrand/Johanna and Captain Alving/Mrs Alving?
3 What does Pastor Manders consider to be the advantages of illusions and ideals?
4 What arguments does Mrs Alving use to approve of a possible marriage between Oswald and Regina?
5 What are the 'ghosts' referred to by Mrs Alving in her speeches (pages 163–4)?
6 Why is Engstrand's explanation of the background to his marriage to Johanna ironic?
7 What is the irony in Oswald's description of his illness?
8 Why does Oswald feels his salvation lies with Regina?

Act 3

186 *The bird's limed* he's caught now – referring to Pastor Manders.

plain as a pike-staff as plain as could be.

180 *benevolent Institution* meaning the Orphanage.

malignant evil.

Inaugural Address the speech to open the Orphanage.

Power of Attorney the right to sign all documents on behalf of the person who owns it.

188 *The original destination . . . completely changed* referring to the use of the money for the Orphanage, as discussed in Act 1 by Pastor Manders and Mrs Alving.

shall pass to the parish the property will belong to the church.

benefactor one who gives financial aid to another.

189 *I know a man ... sins upon himself* referring to himself.

190 *Everything will burn ... burning down* in direct contrast to his 'joy of life'.

191 *exuberant* overflowing.

192 *Everything was marked out into duties* her dilemma of having to stand by her husband in the eyes of society.

193 *So mother was that kind of woman* Regina has her suspicions confirmed.

I, too, have the joy of life in me a very hollow repetition of Oswald's phrase.

194 *'Captain Alving's Home'* by deciding to join her father at the sailors' home, Regina will do whatever her father wants her to do there.

197 *The disease ... is seated here* by pointing to his forehead, Oswald explains that the next stage of the illness for him will be a descent into actual insanity.

198 *To become a little baby again!* his illness will mean loss of all bodily control.

Morphia a very strong addictive pain-killer which, if taken too much, can kill.

199 *pilules* capsules.

200 *Brilliant sunshine!* the irony of the sun coming up at the point of Oswald's impending darkness is an apt climax to Ibsen's use of the light/dark contrast throughout the play.

give me the sun meaning the morphine.

201 *No; no; no! Yes! – No; No!* Ibsen intended creating the uncertainty as to whether Mrs Alving would or would not administer the fatal dose of morphine to put Oswald out of his misery.

1 What agreement is made between Engstrand and Pastor Manders?
2 What are Pastor Manders's plans now that the Orphanage has burned down?
3 How does Mrs Alving reveal the truth about Captain Alving to Oswald and Regina?
4 What will happen to Oswald because of his illness?
5 Why does Regina make the decision to leave and join her father?
6 How does Oswald want his mother to help him?
7 What do you think Mrs Alving will do at the end?

A Doll's House

Act I

205 *porcelain stove* (s.d.) the main means of heating the house. There would have been no central heating in those days.

what-not (s.d.) a piece of furniture to display things.

bric-à-brac (s.d.) ornaments.

lark one of the many bird and animal names Helmer calls his wife.

206 *spendthrift* someone who spends all the money which has been saved.

you made ducks and drakes of them a game of throwing flat stones into water.

creditors people asking for money to be paid on items bought on credit payments.

208 *It's a sweet little lark* Helmer talks about Nora in the third person as if she is not there.

209 *that sort of thing is hereditary* a theme common to all three plays. The inference is that Nora's father let money slip away and so Nora has inherited the problem from him.

confectioner's sweet shop.

210 *For three whole weeks* these weeks become important as events unfold.

hard times the family had obviously not always been as financially well-off as they appear to be now.

212 *egotistical* self-centred.

213 *manager of the Joint Stock Bank* an important position.

A lawyer's position . . . Torvald never would Helmer had been a lawyer and has gained promotion in the banking world. Nora refers to his great sense of honesty.

and other work too Nora makes this very unclear on purpose.

214 *You spent a whole year in Italy* this would have cost a lot of money.

He died just about that time Mrs Linden's comment fills in information about the past.

215 *My mother was still alive . . . for me to refuse him* Nora makes it sound as though she married Helmer out of a sense of duty.

drudgery hard, boring work.

216 *You think Torvald can perhaps do something for you?* the plot and sub-plot link.

217 *It was I that found the money* how Nora obtained the money becomes important.

218 *a wife can't borrow without her husband's consent* a wife would have been considered as subordinate to her husband in matters of finance and would not have been allowed to borrow money without his consent at the time the play was written.

Is it rash to save one's husband's life? Nora feels her motives were honourable.

219 *loathing of debt* an important comment in view of the plot.

That time will never come Nora feels extremely confident that she can control matters.

my grand secret Nora will be only partly honest with Mrs Linden.

instalments Nora has to pay back the money she has borrowed plus interest in regular amounts.

220 *I almost felt as if I was a man* her comment shows how little women were usually allowed to be involved regarding finance.

221 *You? What is it?* Nora's tone and Mrs Linden's reaction when they each see Krogstad creates tension.

222 *round of dissipation* trivial amusements.

223 *mania* mad passion, craving.

moral incurable referring to Krogstad.

It's that notion that makes society a hospital Rank comments on whether society should look after those who have committed crimes.

224 *we – that Torvald* Nora corrects herself, realising that she must make it sound as if her husband is the only one of importance.

contra-band forbidden.

Christina brought me these the audience knows Nora bought them herself.

227 *adjacent* (s.d.) next to.

228 *But it's not the first yet –* the feeling is that Nora is going on to say 'the first of the month' – normally when payments would be due. She stops herself.

229 *I used to know her too* all plots and events from the past are now linked.

one has Nora is trying to speak formally in the third person.

230 *How can you imagine . . . influence over my husband?* the audience has already seen many examples of Nora being able to 'get round' her husband.

231 *You won't tell my husband . . . you money?* the truth is revealed about how Nora got the loan (see pages 218–21).

wherewithal financial means.

232 *note of hand* an official and legally binding IOU.

making your father security for the debt according to the terms of the IOU, if Nora were unable to pay the instalments and interest on the money borrowed then her father would have to pay.

233 *I wrote father's name* it becomes apparent that Nora not only forged her father's name but also signed the document in his hand *after* he had died – both criminal offences.

It was impossible Nora reveals her genuine dilemma at the time.

234 *it was nothing worse . . . outcast from society* Krogstad makes the point that Nora and he have both committed the same kind of offences against the law.

if I am flung . . . keep me company there is the feeling that he will blackmail her.

I did it for love! Nora feels her motive excuses her.

237 *Forgery . . . driven to it by need?* the significance of Nora's reaction would be understood by the audience but not by Helmer.

morally ruined him therefore, that Nora would be thought of in the same way.

238 *canting and shamming* talking rubbish and living a life of pretence.

in such an atmosphere of lies . . . germ of evil this idea is common to all three plays.

Nearly all cases . . . to lying mothers Helmer harshly assumes inheritance of bad traits comes from mothers only.

lies and hypocrisy again – Nora's faults.

physical discomfort this idea of not being able to be near someone who is 'morally ruined' recurs towards the end of the play – hence the significance of the next important stage direction.

1 Up to the entrance of Mrs Linden (page 211), what impression do you get of the relationship between Nora and Helmer?
2 Why did Nora need money, and what explanation does she give to Mrs Linden about how she obtained the money?
3 What were Nora's dilemmas in the first year of her marriage?
4 Why does Krogstad have power over Nora?
5 What is ironic about the way Helmer talks about Krogstad's former actions?
6 How does Krogstad blackmail Nora?
7 How do Nora and Helmer behave towards each other throughout the act?

Act 2

240 ***Christmas tree, stripped*** (s.d.) it was customary to exchange presents on Christmas Eve.

nothing in the letter box the letter box becomes a central feature, as Nora searches to see if there is a letter from Krogstad.

241 ***I can't have them . . . in the future*** Nora has taken Helmer's comment (Act 1, page 238) to heart.

your child up to strangers significant conversation in view of the subject matter.

242 ***Neapolitan*** from Naples in southern Italy.

tarantella a particularly fast Italian dance.

Capri an island off southern Italy.

243 ***spinal consumption*** one of the illnesses associated with syphilis.

245 ***Something has happened since yesterday morning*** Nora is behaving differently because of anxiety since her meeting with Krogstad.

246 ***If your little squirrel . . . so prettily*** Nora reverts to the 'act' from Act I to get something from Helmer.

you could dismiss some other clerk she shows no real thought for anyone else in her desperate need to have Krogstad employed at the bank.

scurrilous wicked, unscrupulous.

247 ***unimpeachable*** blameless from prosecution.

he was a college chum of mine linking Krogstad and Helmer.

248 ***wretched scribbler's spite*** referring to the fact that Krogstad writes for a 'scurrilous' paper (see note to page 246).

249 ***my shoulders are broad enough . . . never, never do!*** these words become significant in the last act.

avail myself benefit from.

250 ***auditing my life account – bankrupt!*** taking stock of what I have in life – nothing. The financial metaphor used by Dr Rank is apt.

to suffer thus for another's sin the same idea as in ***Ghosts*** – of an illness inherited as a result of his father's sexual promiscuity.

251 ***inexorable retribution*** a repayment given which is unstoppable.

wild oats to 'sow one's wild oats' is a saying meaning to indulge in youthful excesses – associated often with sexual activity and drinking.

asparagus . . . Strasbourg pâté . . . truffles . . . oysters . . . port . . . champagne very expensive food and drink associated with fine living.

252 ***taking time by the forelock*** an expression meaning to seize the opportunity.

I suppose you may look at the rest too Nora flirts with Dr Rank. (See the conversation between Nora and Mrs Linden pages 243–5.)

254 ***I have loved you as deeply*** following this remark Nora's attitude changes completely.

I am at your service . . . I can tell you nothing now knowing that Rank loves her, Nora feels she can't ask him to help her.

256 *slips the bolt* (s.d.) Nora ensures that Helmer is locked in his room so that she won't be disturbed.

257 *you should not get back your I O U* Krogstad feels he has power over Nora so long as he has the IOU in his possession.

258 *something worse* meaning suicide.

regain my footing in the world Helmer had described Krogstad as an outcast of society.

259 *petted* spoiled, looked after excessively.

your reputation remains in my hands! the blackmail is relentless.

260 *In the letter box!* this would be a *locked* box attached to the inside of the front door for which only Helmer would have the key.

261 *he would have done anything for me* referring to their past relationship.

263 *I can't dance tomorrow... with you first* Nora uses as many delaying tactics as possible to prevent Helmer reading the post.

Nora dances more and more wildly (s.d.) her manner of dancing reveals the tension she is undergoing.

264 *you're dancing as if it were a matter of life and death* an ironic comment.

The child shall have her own way Helmer is influenced both by Nora's pleading and Rank's helpful comment.

1 Why is the brief conversation between Nora and Anna significant?
2 What actions of Nora's and reactions from Mrs Linden and Rank show the changes in Nora since the previous day?
3 What is learned about Dr Rank and his relationship with Nora from the conversation between Nora and Mrs Linden?
4 In what ways does Nora try to get Krogstad reinstated at the bank? What are Helmer's reasons for not doing so?
5 How does Nora behave towards Rank when they are alone? What makes her not ask for any favours?
6 How does Krogstad maintain the blackmail?
7 In what ways does Ibsen show Nora's psychological state?
8 How does Ibsen's use of stage directions add to the tension in this act?

Act 3

268 ***a heartless woman ... better match offers*** revealing the depth of their previous relationship.

269 ***prudence*** cautious wisdom.

shipwrecked man Krogstad uses a dramatic image to show how he has been made an outcast of society.

270 ***Don't you hear the dancing overhead?*** their conversation occurs at the same time as the party upstairs being attended by Nora and Helmer.

271 ***you must not recall the letter*** perhaps a surprising reaction.

Helmer must know everything ... shifts and subterfuges very much the same idea as the one used by Gregers in *The Wild Duck*.

To have someone ... if I fail at least these two now have some hope, thus increasing the tension about what will happen when Helmer discovers the truth.

272 ***domino*** (s.d.) cape – for formal occasions.

273 ***a little too much nature*** suggesting Nora danced with frenzy, abandon.

my capricious little Capri girl changeable girl from Capri. (See also note to page 242.)

275 ***Don't look at me in that way, Torvald*** the meaning becomes clear along with his reason for bringing her home early.

goes to the other side of the table (s.d.) in doing so she moves away from him.

more enticing he is becoming very aroused at the sight of her.

276 ***won't! Am I not your husband – ?*** an example of Helmer's belief that a husband must be able to have sex with his wife if he wants.

A knock at the outer door (s.d.) brief relief from the tension.

277 ***nothing is to be had for nothing*** Nora would understand the significance of this.

masquerades disguises, fancy dress.

278 ***Havanas*** expensive Cuban cigars.

279 ***a broken hairpin*** obviously Nora has tried to break open the lock of the letter box.

black cross over the name meaning the impending death of Dr Rank.

280 ***I often wish . . . for your dear sake*** the irony soon becomes apparent – even to Helmer.

281 ***How I am punished . . . I did it for your sake*** Helmer's feeling of sacrifice is different from Nora's. In direct contrast to the comments made by Helmer on the previous page, this speech leads to a clash of attitudes and ultimately to the climax of the play.

282 ***collusion*** having been knowingly part of Nora's crime.

Henceforward from now on.

283 *I am saved!* a self-centred reaction to say I, not we.

sends you back your promissory note Krogstad returns Nora's IOU.

I understand . . . I have forgiven you Ibsen uses Helmer's condescension and arrogance to ensure the audience's sympathy for Nora.

I should be no true man . . . dear in my eyes Ibsen exposes what he felt to be a predominantly male attitude.

284 *There is something indescribably sweet . . . his wife and his child* Helmer is obviously concerned with Nora as his property and with his own reputation so he feels he has the right and the power to forgive her.

I have changed my dress the sudden change shocks Helmer. His long speeches have made her even more determined to leave.

285 *this is the first time . . . together seriously?* the ultimate moment of truth for them both.

286 *He used to call me . . . live in your house –* Nora's position has simply been as property to men.

our house has been nothing but a playroom reference to the title of the play.

287 *now comes the time for education* Helmer believes he must teach his wife.

I must try to educate myself Nora is determined to live her own life.

I must stand quite alone . . . so I cannot stay with you this sentiment shocked contemporary audiences.

288 *My duties towards myself* something of the 'spiritual emancipation' with which Ibsen was so concerned.

I don't really know what religion is this would be even more of a shock.

289 *let me appeal to your conscience* having appealed to her sense of duty as a mother, then her religion, Helmer now tries to appeal to her sense of right and wrong.

You no longer love me Helmer cannot understand Nora. His reaction is self-centred.

290 ***when the miracle did not happen*** Nora had hoped Helmer would stand by her from the first moment the truth was revealed.

no man sacrifices his honour ... Millions of women have done so the central difference – which still provokes a reaction from today's theatre audiences.

293 ***the reverberation of a heavy door closing*** (s.d.) the famous final stage direction which caused such shock amongst audiences and critics throughout Europe, as Nora leaves her husband and children.

1. What is revealed about the past relationship and future plans of Krogstad and Mrs Linden?
2. Why does Mrs Linden not want Krogstad to ask for the return of his letter?
3. How do Nora and Helmer behave towards each other when they return early from the party?
4. What comments from Dr Rank appear to have particular depth?
5. What is Helmer's immediate reaction when he reads Krogstad's letter?
6. In what ways do Helmer's attitudes change when he receives the return of Nora's IOU?
7. What does Nora intend to do and what reasons does she give?
8. How does Helmer try to appeal to Nora to stay?

Study programme

The Wild Duck

Structure

1 Make a chart to show the on-stage plot line and information revealed about the past in each act. It could look something like this:

	Plot/stage action	Information about the past
Act I	Hialmar at Mrs Sörby's dinner party. Old Ekdal appears to get some copying. Discussion about wine.	Werle's reputation with women. Business partnership between Werle and Old Ekdal. Old Ekdal imprisoned for fraud. Werle provided money for Hialmar to start photography business.

Now continue with the rest of this act and the others.

2 There are many moments of suspense and tension throughout the play. Note down:

- what they are;
- where they come (e.g. start, middle of act; when someone exits, etc.);
- how they are written (e.g. as action, speech, stage direction, etc.).

Use your notes to write an essay on how Ibsen uses suspense and tension in the play. Your plan should include:

- a brief explanation of the examples;

- reasons as to why and how they work in the play;
- how the tension is sustained throughout the play;
- how they arise naturally from the plot and the characters.

One example might be the sound of the shotgun coming from the garret in Act 5. This creates suspense because no one on stage is quite sure what has happened and so they all think it is Old Ekdal. The audience knows, however, that Old Ekdal is in his room and only Hedvig is in the garret with the shotgun. It is tense because Gregers has suggested Hedvig could make the supreme self-sacrifice for Hialmar by shooting the wild duck. She believes Gregers but the tension mounts further after Hialmar's reaction towards her on discovering she is not his real daughter. There is further suspense when wondering just what could have happened.

3 Ibsen uses the device of *irony* many times. Find as many examples as you can – they can be words, actions, stage directions. Use your notes for a piece of writing on Ibsen's use of dramatic irony in the play.

Character

1 Look for all the connections between Mr Werle and the other characters, past events and present action. Chart your findings on a spider graph, for example:

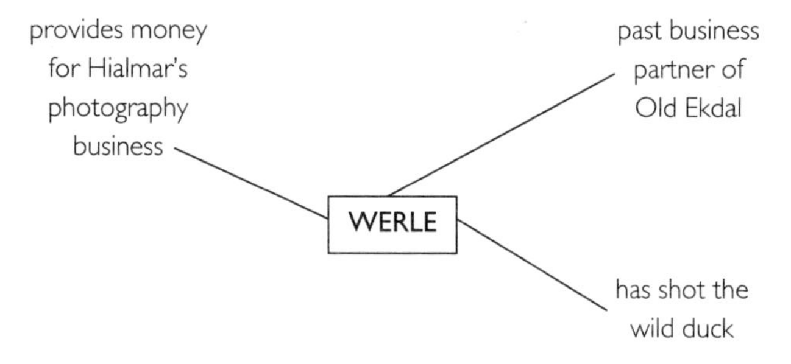

2 In pairs, prepare speeches to present as an oral assignment in role as Mr Werle:

- one speech defends all his past and present actions;
- the other speech admits his faults and a kind of apology.

You will need to use information from the play to be as accurate as possible.

3 Think about Gina's actions and whether or not she was right in keeping the past a secret and in the way she runs her family.

In pairs or in a group write down as many ideas as you can under these headings:

In defence of Gina's actions **Attacking Gina's actions**

4 Ibsen makes Gina a sympathetic character. Try to write down how he does this. Think about:

- Gina's actions;
- her character in contrast with Hialmar;
- the photography business;
- her speeches;
- her relationship with Gregers.

5 In a letter of 14 November 1884, Ibsen wrote:

> *Hialmar must not be acted with any trace of parody. The actor must never for a moment show that he is conscious that there is anything funny in what he says. His voice has, as Relling observes, something endearing about it, and this quality must be clearly brought out. His sentimentality is honest, his melancholy, in its way, attractive; no hint of affectation… Gregers is the most difficult part in the play, from the acting point of view…*

Imagine you are casting the play.

EITHER Write notes explaining how you see the characters of Hialmar and Gregers. Think about the following questions:

- how should each be played?
- which are the most important scenes?
- which speeches are the most significant?
- what should the characters look like?
- how do the other characters react towards them?
- how do they act towards each other?

OR Write a character study either on Hialmar or Gregers. Remember to include:

- what they are like based on their role in the play;
- how their speeches help to convey their character;
- what other characters say about them;
- what they think and say about other characters;
- their actions;
- short, important quotations which can illustrate the points you make.

6 You have been told that to cut costs in a new production the following characters will not be cast: Hedvig, Old Ekdal and Mrs Sörby.

Either write a letter or prepare a speech arguing against cutting out their characters in the production. Give detailed reasons why each one must be included.

Symbols and images

1 Remember: a symbol represents something as well as being an object in its own right; an image is a picture painted in the mind by the use of language (sometimes figurative language such as *metaphors* and *similes*).

Brainstorm how the symbol of the wild duck works in the play.

Here are some ideas to start you off:

2 What images can you find in the play which convey ideas of the following?

- sight and blindness
- hunting
- money

Themes

1 Look at the following list of themes:

marriage	family life	inheritance
truth	lies	illusions
light	dark	blindness

In a group, brainstorm ideas on how these themes are dealt with in the play. You may feel there are other themes not listed here.

2 In pairs argue for and against the following statement:

'The Ekdal family should not have been forced to face the truth.'

You can use any of the comments and speeches made in the play, but you must acknowledge where they come from.

3 Either prepare a speech or write an essay on what you think ***The Wild Duck*** is about. For this assignment you must not spend too much time on the plot itself; concentrate on the themes.

In performance

Read the following review of a production of the play:

Thrills and Bills

We have heard a lot about Peter Hall's intention of restoring the comedy to Ibsen's **The Wild Duck**. *In fact it has always been there... The greatness of* [the] *production is that it puts the tragedy back into the play. As we sit spell-bound watching the destruction of the Ekdal family by the meddling idealist Gregers Werle, we feel we are watching something both particular and universal.*

Particularity is shown by fanatical attention to detail, such as the fear everyone has of being touched: just as Gregers shies away from contact with his father so Gina flinches at Gregers's touch as if she feared contamination. But the sense of the cosmic tragedy is conveyed by the astonishing device of prefacing each act with the sound of a duck's wings vainly flapping: an aural extension of Ibsen's central symbol of wounded humanity's tendency to hide itself in illusion.

Hall also intensifies the tragedy by casting the key roles much younger than usual. Alex Jennings plays Hialmar not as a dithery middle-aged buffoon but as a youngish man shrouded in self-pity and anger... what you see... is the tragedy of a man who is prey to Gregers's idealism and to doubts about his child's paternity. Mr Jennings illuminates the part by suggesting that Hialmar is cursed with the rage of the insecure.

Gregers is an even tougher part which David Threlfall plays superbly as a soft-spoken zealot. He looks like an El Greco Christ in urgent need of psychiatric attention: everything he does has a terrifyingly quiet intensity...

Nicola McAuliffe is also, for me, the definitive Gina: a loving woman, who has a sharper hold on reality than anyone in the play. She also sends a thrill down the spine at the moment when it is revealed that Werle, like Hedvig, is going blind . . .

Michael Billington, ***The Guardian***, 19 May 1990

1 Take any phrase or comment from the above review for the basis of a piece of writing on the play. For example, discuss the comment: '. . . we feel we are watching something both particular and universal.' Or explain why it might be true to say that 'Gina has a sharper hold on reality than anyone in the play'.

2 If you can see a production of the play, write your own review. Remember to comment on the play, production, acting, set, characterisation. If you think any of the actors have got it wrong, say so!

Ghosts

Structure

1 Make a chart to show the on-stage plot line and information revealed about the past in each act. It could look something like this:

	Plot/stage action	Information about the past
Act 1	Engstrand – to establish sailors' tavern and wants Regina with him. Pastor Manders and Mrs Alving discuss plans for the Orphanage – in memory of Captain Alving (dead for 10 years). All money from estate to go into Orphanage. Orphanage to be uninsured.	Regina has tried to get an education. Oswald has returned home. Pastor Manders and Engstrand have known each other in the past.

Now continue with the rest of this act and the others.

2 The figure of Captain Alving is central to the structure of the play although he has been dead for ten years as the play opens.

Note down all the reasons why he is central to the present action, characters and past events, charting your findings in a spider graph.

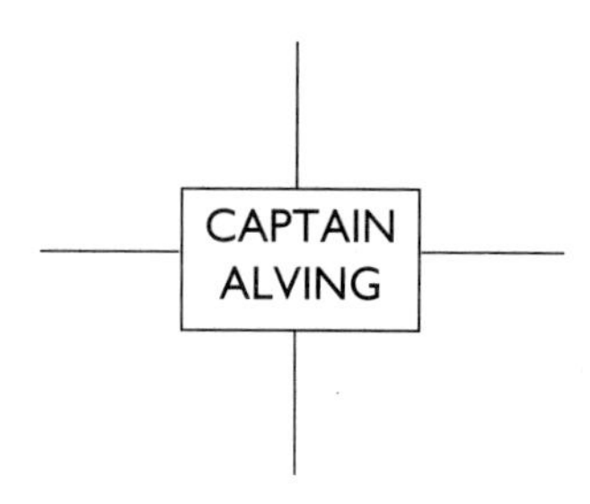

3 Oswald's belief that it is own fault that he has become so ill is ironic because, unlike the audience, he is unaware of the truth about his father; and when Mrs Alving says: 'Oswald takes after me' (Act 1, page 144) her words are ironic because of Oswald's 'inheritance' – of which at that stage *she* is unaware.

Find as many examples of irony in the play as you can:

- from the things people say;
- from their actions;
- from the stage directions.

Use your notes for a piece of writing on the use of irony in the play.

4 The play is called ***Ghosts***. What ghosts are there in the play? Make a list. Try to find examples:

- in what people say;
- in what they do;

- in what they mean;
- in stage directions.

One example could be that when Oswald makes his first appearance with the pipe there is a sense of the late Captain Alving.

Character

1 Mrs Alving is the one character who knows everything that has happened in the past. What kind of character is she?

Discuss the character of Mrs Alving under the following headings, looking particularly at the way she responds to the different characters. Make notes on your discussion. Consider:

- her reading habits;
- the way she treats Regina;
- her relationship with Oswald;
- her past and present relationship with Pastor Manders;
- her dilemma regarding her duty in the past;
- her thoughts on money;
- her attitudes towards her husband and the Orphanage.

Use your notes to write a character study of Mrs Alving.

2 Read the following review of a production of ***Ghosts***. It concentrates on the portrayal of Oswald and Pastor Manders.

> *Simon Russell Beale's brilliant depiction of Oswald – the boy whose mother sent him away to Paris to shelter him from the knowledge of his father's degeneracy and who now returns harbouring the syphilis which is his paternal inheritance – gets you in the guts.*
>
> *Notice how his hand strokes his mother's hair with an abstracted tenderness that makes it look as if he's still doing this more in yearning imagination than in actuality, and notice how the hand is instinctively snatched away when Jane Lapotaire's gamut-spanning Mrs Alving attempts to*

touch it. His eyes, too, convey a man torn between the desire to appeal to this woman for help and the urge to punish her for what he regards as years of pointless estrangement. Squirming with shame at his condition, he may conceal his eyes behind a pudgy hand, but then whenever he manages to blurt out the next scalding instalment of the truth, those frightening eyes bulge in goggling curiosity, monitoring every twitch of how his mother registers the shock. It's an inquisitiveness that seems inseparably bound up with the thwarted intensity of his love.

John Carlisle's [is a] *masterly portrayal of Pastor Manders, the cleric whose rigid advocacy of society's false ideals has had such a disastrous effect on this household. Confronting the world with a face of grimly ashen aquilinity, Carlisle's Manders is a wonderfully comic creation and a seriously disturbing one, both qualities stemming from the same source: the utter benighted sincerity and intransigence that sharply separate this man from a Tartuffe* [from Moliere's *Tartuffe*] *or an Angelo* [from *Measure for Measure* Shakespeare's].

Carlisle inflects a line like 'I can't think how I could get down a morsel of dinner' [Act 2, page 157] *so that Manders seems severely oblivious to the incongruity of the words... It's at once amusing and infuriating to watch this figure being taken in by John Normington's transparently disingenuous Engstrand, who here, is all cap-in-hand unction and inclined to move himself to crocodile tears at the least provocation.*

But if Manders's failure to cotton on to the pert overtures of Alexandra Gilbreath's determined Regina causes more of a grin than a grimace, the obduracy with which he refuses to unbend before Lapotaire's [Mrs Alving's] *mixture of piteous entreaties and sardonic wiles is shattering in its cold preference for lofty principle over intimate human detail. Yet it is also Carlisle's achievement to make you aware at moments, how it must feel from the inside of this kind of person.*

Paul Taylor, ***The Independent***, 8 April 1994

Think carefully about how you would play Oswald and Pastor Manders. Write detailed notes about how each part should be played. You could do this from the point of view of a director or actor, but remember to include the following:

- what kind of characters they are (they are both complex);
- their beliefs (look in particular at the discussion between them both in Act 1, pages 146–8);
- their relationships with other characters, in particular with Mrs Alving;
- their views on Captain Alving;
- references to the text – even short quotations explaining how they should be delivered by the character;
- perhaps even a physical description of how they might look in a production.

3 Why are Engstrand and Regina so important in the play? Brainstorm ideas connected to the function of each, setting out your your ideas on a spider graph.

Images

1 Find as many examples as you can of images to do with:

- light and dark
- illness
- inheritance.

Explain:

- where they come in the play;
- how they connect with other images;
- why they are appropriate images for this play;
- whether there are any other important images.

Themes

1. Consider the following themes:

   duty   joy of life   love   beliefs
   children/parent relationships   marital relationships
   inheritance   spiritual emancipation
   truth   illusions   sight

   In a group take each one in turn and discuss how each theme is examined in the play. You might start by brainstorming ideas around each word. Remember to think about *all* the characters in your discussion.

   Are there other themes which you think are explored in the play?

2. In pairs, prepare speeches for and against the following statements:

   - 'Mrs Alving had to conceal the truth about Captain Alving from everyone.'
   - 'Pastor Manders is right in his beliefs about duty.'

   You could present these for a debate or an oral assignment. Use comments and quotations from the play but make sure you acknowledge where they come from and who says them.

3. What do you think ***Ghosts*** is about? With only the briefest reference to the actual plot think about the main theme of the play. Write down your ideas in the form of a speech or an essay.

In performance

Read the extract of the review written just after the first London production of ***Ghosts*** in 1891 by A. B. Walkey ('Introduction' page xvii) and the following review of the play which concentrates on the central plot and theme:

Ibsen's trail-blazing drama was for its time an unconventional play about a conventional woman whose commitment to duty, obligation, morality and the ghosts of outmoded ideas gave her dignity but robbed her of the life force.

It also robbed her son Oswald of the knowledge that his father was a degenerate, the price of whose 'secret dissolutions' was to contract, and pass on to Oswald, syphilis.

The theme of the play – the stifling of individuality, allied to the grim reminder that the sins of the fathers are visited on the children – is explored with Ibsen with breathtaking economy.

The result is an austere and decidedly bleak drama, whose wintry atmosphere and highly charged psychological nooks and crannies are thrillingly explored by the director Katie Mitchell for the Royal Shakespeare Company.

Clive Hirschhorn, ***Sunday Express,*** 10 April 1994

1. Take any phrase or comment from the reviews for the basis of a piece of writing on the play. For example, how true is it to describe ***Ghosts*** as 'An unconventional play about a conventional woman whose commitment to duty, obligation, morality and the ghosts of outmoded ideas gave her dignity but robbed her of the life force'?
   Or, discuss ***Ghosts*** as a play about 'the stifling of the individual'.

2. If you can see a production of the play, write your own review. Remember to comment on the play, production, acting, set, characterisation. If you think any of the actors have got it wrong, say so!

A Doll's House

Structure

1. Make a chart to show the on-stage plot line and information revealed about the past in each act. It could look something like this:

	Plot/stage action	Information about the past
Act 1	Helmer family preparing for Christmas. Nora returns from shopping. Nora and Helmer discuss money. News of Helmer's promotion. Mrs Linden visits. Nora talks about her husband's illness.	Suggestion about Nora's father's bad habits with money. Explanation of Helmer's illness during first year of marriage. Reference to death of Nora's father at about the same time.

Now continue with the rest of this act and the others.

2 The play is called ***A Doll's House***. Nora makes an explicit reference to having been treated like a doll:

> *He used to call me his doll-child, and played with me as I played with my dolls... But our house has been nothing but a playroom.*
>
> Act 3, page 286

How does Ibsen use the idea of a doll's house in the structure of the play? Think about:

- games being played.
- who might be the doll in any given act;
- who is in control at different times;
- whether the doll's house is needed to give the characters security;
- whose doll's house it is.

Set out your thoughts in the form of a spider graph:

3 The tension and suspense of the play hinge on the fact that the only character who does not know the whole truth about Nora's past actions is Helmer.

At which points in each act does Ibsen use the techniques of tension and suspense? In identifying these moments, think about:

- plot
- words
- action
- stage directions
- character

Character

1 Nora is a complex character. The way she is first portrayed in her dialogue with Helmer is completely different from their final confrontation at the climax to the play.

Make notes on how Nora behaves with the following characters and think carefully about her motives. Remember, she may behave in different ways with each character. It may be helpful to use spider graphs to organise your thoughts.

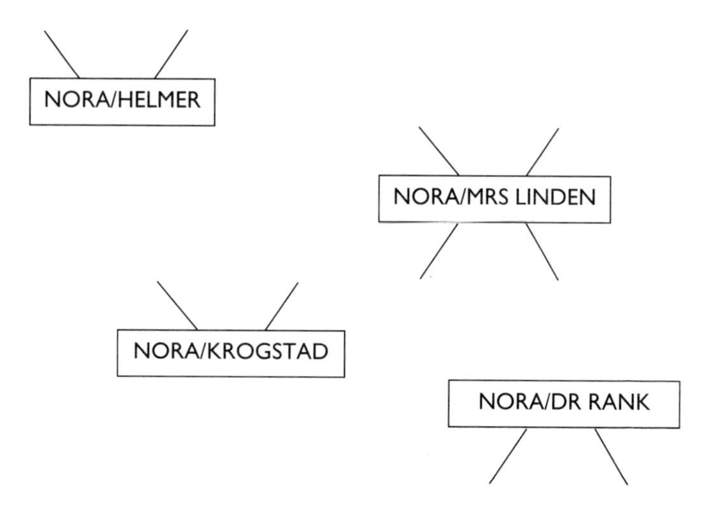

Use your notes to write a character study of Nora. Include references to her:

- words
- actions
- motives
- society
- relationships with others

2 In pairs, place Nora in the Psychiatrist's Chair. Think about the questions you would ask her and what her replies would be.

Some of her answers might be taken directly from the text. You could also refer to Ibsen's own ***Notes for a Modern Tragedy*** (see 'The writer on writing', pages x–xi). Take it in turns to be the psychiatrist and Nora.

3 In a small group prepare speeches or written assignments for and against the following statement: 'Torvald Helmer is a sympathetic character'.

4 Think about the way Ibsen uses Mrs Linden, Krogstad and Dr Rank in the play. Make your own version of the chart below using a large piece of paper.

	Mrs Linden	**Krogstad**	**Dr Rank**
Relationships with the others			
Part played in plot			
Motives			
Important comments			
Importance of character			

5 Think about all the characters in the play. Ibsen does not make any one character all good or all bad – just like in real life!

For each character write down their sympathetic and unsympathetic points. Explain what your findings tell you about the way Ibsen portrays his characters.

Images

1 From the words or action of the play find as many images as you can to do with:

- animals
- games
- illness
- disguise
- money

Make these into a wall collage.

Themes

1 Consider the following themes:

marriage	power	freedom
money	fraud	heredity
games	truth	illusions

In a group, brainstorm how these themes are explored in the play. Remember to think about all the characters and all strands of the plot. You may want to include other themes not listed here.

2 Arrange a debate to discuss the following proposition:

This house believes that Nora was justified in leaving her home at the end of the play.

You will need speakers for and against the proposition as well as others who are prepared to ask questions and put forward other points of view.

In performance

1. Make a list of stage directions which are particularly important to the play. Make sure you think about ones which might easily be lost in a read-through only.

2. Read the following review of ***A Doll's House***.

Adrian Noble [director] *sees the play as infinitely more than a pioneering feminist tract about a doll-wife who finally achieves liberation. In this production it is about a whole group of people struggling to free themselves from either the burden of the past or their own natures. For Nora this is done through historic domestic exit and for her husband, Torvald, through being shocked into awareness of the cosseting, protective role he has long played. But the blackmailing Krogstad and the widowed Mrs Linden achieve a different kind of freedom through the pooling of their solitude in marriage.*

[Cheryl Campbell] *takes huge risks playing the whole of the first act on a high-pitched note of giggling, gurgling, coquettish, even petulant, near-frenzy: she is dangerously vivacious as if the strain of living a constant lie (playing the kitten-wife while having engineered her husband's recovery) were tearing her assunder. She catches brilliantly the riven complexity of Nora who is both in thrall to others (Krogstad) and who at the same time enjoys wielding sexual power over Dr Rank: never before have I seen the moment in which she allows him to caress and fondle her silk stockings, delicately running his fingers through them, played with such Pinterish finesse. But it is precisely because Ms Campbell's Nora is such a schizoid, suicidal, near-hysteric that the final discovery of her real self becomes not merely moving but cleansing.*

Stephen Moore offers us an almost definitive Torvald: no paternalist villain but someone trapped inside the role of the doll-husband.

> *Mr Moore wonderfully suggests patronising kindliness. But his real strength comes when Nora presents him with the truth of their relationship.*
>
> *The great strength of this production is that every character is seen from his or her point of view. Bernard Lloyd's Krogstad is no satanic heavy but a reformed criminal yearning for status and recognition. John Franklyn-Robbins's Dr Rank is an astonishing study of a man approaching death with the formal suavity of going to a wedding. And Marjorie Bland's Mrs Linden brings on with her the melancholy aura of provincial solitude and a passionate need for contact.*
>
> Michael Billington, ***The Guardian***, 19 June 1982

Take any phrase or comment from this review as the basis for a piece of writing on the play. For example, discuss the statement that ***A Doll's House*** is about 'a whole group of people struggling to free themselves from either the burden of the past... or their own natures.'

Or, how true is it to think that Torvald Helmer is 'no paternalist villain but someone trapped inside the role of the doll-husband'?

3 If you can see a production of the play write your own review. Remember to comment on the play, production, acting, set, characterisation. If you think the actors have got it wrong, say so!

Further assignments on the three plays

1 Think about what all three plays have in common in the following areas:

- themes
- images
- structure
- character
- plot

Take each in turn and in a group brainstrom as many ideas as you can for all three plays.

2 Working in a small group, with one of you as the director, act out a short extract from each play. Depending on the size of your group, choose a scene which is tense dramatically so that you can concentrate on:

- how to say the lines;
- characterisation;
- gestures, movements;
- stage directions.

Here are some suggestions from which to choose:

The Wild Duck	Act 1, pages 6–10 (Hialmar and Gregers)
	Act 1, pages 16–23 (Gregers and Mr Werle)
	Act 2, pages 41–8 (Ekdal, Gregers, Hedvig, Hialmar, Gina)
	Act 3, pages 70–4 (Gina, Gregers, Mr Werle, Hialmar, Relling, Hedvig)
	Act 4, pages 75–81 (Hedvig, Gina and Hialmar)
	Act 5, pages 102–6 (Gregers and Relling)
	Act 5, pages 110–21 (Hialmar, Gina, Gregers, Relling, Ekdal, Hedvig)
Ghosts	Act 1, pages 125–31 (Regina and Engstrand)
	Act 1, pages 134–42 (Mrs Alving and Pastor Manders)
	Act 1, pages 144–8 (Mrs Alving, Oswald and Pastor Manders)
	Act 1, pages 149–55 (Mrs Alving and Pastor Manders)
	Act 2, pages 157–65 (Mrs Alving and Pastor Manders)
	Act 2, pages 173–81 (Mrs Alving, Oswald, Regina)

	Act 3, pages 192–201 (Mrs Alving, Oswald, Regina)
A Doll's House	Act 1, pages 211–21 (Nora and Mrs Linden)
	Act 1, pages 228–34 (Nora and Krogstad)
	Act 2, pages 249–55 (Nora and Dr Rank)
	Act 2, pages 262–66 (Nora, Helmer, Dr Rank, Mrs Linden, Ellen)
	Act 3, pages 272–8 (Nora, Helmer, Dr Rank, Mrs Linden)
	Act 3, pages 281–93 (Nora, Helmer)

3 If you had to choose one major theme common to all three plays that has particularly interested you, which would it be? Explain your reasons with references to each play and illustrations from the texts.

4 You have the chance of playing any character from the plays. Who would you choose?

Write a letter asking a production team to let you play that character. Explain in detail your reasons for wanting to play the role and why you think you would be just right in the part.

5 Write the next act to each play. You can choose to:

- set the play as much as five years into the future from the point of the last act;
- use as many characters from the play as you think necessary;
- use as much of the past information as necessary;
- end the act in a final resolution or keep it open-ended;
- not introduce any new characters to the play.

6 Think about the idea of 'life-illusions' from all of the plays. In a group discuss how honest you think people can be (or ought to

be) in any family. Write an essay entitled: 'It is not always possible for a family to be entirely honest.'

Study questions

Many of the activities you have already completed will help you to answer the following questions. Before you begin to write, consider these points about essay writing:

- Analyse what the question is asking. Do this by circling key words or phrases.
- Use each part of the question to 'brainstorm' ideas and references to the plays which you think are relevant to the answer.
- Decide on the order in which you are going to tackle the parts of the question. It may help you to draw a flow-diagram so that you can see which aspects of the question are linked.
- Organise your ideas and quotations into sections to fit your flow-diagram. You can do this by placing notes in columns under the various headings.
- Write a first draft of your essay. Do not concern yourself too much with paragraphing and so on; just aim to get your ideas down on paper and do not be too critical of what you write.
- Redraft as many times as you need, ensuring all the time that:
  - each paragraph addresses the question;
  - each paragraph addresses a new part of the question, or at least develops a part;
  - you have an opening and closing paragraph which is clear and linked to the question set;
  - you have checked for spelling and other grammatical errors.

1 'There are no heroes and villains in ***The Wild Duck***.' Discuss this statement.

2 Why do you think ***The Wild Duck*** is considered to be a 'well-made play'?

3 Discuss Ibsen's use of the symbol of the wild duck and other images in ***The Wild Duck.***

4 Ibsen once said in an interview: '***The Wild Duck*** is to be a tragi-comedy…or else Hedvig's death is incomprehensible.' What elements are there of the tragic and the comic in the play?

5 What arguments can you find in ***The Wild Duck*** for and against the 'claims of the ideal' and the 'life-illusion'?

6 What do you consider to be the central theme of ***Ghosts***? Explain your reasons.

7 How sympathetic do you find the character of Mrs Alving?

8 In what ways do you think the figure of the deceased Captain Alving is central to the structure of ***Ghosts*** even though he does not appear?

9 'It's all sorts of dead ideas, and lifeless old beliefs, and so forth. They have no vitality, but they cling to us all the same, and we can't get rid of them.' (Mrs Alving, Act 2, page 163). Explain why this speech is central to ***Ghosts.***

10 Discuss ***A Doll's House*** as a play which examines all kinds of power games.

11 How sympathetic do you find Torvald Helmer as a character?

12 How does Ibsen portray the character of Nora throughout ***A Doll's House***?

13 'No man sacrifices his honour, even for one he loves…Millions

of women have done so.' In what ways does ***A Doll's House*** examine the relationships between men and women?

14 'Every new work has had as its purpose for me that of serving as a process of spiritual emancipation . . .' In what ways do Ibsen's plays explore individual spiritual emancipation?

15 How is the device of irony successfully used in Ibsen's plays?

16 Examine the importance of the past in Ibsen's plays.

17 Discuss the importance of the secondary characters in the three plays.

Suggestions for further reading

Other plays by Ibsen

Brand
A verse play about a young priest who believes religion has lost its way, and whose mission in life is based on the ideal of 'all or nothing' and a refusal to compromise in anything.

Peer Gynt
A verse play about a man who constantly compromises, lies, invents truth, daydreams and travels the world to feed his quest for experience.

An Enemy of the People
A medical officer in a small spa town discovers that the local baths are contaminated and finds himself at the centre of the town's dilemma: to publicise the contamination and lose the livelihood of the town or to keep quiet and suffer the consequences.

Hedda Gabler
Another of Ibsen's middle-period 'domestic' dramas in which Hedda

makes a loveless mariage when a former admirer re-enters her life with tragic consequences.

Plays by other playwrights

An Enemy of the People by Arthur Miller
An adaptation of Ibsen's play.

Death of a Salesman by Arthur Miller
An American play looking at a tragic hero and the effects of the past on his life and the lives of his family.

Long Day's Journey into Night by Eugene O'Neill
An American play exploring the self-destruction of a family with its own past secrets and illusions.

Look Back in Anger by John Osborne
A play which in its time (1956) shocked the London stage with its depiction of the 'angry young man' and contemporary life.

Heartbreak House by George Bernard Shaw
A study of a family written by an admirer of Ibsen's drama.

Mrs Warren's Profession by George Bernard Shaw
Written seven years after ***The Wild Duck*** and refused a licence for many years, it is a play concentrating on the hypocrisy regarding women in society.

Cat on a Hot Tin Roof by Tennessee Williams
An American play looking at the nature of family life in the Deep South.

Wider reading assignments

1 Read ***Hedda Gabler*** by Ibsen. What does it have in common with ***The Wild Duck***, ***Ghosts***, or ***A Doll's House***? Think about its structure, plot, themes, central images, and characters.

2 Read either ***Brand*** or ***Peer Gynt*** by Ibsen. How is either one of them a forerunner to the three plays in this volume?

3 Read the Ibsen and the Arthur Miller versions of ***An Enemy of the People.*** Examine the similarities and differences between the plays.

4 Read any other play from the suggested list. Discuss what devices, themes and images are central to the play and compare it to any one of Ibsen's plays.

5 From a reading of any of Ibsen's and George Bernard Shaw's plays, discuss what their drama has in common.

Longman Literature
Series editor: Roy Blatchford

Novels

Jane Austen ***Pride and Prejudice*** 0 582 07720 6
Nina Bawden ***The Real Plato Jones*** 0 582 29254 9
Charlotte Brontë ***Jane Eyre*** 0 582 07719 2
Emily Brontë ***Wuthering Heights*** 0 582 07782 6
Marjorie Darke ***A Question of Courage*** 0 582 25395 0
Charles Dickens ***A Christmas Carol*** 0 582 23664 9
Great Expectations 0 582 07783 4
Oliver Twist 0 582 28729 4
Berlie Doherty ***The Snake-stone*** 0 582 31764 9
George Eliot ***Silas Marner*** 0 582 23662 2
Josephine Feeney ***My Family and Other Natural Disasters*** 0 582 29262 X
Anne Fine ***The Book of the Banshee*** 0 582 29258 1
Flour Babies 0 582 29259 X
Goggle-Eyes 0 582 29260 3
Madame Doubtfire 0 582 29261 1
A Pack of Liars 0 582 29257 3
Step by Wicked Step 0 582 29251 4
F Scott Fitzgerald ***The Great Gatsby*** 0 582 06023 0
Graham Greene ***The Captain and the Enemy*** 0 582 06024 9
Thomas Hardy ***Far from the Madding Crowd*** 0 582 07788 5
The Mayor of Casterbridge 0 582 22586 8
Susan Hill ***The Mist in the Mirror*** 0 582 25399 3
Lesley Howarth ***MapHead*** 0 582 29255 7
Aldous Huxley ***Brave New World*** 0 582 06016 8
Robin Jenkins ***The Cone-Gatherers*** 0 582 06017 6
Joan Lindsay ***Picnic at Hanging Rock*** 0 582 08174 2
Joan Lingard ***Night Fires*** 0 582 31967 6
Bernard MacLaverty ***Lamb*** 0 582 06557 7
Michelle Magorian ***Goodnight Mister Tom*** 0 582 31965 X
Jan Mark ***The Hillingdon Fox*** 0 582 25985 1
Dalene Matthee ***Fiela's Child*** 0 582 28732 4
Beverley Naidoo ***Journey to Jo'burg*** 0 582 25402 7
George Orwell ***Animal Farm*** 0 582 06010 9
Alan Paton ***Cry, the Beloved Country*** 0 582 07787 7
Ruth Prawer Jhabvala ***Heat and Dust*** 0 582 25398 5
Catherine Sefton ***Along a Lonely Road*** 0 582 29256 5
Robert Swindells ***A Serpent's Tooth*** 0 582 31966 8
Daz 4 Zoe 0 582 30243 9
Follow a Shadow 0 582 31968 4
Anne Tyler ***A Slipping-Down Life*** 0 582 29247 6
Robert Westall ***Urn Burial*** 0 582 31964 1
Edith Wharton ***Ethan Frome*** 0 582 30244 7

Other titles in the Longman Literature series are listed on page ii.

Addison Wesley Longman Limited
Edinburgh Gate, Harlow,
Essex CM20 2JE, England
and Associated Companies throughout the world.

This educational edition first published 1995
Fourth impression 1998

Editorial material set in 10/12 point Gill Sans Light
Printed in Singapore (PH)

ISBN 0 582 24948 1

Consultants: Geoff Barton and Jackie Head

Acknowledgements
We are grateful to the following for permission to reproduce photographs: Donald Cooper (Photostage), pages 1 and 123; John Timbers, page 203.

We are grateful to the following for permission to reproduce copyright material: Express Newspapers Ltd for the review on 'Ghosts' by Clive Hirschorn in *Sunday* Express, 10.4.94; The Guardian Media Group plc for the articles 'Thrills and Bills' by Michael Billington in *The Guardian* 19.5.90 and 'Frenzy at Home' by Michael Billington in *The Guardian* 19.6.92; Newspaper Publishing plc for the review 'Sins of the father' by Paul Taylor in *The Independent* 8.4.94.

Cover illustration by Ramsay Gibb

The publisher's policy is to use paper manufactured from sustainable forests.